P9-CFN-753

SYLVIA DIPIETRO MAKES IT AS EASY AS TWO PLUS TWO TO DISCOVER:

—The job that will give you satisfaction and success

—The mate who will bring you happiness

—The foods that will assure your health

The days to take risks and the days to be careful

—The colors to wear and those to shun

—The lottery numbers that give you the best chance to win millions

—And above all, the personal number derived from your birthday and given name that vibrates through every part of your life your whole life long

LIVE YOUR LIFE BY THE NUMBERS
Your Guide to Numerology

SYLVIA DIPIETRO has attained both fame and acclaim through her celebrated national cable TV show. Based in New York, she also has a private practice in which she advises some of the world's most powerful and wealthy people on personal business decisions.

⊘ SIGNET   (0451)

KNOW THE PAST, THE PRESENT AND THE FUTURE!

☐ **THE TAROT REVEALED by Eden Gray.** The essential, fully illustrated guide to uncovering the mysterious powers of the Tarot. When properly understood, the symbols of the Tarot have a message for all men and women—of all ages. With this completely revised and updated edition of the classic *The Tarot Revealed*, you can uncover more of the timeless wonders of this mysterious art of the New Age.   (156730—$4.50)

☐ **SYDNEY OMARR'S ASTROLOGICAL GUIDE FOR YOU IN 1992 by Sydney Omarr.** Monthly forecasts for every zodiac sign from America's most accurate astrologer! Let the power of the zodiac chart your destiny in love, health, and fortune for the coming year.   (170229—$4.50)

☐ **WRITE YOUR OWN HOROSCOPE by Joseph F. Goodavage.** A leading astrologer tells how you can chart your individual horoscope with the accuracy of a trained professional. This ancient science is explained with explicit details and rare clarity that will unlock the secrets of your character—and your future—as no other book can.   (160282—$4.95)

☐ **YOU CAN ANALYZE HANDWRITING by Robert Holder.** Here is the fascinating book that explains, stroke by stroke, the significance of every type of handwriting including that of famous public figures like Richard Nixon, Helen Gurley Brown and Walter Cronkite. A practical tool for self-knowledge and personal power.   (162447—$4.95)

☐ **FORTUNE IN YOUR HAND by Elizabeth Daniels Squire.** Let this world-famous authority guide you into the realm of fascinating perceptions about the past and future, about yourself and others through the science of palmistry.   (164067—$4.95)

Prices slightly higher in Canada

Buy them at your local bookstore or use this convenient coupon for ordering.

NEW AMERICAN LIBRARY
P.O. Box 999, Bergenfield, New Jersey 07621

Please send me the books I have checked above. I am enclosing $_____
(please add $1.00 to this order to cover postage and handling). Send check or money order—no cash or C.O.D.'s. Prices and numbers are subject to change without notice.

Name_____

Address_____

City _____ State _____ Zip Code _____
Allow 4-6 weeks for delivery.
This offer, prices and numbers are subject to change without notice.

LIVE YOUR LIFE
BY THE
NUMBERS
Your Guide to Numerology

Sylvia E. Di Pietro

A SIGNET BOOK

SIGNET
Published by the Penguin Group
Penguin Books USA Inc., 375 Hudson Street,
New York, New York 10014, U.S.A.
Penguin Books Ltd, 27 Wrights Lane,
London W8 5TZ, England
Penguin Books Australia Ltd, Ringwood,
Victoria, Australia
Penguin Books Canada Ltd, 10 Alcorn Avenue,
Toronto, Ontario, Canada M4V 3B2
Penguin Books (N.Z.) Ltd, 182–190 Wairau Road,
Auckland 10, New Zealand

Penguin Books Ltd, Registered Offices:
Harmondsworth, Middlesex, England

First published by Signet, an imprint of New American Library, a division
of Penguin Books USA Inc.

First Printing, September, 1991
10 9 8 7 6 5 4 3 2 1

Copyright © Sylvia E. Di Pietro, 1991
All rights reserved

REGISTERED TRADEMARK—MARCA REGISTRADA

PRINTED IN THE UNITED STATES OF AMERICA

Without limiting the rights under copyright reserved above, no part of this
publication may be reproduced, stored in or introduced into a retrieval system, or transmitted, in any form, or by any means (electronic, mechanical,
photocopying, recording, or otherwise), without the prior written permission
of both the copyright owner and the above publisher of this book.

BOOKS ARE AVAILABLE AT QUANTITY DISCOUNTS WHEN USED TO PROMOTE
PRODUCTS OR SERVICES. FOR INFORMATION PLEASE WRITE TO PREMIUM MAR-
KETING DIVISION, PENGUIN BOOKS USA INC., 375 HUDSON STREET, NEW YORK,
NEW YORK 10014.

If you purchased this book without a cover you should be aware that this
book is stolen property. It was reported as "unsold and destroyed" to the
publisher and neither the author nor the publisher has received any payment
for this "stripped book."

For my husband,
Richard A. Rehbock
and in memory of my parents,
Flora and Silvio Di Pietro

ACKNOWLEDGMENTS

Writing a book is indeed a group endeavor and it is difficult to name everyone who gave aid and comfort during its year of birth. I would be remiss, however, not to thank my editor, Matthew Sartwell, whose active support and efforts made this work possible.

I am also eternally grateful to my clients and friends who, by sharing their personal experiences allowed me to learn and grow, both as a numerologist and as an individual.

A special note of love and appreciation goes to Ruth Hersh, my second mother, who has always been there for me, adding encouragement and moral support when I needed it the most.

As always, I count myself a lucky person to have attracted into my life such a warm and loving family and blessed to have such a wonderful son. Here's to you, Charles.

CONTENTS

PART II: THE LETTERS

INTRODUCTION

The Spirit of Numerology and What It Can Do for You

We live in an age when self-discovery through inner growth is not only emphasized and encouraged but has also found a warm, receptive audience. As people become more cognizant of their own personal power and potential and understand their inner world, they manifest and materialize their creative visualizations, ambitions, and desires in their outer world.

It is no wonder that in this environment numerology, the science of numbers, is experiencing a rebirth of interest, for by simply adding and subtracting the numbers 1 through 9, much insight and guidance can be gleaned—more by this method than by any other—not only about ourselves and our loved ones, but also about how to live every day, month, and year of our lives with peace and harmony.

Numerology, the science of numbers, is based on vibration. Today scientists tell us that everything in the universe vibrates, and that in one way or another, we are all affected. The numbers that make up your birthday, month, and year, as well as the letters in your name at birth, constitute the architectural blueprint of these vibrations. These numbers and letters represent your starting point in this life, the plans upon which you will construct your life, the source of all your personal power.

With the aid of numerology, you can tap into this source and use the numbers to guide you in any area of your life, whether it be personal, business, or spiritual. In our study of numerology, these vibrations are given to the numbers 1 through 9. Eleven and 22 are *Master* numbers, with a higher vibrational rate.

In this book you will discover the many wonderful ways that numerology can harmonize stress points in your life. Just by adding a few numbers you can select a new profession, pick your wedding day, name your baby, or choose a new home. Numerology will also help you understand instantly why you and some friend or beau are so attracted or dissimilar to each other.

By discovering your *Life Path* number (the road you chose to take at birth) you will further uncover what to expect during the three major cycles of your life. You will be able to express perfectly your own dynamic talents, gifts, and challenges in conjunction with your *Birthday* number.

Your *Achievement* number can show you what you *must* accomplish in order to be successful. Your *Pinnacles of Attainment* can guide you to greater growth and success during major periods of your life. Your *Challenges* can act as signposts, warning of the type of obstacles that you can expect along the way and alerting you to constructive ways of overcoming them in a joyous and productive manner.

It is easy to let numerology work for you. Use it in selecting your lucky lotto numbers, your most effective colors, and the most beneficial foods to eat. Whether you are buying a car or selling your home, numerology will hold the key to the most beneficial timing in your life. Undoubtedly, you will discover that a decision made against the tide will be fraught with problems and disappointments. If you go back and check out your numbers, you are sure to discover that you made a move at the wrong time.

If we are to live in harmony with life and our universe, we must determine first our own rate of vibration and what urges and desires it attracts. Then we can develop an effective way to adjust and heighten the many different vibrations around us.

PART I

THE NUMBERS

CHAPTER 1

Your Highway to Success—The Life Path Number

No matter who you are, you've got a *Life Path*, or birth force, number. Your Life Path number is determined subconsciously before your birth as a foundation upon which to build your life. It symbolizes all the positive lessons you have already learned from past lives, as well as the character attributes that you can successfully utilize and count on in this life.

Your Life Path number is the number around which most of the important experiences of your life revolve. It is important that you build upon it, therefore, for the realization and perfection of this number will lead you to greater fulfillment. It is the single most important number to compute in numerology, and it is found by adding the month, day, and year of your birth.

Computing your Life Path number is simple and can be found in two ways. I suggest that you employ both methods in order not to miss important Master numbers, which will be discussed later. The easiest method is to set up an addition equation. Just add together the month, day, and year you were born, and reduce your answer to a single digit. Before you do so, however, it is important to understand that as a Life Path number, the Master numbers 11 and 22 are never reduced to a single digit. If you arrive at these two numbers, do not reduce your answer further.

Method number 1

Now let's set up our equation for Flora, born on December 28, 1948. Just add together the numbers $12 + 28 + 1948$. The addition looks as follows:

```
  12     Number of month
  28     Number of day
1948     Number of year
1988 =   1+9+8+8=26=2+6=8
```

Flora's Life Path number is 8.

There is a faster way to compute the Life Path number, but if you use this method, caution must be exercised so that you don't drop a Master number unknowingly.

Method number 2

In method number 2, first reduce the numbers of the month, day, and year, and then add the three totals together. Using Flora's birthday again, let's compute the Life Path number employing method number 2:

MONTH	DAY	YEAR
12	/ 28	/ 1948
1+2=3	2+8=10=1+0=1	1948=1+9+4+8=22=2+2=4
3	+ 1	+ 4=8

It is strongly recommended that you compute the Life Path number using both techniques. Frequently you will observe when computing the Life Path number for the numbers 2 and 4, employing the first method, that your numbers will be 20 or 40 before you reduce them. Using the second technique, the Life Path numbers will show up as 11 and 22. When this occurs, keep in mind that, with Master numbers 11 and 22, often the individual cannot always carry the heavy vibratory rate and awesome power that the Master numbers, 11 and 22, hold. In many instances, the person unconsciously reduces these vibrations to their lower interpretations. Numerologists often write them as 11/2 and 22/4. In this case the general meanings of both 11 and 2, and 22 and 4, must be read.

Now let's discuss the meaning of the Life Path numbers 1 through 9, and the meaning of the Master numbers 11 and 22. Always remember that the Life Path number is a number that you selected to follow. You can take advantage of the benefit and purpose behind it. It will point in the direction of where you will succeed naturally and easily.

Each Life Path number has positive, passive, and negative qualities, as well as signifying an introverted or extroverted personality. Numbers that point to introverted qualities include all the odd numbers: 1, 3, 5, 7, and 9. People characterized by these numbers like to do things alone. The numbers that claim extroverts are the even numbers: 2, 4, 6, 8, as well as 11 and 22. People characterized by these numbers work and play best with others. Those with introverted numbers and corresponding personalities look within to find the answers to life, while the extroverts—both in number and personality— look outside themselves in order to find their way.

The following section discusses the Life Path numbers 1–9, 11, and 22, and also includes a small section on what some numerologists consider the newer Master numbers, 33 and 44. The 33 can be viewed as a higher octave and Master number of the number 6, and 44 as a higher octave and Master number of the number 8. These Master numbers are mentioned just to enhance your knowledge of them.

The Number 1 Life Path

An odd number, introverted, masculine, ruled by the Sun, there is the possibility of Aries and Leo significantly placed in the natal astrological chart.

Key words: Courage, individualism, leadership, independence, and achievement.

Favorite saying: I'm number one!

Famous people: Betty Friedan   2/4/21

              William J. Fulbright   4/9/05

              Carl Sagan   11/9/34

POSITIVE	PASSIVE	NEGATIVE
original	indifferent	aggressive
active	lazy	arrogant
assertive	changeable	antagonistic
assured	insecure	boastful
courageous	helpless	dictatorial
determined	wimpy	quarrelsome
authoritative	procrastinating	self-centered
inventive	subservient	egotistical
self-reliant	wavering	egocentric
independent	fearful	autocratic
venturesome	indolent	pompous
powerful	weak	conceited
individualistic	impotent	impatient
creative	lacking application	greedy
ambitious	unmotivated	willful
direct	submissive	proud
energetic	reticent	overly talkative

PURPOSE: The purpose of the number 1 Life path is the development of positive goals that will aim you toward achievement and attainment by acting upon original and creative ideas, learning to work alone, learning to discriminate, and lead. In trying to attain and improve upon these qualities, you must develop a realistic and down-to-earth attitude, and depend on your own inner resources to solve life's problems instead of becoming lazy and helpless, leaning on others. Standing tall, acting in a courageous and brave manner, and playing the role of leader will not always be easy. Success will most likely be roadblocked by impatience, boasting, bullying, egotism, egocentrism, and a tendency to vacillate between passive and dependent postures. Do not allow others to make decisions for you by refusing to take responsibility for yourself.

VOCATIONS: inventor, director, writer, engineer, salesperson, promoter, aviator, executive of all types, doctor, entrepreneur, lawyer, administrator.

HOW TO SPOT A PERSON WITH A NUMBER 1 LIFE PATH: With the number 1 personality, don't be misguided by the initial picture of softness or shyness in youth, for regardless of appearance, there's nothing easygoing or wimpy about this number. Underneath, the number 1 is courageously daring, possessing a sense of ironclad determination to lead and succeed. And lead and succeed the number 1 will do, once it gets a handle on its power. Appearing more like a steam roller, the number 1 will charge ahead with lightning speed once it has harnessed its ferocious energy.

The most dynamic and compelling of all the numbers, the number 1 possesses the individuality and creative force that lights the way to courage and greatness. Driven and motivated, it gets what it sets out to do. Conscious of itself but often appearing self-centered, willful, and secretly arrogant, the needs of the number 1 come first. Don't make the number 1 wait—it must have instant gratification.

The number 1 personaltiy type is so headstrong, it could have been a head banger as a tot. Scars in and about the head and forehead may be sure signs of this type of individuality coming to the fore. But nothing keeps the number 1 down for long, not even fear of failure. The number 1 may be shaken more than most people, but no one will ever know it. It prefers a fearless image and would rather be caught dead than weak. It's the momentum of charging forward that allows the number 1 to work with and overcome the fear that may exist within.

By now you've guessed correctly that there are two sides to this critter. At times the number 1 is said to be introverted, but there is nothing passive about it, only the image projected by those 1's that like *pretending* to be introverted, passive, meek, and helpless. Committed to a cause, the number 1's forceful, friendly manner will take it straight to the top. Remember, this type of personality leads from the forefront. That includes barking out the orders and directives of the day. As a number 1, it may not take advice well—because it's being in control that counts.

The number 1 represents the birth of new ideas and all that is unique and different in our world. It hates the dull and boring aspects of living. You'll find this kind of temperament generally in a profession of its own or at the head of a chosen career. The leader of broad undertakings, the make-up of the number 1 Life Path is such that it sets the standard that others will follow.

Without the number 1, there are no beginnings. No matter where its strength takes you, it possesses the hidden knowledge of what is to be. It thinks and plans on a mental level, fortified by a natural quality to be the boss and work alone, even as it cultivates the qualities of design and engineering needed to launch worthwhile enterprises.

One is the number of motion. It represents the doer, the self-starter. The number 1 is often consumed by the action of the moment, dashing here and there to get some project off the ground. A word to the wise, if you live or do business with this kind of prototype, patience and follow-up are not among its sterling attributes, so make sure that a strong backup detail is in place.

Show it respect, stroke its strong ego, let it know you understand its lofty purpose, and you'll find no one more loyal and generous than the dashing, daring, courageous number 1.

The Number 2 Life Path

An even number, an extrovert, feminine, ruled by the Moon, there is the possibility of Virgo, Libra, or Scorpio significantly placed in the natal astrological chart.

Key words: Cooperation, peacemaker, diplomacy, tact, persuasion, and adaptability.

Favorite saying: Join me—I hate to do anything alone.

Famous people:		
John Glenn		7/18/21
Roone Arledge		7/8/31
Henry Kissinger		5/27/23

POSITIVE	PASSIVE	NEGATIVE
agreeable	tactless	blunt
considerate	discourteous	scheming
cooperative	unsure	cold-hearted
responsive	wimpy	bull-headed
tolerant	spineless	disparaging
sincere	unconcerned	callous
flexible	unambitious	overly sensitive
musical	careless	spiritless
gregarious	sluggish	intolerant
contributor	disinterested	reproachful
diplomatic	ill-mannered	disapproving
tactful	insensitive	crass
persuasive	aloof	quarrelsome
statistical-minded	sloppy	duplicitous
cordial	fearful	inhospitable

PURPOSE: Your purpose as a person who chose a number 2 Life Path is to develop diplomacy: the ability to bring inharmonious factions together, weigh both sides of an issue, and bring about a peaceful solution. As an exemplar of the number 2 Life Path, you must cultivate being a good follower and companion, while working in a peaceful manner with others. One of the numbers you work well with is the number 1 type, from whom you can take orders and effectively and persuasively pass them along to others.

As a number 2 personality, you must overcome a periodic sense of shyness and insecurity in order to become an effective companion and coworker. Remember, absolutely nothing worthwhile in this life is possible without the assistance of a number 2, who smoothes out the rough edges as it gets things done. Always remember, your assets are needed by others.

VOCATIONS: musician, entertainer, statistician, all forms of banking, mechanic, technician, artist, programmer, host, mediator.

A TYPICAL NUMBER 2: Trying to describe the dual nature of the number 2's Life Path can be difficult at times. It may thoroughly surprise you to discover that beneath many a 2's character is the sincere intention to make peace. To the observer, the number 2 may seem arbitrary, cranky, and overly "picky," but if you're around this type of temperament for any length of time, you'll understand that it's just trying not to provoke, to be supportive in some way or another—even if you don't understand what the "other" is.

Since they are generally modest and tactful, you will not find these sensitive, harmonious sweethearts riding naked and bareback down the center of town or being shot headfirst out of a cannon. The number 2 is not geared for showy emotional displays or for challenging the Big Bang theory, but should the "tender-hearted" maiden be considered or told outright that she's less than perfect, fastidious, and fair, it very well could ignite the fuse that shoots off a barrage of verbal whiplashing possible only from the sour mouth of the "terrible 2." This type does not take criticism well. On a more delicate note, offend its sensitive feelings and one might as well put out a flood watch. Not even overflow valves will save the bystander from being emotionally moved when the tears come.

Either way, it will be instantly apparent that the number 2 does not appreciate being thought ill of, and if one wants to maintain a friendship, it's better to comment on its rather meticulous, clean, spick-and-span, well-groomed appearance. That way harmony will reign, and everyone will breathe easier.

Number 2's do not like to do anything alone, and seldom will they volunteer for top leadership positions, but if you've found one that does, you had better check again—you may be viewing an 11.

As an observer of this type of nature, you will notice that it shines in the art of tactful diplomacy. On the governmental, corporate, and institutional ladders of success, the 2 finds success as an artful mountain climber, stepping straight up to receive recognition all the way. Perhaps the 2's greatest achievement is in the manner in which it brings conflicting parties together.

A 2 personality seems to have an innate sense of just when to don its velvet gloves. It possesses knowledge of how to handle even the most unmanageable of monsters. Without fire-and-brimstone speeches, it can turn all warring factions into kissing cousins—or close to it.

Mostly unhappy when left alone, the vital forces of the number 2 come alive when utilizing the art of persuasion to accomplish what others cannot do. Slowly, but surely, it will gather up all the facts, statistics, and information necessary to change the opinions of those who count. Then it becomes the natural leader, sought after by all.

You could say that it possesses impeccable timing, as well as a sense of rhythm. Confronted by a decision, it will pick two from column A and one from column B, dance through all the arguments, listen attentively, and then, at the precise moment, arrive at a decision that is fair and equitable, one that even Solomon wouldn't question.

Psychically, this personality type is attuned to even the smallest of details—it doesn't miss much and is famous for snatching success from the jaws of failure. It may be harder as a number 2, however, to look away; at times a 2 may prefer to make a snappy, sharp comment. Moreover, the comments can have a stinging quality—the type that leaves others hurt and bleeding without knowing why. When this happens, even its friends will not always know how to take the number 2.

Those who have chosen the 2 Life Path have great technical ability and are masterful in professions that require golden hands and precision. They also excel and can expect success in professions that cater to the laws of sound, space, and light. The number 2 can achieve status in the radio and TV industry as a technician, or as a host of talk shows dealing with the latest issues, giving full play to both sides of the story.

So, the next time you think you see a methodical, rather dandy, soft, shy, and pleasing type of individual, beware: It would be wiser not to comment in haste or jump to any conclusions. Wait patiently and peer behind the veil of secrecy. You could be viewing a 2 who has friends in some very high places.

The Number 3 Life Path

An odd number, an introvert, ruled by Jupiter, there is the possibility of Sagittarius or Libra significantly placed in the natal astrological chart.

Key words: Joy, creativity, self-expression
Favorite saying: Where's the party?

Famous people: Edward M. Kennedy   2/22/32
               Jeane Kirkpatrick   11/19/26
               Ann Landers   7/4/18

POSITIVE	PASSIVE	NEGATIVE
creative	bored	faddish
happy	indifferent	gloomy
optimistic	melancholy	pessimistic
imaginative	unmoved	ostentatious
effervescent	cheerless	verbose
appreciative	petty	complaining
friendly	distant	hostile
sociable	timid	gossipy
enthusiastic	reserved	snobbish

PURPOSE: Your purpose as a number 3 Life Path participant is to develop a sense of joy and exuberance for life and for people; to develop the special creative talents that you possess in the fields of artistic expression, such as writing, acting, public speaking, and music. Three must learn to shed happiness and joy everywhere it goes and to help others cultivate the value of open communication in a warm and friendly atmosphere. It is the job of the 3 to make life a source of hope for others.

VOCATIONS: artist, cosmetician, musician, actor, writer, speaker, advertiser, public speaker, the drama field, all forms of psychic pursuits.

A TYPICAL NUMBER 3: It doesn't necessarily take dancing with a chicken or wearing a lamp shade to make the point: A number three in action is hard to miss. Bubbling over with self-expression, probably talking a blue streak, the number 3 is the quintessential joy-giver, dedicated to educating the earthbound by making them aware of brilliance and beauty.

A dreamer by nature and never truly practical, the number 3 paints visions of heaven on earth with broad strokes. No matter how the story is told, it's bound to be colorful. Forever young, a curious child at heart, the number 3 sells love and enthusiasm the way fairies sell dew drops. This inspiration and merriment has great commercial value, for the number 3 possesses the skill and power to attract the rewards without the work. Moreover, it possesses more luck than the other numbers and is usually the one who finds the $100 bills flying in the wind.

Born with the gift of prophetic vision, this Life Path sparkles as a writer, comedian, or actor. Its artistic soul flourishes in the areas of lecturing, speech writing, and advertising. This is no surprise, since the 3 vibrates to the written and spoken word.

Open and friendly, blessed with the "gift of gab," the number 3 is a natural promoter. But don't be hoodwinked into thinking that something is wrong if the lips and tongue stop moving, however infrequently that may be. You can bet on the fact that the 3's creative brain will soon be charging full speed ahead again.

Sometimes it can be difficult to forgive the 3. Statistically more 3's suffer from foot-in-mouth disease than any other number. But beneath that nonstop chattiness lies a warm, good-natured heart that rings with joy and laughter. If you peek beyond the restless and periodic "down" moods, not to mention the bouts of sweeping exaggeration and extravagance, you will discover a real inner glow. The glow comes from the iridescent reflective quality of the angel dust that the 3 sprinkles everywhere it goes.

Don't be sidetracked, either, by the mild and overall gentle nature of some 3's. This personality makes for a quick, clever, and shrewd businessperson. Ambition can be fierce. Naïve or vulnerable the 3 is not. This type will use its psychic senses to know just when to hold and when to fold on any projects or deals that are in the works.

Some of the most creative 3's can be seen working for America's top advertising, cosmetic, and fashion giants. These fields are famous for attracting fistfuls of 3's, guiding the masses toward this or that color, product, or style. The 3 is an expert when it comes to luxury.

If you think you are beginning to understand the number 3, there's more. Although gifted with the magic power of the word and apt to speak out of turn now and then, this type may turn its unforgiving back and walk away for a lifetime for what is said to it. If you want to stay friends, accept the contradictions and character flaws. Let the 3 do the talking, and keep your banter on the light side. Whatever the cost, humanity will always be quick to forgive and love the number 3, for without it we are sure to lose all that is creative, funny, magical, and charming in our very existence.

The Number 4 Life Path

An even number, an extrovert, ruled also by the Sun, there is the possibility of Taurus or Capricorn significantly placed in the natal astrological chart.

Key words: Order, work, discipline, limitations, practical.
Favorite saying: Who has time? I'm working.

Famous people: Edward I. Koch   12/12/24
              George McGovern   7/19/22
              Howard Cosell   3/25/20

POSITIVE	PASSIVE	NEGATIVE
dedicated	haphazard	inflexible
confident	careless	narrow-minded
disciplined	lazy	crude
methodical	slipshod	dogmatic
dignified	lax	discourteous
economical	impractical	restricted
constructive	unaccountable	unyielding
reasonable	indifferent	headstrong
serious	uncommitted	thick-skinned
trustworthy	incompetent	dishonest

PURPOSE: Your purpose as a number 4 is to construct, adjust, and organize your life, home, and business activities in an orderly fashion. As a number 4, your talent lies in your ability to labor slowly and efficiently over details, building your life brick by brick, upon a solid foundation, making as few mistakes as possible and improving upon the old.

You may not move swiftly, as it is against your inner nature to jump into things haphazardly. Patiently taking time to smooth over all the edges of any project seems to a number 4 like the only correct way of achieving anything worthwhile and lasting in life.

As a number 4, you are undaunted by the long haul. The thought of working hard and in a systematic fashion is not frightening or burdensome to you. To the outsider, however, it can appear to be a restricting, limiting, monotonous, and boring process. To you, redoing a project is just a step toward creating something perfect. Your gift is your staying power.

Following your Life Path, you are a builder of home, community, business, and country. You display great honesty and integrity, perseverance and determination. You offer rock-solid dependability. Your pronounced mathematical talents can place you in positions requiring exactness and an ability to call forth form in a tangible way. Your feet are always firmly planted on the ground.

VOCATIONS: builder, contractor, mechanic, accountant, business owner, manager, real estate agent, architect, manager and laborer.

A TYPICAL NUMBER 4: Examine the clothes closet of a typical number 4 and you'll find Old World classics: herringbones, medium lapels, and conservative styles. Moreover, check the threads on the garments—they're strong and durable. Need more proof? Check the 4's attitudes, outlooks: The body may be slow-moving, but the brain is fast, spitting forth calculations with lightning speed. Still, don't expect the number 4 to decide anything quickly. It may be looking for an angle. It will churn the facts and figures over a few times just to be sure.

The number 4 likes to regulate and engineer the machinery that runs humanity. The salt of the earth, the earth-plane director, it moves forward with hidden strength, step by step, inching toward stability. The most fixed and stubborn of all the Life Paths, try to push this number into quickening its pace, and expect to witness the bull's blind rage. The number 4 does not like to be rushed. It's not inclined to take many chances, either, especially with money. The 4 is careful and economical, and enjoys saving money and accumulating power. A good round of golf on Saturday is a perfect way for this type to tie together all the facets of the money-power stakes. Number 4's can attain supreme happiness watching the bank account grow. The grass in its backyard could also bring enjoyment: It's the same color as money—green. The connection may be deeper than expected: The 4 is as bonded to land as it is to money, so don't expect it to part with either easily. An ultimate bargain hunter, the 4 has plans for its wealth: more often than not, it's buying more land.

Conscientious, serious, and a bit bullheaded, right or wrong, the number 4 glues himself to a secure position and inflexible opinions. If you want to win with this personality type, attack the foundation of your opponent's argument first. By doing so, you'll catch the 4 at a weak spot, and at least it may listen—may!

Dedicated and strongly attached to home and family, the number 4 will handle domestic responsibilities with the same loyal devotion, thrift, and practicality that it displays in its business dealings, PTA involvement and Elks Club membership.

Typically a health nut, 4's don't get sick often unless it's due to overwork. Moreover, you can anticipate that a 4 probably wrote the latest vitamin or "how to" book. Sickness is taboo: It keeps the 4 away from the mansion or business it's building brick by brick.

It's true, the 4's actions are predictable. This type does move along at a snail's pace, but it's the only tempo that makes good sense to the 4. Like the tortoise, it knows that Haste makes waste; getting carried along by the drama of life just isn't the 4's style.

An exemplary 4 is industrious, honest, traditional, and practical. With a well-defined sense of established order, a 4 in your corner is a good friend. Its thoroughness will save you a lot of headaches. The fireworks may not go off daily, but down the road the individual in this Life Path will have a strong financial base and an established security unrivaled by any other number.

The Number 5 Life Path

An odd number, an introvert, ruled by Mercury, there is the possibility of Gemini or Leo predominantly placed in the natal astrological chart.

Favorite saying: I can do anything you can do, better.
Key words: Versatile, active, free, independent, progressive, accepting of change.

Famous people: Walter Cronkite   11/4/16
                Harry Blackmun   11/12/08
                Lee A. Iacocca   10/15/24

POSITIVE	PASSIVE	NEGATIVE
independent	inactive	impulsive
intuitive	spiritless	fearful
spontaneous	stagnant	restless
opportunistic	fearful of change	overactive
convivial	colorless	shallow
flexible	undecided	frenzied
enthusiastic	passionless	nervous
versatile	dull	eccentric
unconventional	hesitant	impetuous
enterprising	old-fashioned	frivolous

PURPOSE: Your purpose as a number 5 is to learn to use freedom constructively, to be a go-getter and not fear change. As a number 5, you enjoy a life of travel, adventure, and great versatility, but while doing so you must also guard against being superficial, frivolous and lacking in application or direction. A fluent communicator, adept at promoting a number of projects at one time, you are often envied for your varied life. Mercurial, multifaceted, fun-loving, and always more youthful than the other numbers, you must guard against over indulging in sex, drugs, gambling, and money and must apply yourself resourcefully so that you don't live irresponsibly, a rolling stone gathering no moss.

Positioned at the midpoint in the cycle of numbers, you are capable of experiencing the peaks of greatness and the depths of misery. You engage in activities with zeal and inquisitiveness. Your forward-looking and constructive efforts bring a measure of success unachieved by any other number. When you allow your negative traits to triumph, however, you can expect to be miserable, suffering from your excesses more than most. As a number 5, you must learn not to get stuck in a rut or be foolishly impulsive, but to act when the timing is right and the opportunities present themselves.

VOCATIONS: travel agent, promoter, publicist, investor, newspaper writer, politician, analyst, detective, occultist, salesman, film director, advertising.

HOW TO SPOT A NUMBER 5: Now you see him, now you don't. It's not a magician or a disappearing act you are witnessing, but the antics of the person who has chosen a number 5 Life Path. Here one second and gone the next, the number 5 is the most curious of all the numbers, and, like quicksilver, with the nervous energy of a popcorn machine operated by Jumping Jack Flash, the number 5 can change lovers and life styles more often and more quickly than any other personality.

Since number 5's are attracted to speed and excitement the way a racer takes to the track, you will know you've run into a sixty-year-old number 5 when you are invited to witness the senior division motorcross competition.

Yes, yes, there are quieter 5's who are more subdued and less addicted to walking on the wild side straight into the unknown, but get caught in a traffic jam and even the more stagnant type will treat you to a scenic tour of every bombed-out backstreet in town. Then after arriving home, luckily in one piece, the number 5 will eat and head off to catch the fifth race at the track, where Flora's Boy Gary is predicted to win.

It's one adventure after another with a number 5. Your secret to peaceful coexistence is your ability to carry a long leash, portable phone, or beeper!

Because of the 5's irresistible urge to keep things going, this number makes the best administrators. The 5 may not be truly "executive," but it is a natural leader in the art of wearing more than one hat and juggling several endeavors at once. Excellent powers of observation allow the number 5 to spot trouble with lightning speed—an attribute that can save you trauma and expense in the long run.

There is never a dull moment in the life of a 5 or anyone coexisting with one. Fives have a flair for living and a knack for spotting the new and different. A good talker and fine speaker, the number 5 can always be found promoting and selling some new something. Every day is devoted to one wish: "Let's make a deal!" As you may have already guessed by now, more con artists have chosen the number 5 Life Path than any other number.

The 5 usually wins top honors in human relations. No matter what the profession, the 5 can always be found pushing humanity forward, furthering the boundaries of knowledge on any given subject. While the 5 is not a domesticated animal (swimming through a tidal wave may be easier than getting this tornado to say "I do"), once ball-and-chained, this personality type will spoil the kids and shower them with fun, games, and amusement parks. Baby-sitting and housework will probably be out of the picture, unless your number 5 Life Path participant has a 4 birthday, and even then it's just *maybe*. But taking the kids to the movies while you do the shopping is a piece of cake.

Nothing in life ever changes without the number 5, and existence could prove monotonous without the excitement it engenders. Just remember, the secret is in the leash, the phone, and the beeper!

The Number 6 Life Path

An even number, an extrovert, ruled by Venus, there is the possibility of Cancer or Pisces significantly placed in the natal astrological chart.

Favorite saying: I'll take care of you.

Key words: Responsibility, humanitarianism, justice, harmony.

Famous people: Patricia Schroeder   7/30/40
       Barbara Jordan   2/21/36
       Erma Bombeck   2/21/27

POSITIVE	PASSIVE	NEGATIVE
humanitarian	lax	irresponsible
adjustable	impersonal	unyielding
benevolent	inhospitable	vindictive
sharing	self-seeking	possessive
supportive	indifferent	pessimistic
appreciative	biased	fault-finding
trustworthy	dishonest	suspicious
charitable	unsympathetic	ungracious
dutiful	unaccountable	unreliable
honorable	disloyal	resentful
happy	melancholy	hostile
philanthropic	uninvolved	unfeeling

PURPOSE: Your purpose, having chosen a number 6 Life Path, is to learn to assume responsibility, to share with others, to give freely of wise counsel, and to teach and work toward the betterment of mankind. You must be satisfied to share the fruits of your labors, riches, comforts, and happiness with others, while instructing them in all that is just, honorable, and good. Your creativity as a number 6 is usually at its zenith when you are providing products and comforts for the home or personal adornment.

You may say that you know ten 6's besides yourself and that nobody's a teacher by profession. Take another look. See that line forming around the block? They're people who line up early to seek your advice on everything from garbage to gambling.

As a number 6, you must be aware of your soft side: being overly sensitive to criticism. You prefer giving it to receiving it. This sensitivity, added to your need to be perfect, can let you be knocked out of balance by an unkind word or your own inability to adjust to circumstances. Even a casual observer doesn't have to be a rocket scientist to know that you can be the cause of your own undoing.

Your negative side can lead to romantic problems, divorce, and downright misery. You may prefer to be married, but you may also be unaware that a necessary ingredient of domestic harmony is the ability to adjust to whatever comes your way. It won't hurt you to soften some of your stronger opinions, either.

VOCATIONS: singer, decorator, artist, painter, teacher, educator, nurse, adviser, beautician, social worker, counselor, lawyer, public speaker.

HOW TO SPOT THE NUMBER 6: Listen carefully to the voice! Its tone suggests authority, responsibility, and knowledge. You'll know it's a 6 when you hear pearls of wisdom or catchy phrases like, "I don't want to be rich, I just want to live that way!"

Life usually compensates the number 6 in some way. At times, the 6 will handle large sums of money and responsibility. And, like the 3 and 9 Life Paths, its earning power will be vast. The crowning gift for being the world's greatest social worker will be an overabundance of money and the luxuries that go with it.

The 6, more than any other number, will dedicate its life to doing things for and taking care of others. Its deep-seated desire to make life harmonious, coupled with a strong sense of right and wrong, truth and justice, lands the 6 some sought-after jobs, where duty and service are required. It also sometimes puts the 6 in hot water for objecting at the wrong time or voicing an opinion too strenuously—but never mind about that, we won't be negative.

Like the 3 and the 9, the 6 receives just compensation for what it does, but unlike the other two numbers, it *demands* that it be paid well for services rendered. It's a good thing it does, for this type possesses a mystical reverence for the finest in art, beauty, and luxury items. It needs the money to purchase its "necessities."

Fine foods, clothing, houses, cars, jewels—as in diamonds, rubies, and emeralds—are practically staples for the number 6. After all, it makes sense to buy only the best. If you're a 6's lover, you stand to benefit from its astute business sense, that marvelous quality that makes it possible to purchase only the most brilliant in jewels or furs. Be lavish with praise when the Tiffany boxes arrive and then wait to see if next year's gifts don't top them. As you may have gathered, being praised, noticed, appreciated, and needed are extremely important to the 6.

The six is not called the cosmic parent for nothing. Like a kind mother or wise father, the 6 can be found generously caring for and helping those in need, unselfishly giving of its time and precious advice. At some point in its life you will find it teaching what it knows best: lessons involving truth, justice, and history. Speaking about history, you might become it if you don't absolutely love, adore, and have the same tremendous reverence that the 6 has for its own—family history, that is.

The 6 can give to its friends and loved ones to the point of exhaustion, considering it both a privilege and a pleasure to serve. Remember that the 6's family relationship is never casual. Besides, it's easier to make a big fuss, bite your tongue, and keep all opinions to yourself. When the 6 spouts forth opinions, just listen.

Despite, or because of, shouldering the weight of the world and the burdens of selfless caring and sharing, you should know that 6's are the greatest of lovers, too. Remember the mink? As long as you absolutely love the way you're being showered with attention and affection, you will bear witness to the finest that life has to offer. Providing a secure home and the best of everything forms the necessary backbone so vital to the number 6's existence. Just don't forget that the opinions of this type are fixed and often rigid, not to mention powerful. If you're smart, you will always make the 6 as right as possible, within reason. Remember, the 6's, like the 2's, can't take criticism well. Besides, it is quite a sentimental number, so each year look to more of better and then to the best. It will ultimately pay off.

The 6's artistic talents provide humanity with an elevated style of fine living. Many lines of endeavor call for the 6's superiority in design, providing products fit for a king. Whether it be food, fashion, or flowers, you can bank on the fact that whatever the 6 produces will be of high quality, the latest in conservative chic, and *expensive*.

So, now you've got the secret: Allow the 6 to brighten the corners of your life, love, respect; appreciate the way it handles your life, and then sit back and enjoy it.

The Number 7 Life Path

An odd number, an introvert, ruled by Neptune, there is the possibility of Scorpio or Aquarius significantly placed in the natal astrological chart.

Key words: wisdom, understanding, truth, analysis, spiritual, specialization.

Favorite saying: I analyze!

Famous people:

George Bush		6/12/24
Helen Gurley Brown		2/18/22
Leslie Stahl		12/16/41

POSITIVE	PASSIVE	NEGATIVE
analytical	superficial	incompetent
intuitive	dull	critical
contemplative	short-sighted	agnostic
studious	untrained	impatient
imaginative	lack of depth	bigoted
dignified	aloof	proud
solitary	fear of loneliness	reclusive
precise	illiterate	extremist
learned	simple-minded	eccentric
technical	undeveloped	impractical
calm	awkward	nervous
intellectual	unenlightened	pedantic
dependable	ineffectual	cunning

PURPOSE: Your purpose as a number 7 Life Path participant is to specialize in a chosen field, to appraise and evaluate the worth of all things in a calm, detached, and peaceful environment, and to seek out and develop a sense of wisdom and truth.

As a number 7, you are most often a loner, with a philosophical bent, and not materially inclined. You seek to understand the mysteries of life. You require a quiet, peaceful environment, free from stress and turmoil. The number 7 is considered a sacred number: You may be attracted to spiritual pursuits in one form or another. Basically you gravitate toward and prefer to associate with those involved in deep scientific, analytical, spiritual, or inspired thought.

VOCATIONS: scientist, chemist, mathematician, medicine, law, occult studies, technical analyst, researcher, criminologist, writer, surgeon, dietician, cinematographer.

HOW TO SPOT A NUMBER 7: So your darling looked up, gazed at your face, and asked, "Why is your nose so chiseled? Why are your eyes so blue? Why are your teeth so crooked? Why is your hair so red? Why do you think birds fly?" If you feel cornered, don't panic: You're simply being inspected, dissected, and cross-examined by a number 7 in search of wisdom and truth—your hidden wisdom and truth. You will survive.

The 7 has a charming manner and pleasing personality that hides a secretive vital force in a case hardened like steel. Beneath this cool, calm, and seldom chatty exterior lies the power of nuclear fission.

The number 7 was born to behold in its visions and dreams the realities of powers unseen, to understand all phases of life and death, to investigate, analyze, and then master the facts and reasons of mankind's existence. Care to take another look at the 7 who's staring at your teeth?

Save yourself the aggravation: Accept the fact that the 7 is at heart a thinker, gentle and kind, but usually unemotional and most of the time consumed in deep thought. Think twice before you ask the 7 the truth about your new hairdo; but if you do decide to take the chance, you may need to get your brake linings checked first—

the answer you receive might stop you dead in your tracks. If you're sensitive, it might be wiser to go to a 3 for an opinion, unfortunate as it may seem. The number 7 can be brutally honest.

Most 7's don't engage in much playful talk or superficial activity; their senses are generally tuned in to loftier spheres of influence. Always snooping into some dark corner of the unknown, the number 7 is forever the scientist, the researcher, the inventor, discovering hidden secrets. So while you may have thought that your visionary was building sand castles in the air, the realist was really at work laying the foundation for a solution to the problems of the day. It's therefore no surprise that many of our greatest presidents had number 7 prominent somewhere in their numerological chart.

In human relations the 7 can appear the lone wolf, distant and self-contained, engulfed in its own neurotic concerns and lacking in self-expression. However, it may be that the 7 has just discovered its own imperfection (a curious fact that all 7's find hard to accept) and is quite depressed and uncomfortable.

Whatever you do, don't ask the 7 why—why this, that, or anything! Learn the secret of successful public relations, especially with this type. It asks the questions, and you answer them! It's that plain and simple. Never appear foolish or stupid. A dumb statement can knock you clear out of the ballpark forever.

This personality is a prober, a digger, the one who rows down unexplored waters. It refuses to take life at face value but delves under the surface to see what's really there. As such it often becomes the specialist, an expert in highly technical fields, which can include areas of spirituality and mysticism. When well adjusted, the 7 will be greatly admired and appreciated for its talents, accomplishments, and superior mental powers.

Never interrupt the 7's solitude. While not domestically inclined or conventionally religious by nature, this number does respond to occult and metaphysical thought. It needs time alone in order to plug into altered states of consciousness.

Without a doubt, this silent steel monolith travels on a different wavelength than most people, but then again, the number 7 isn't ordinary. When its true place has been found, mankind will beat a path to the 7's door, eager to receive its pearls of wisdom.

The Number 8 Life Path

An even number, an extrovert, ruled by Saturn, there is the possibility of Capricorn significantly placed in the natal astrological chart.

Key words: Organization, judgment, balance, material success, authority, power.

Famous saying: I rule!

Famous people: Andy Rooney   1/14/19
               Gerald R. Ford   7/14/13
               Robert Dole   7/22/23

POSITIVE	PASSIVE	NEGATIVE
powerful	defenseless	tyrannical
decisive	disorganized	restrictive
judgmental	unreliable	rigid
disciplined	disorderly	unyielding
enterprising	fixed	afraid of failure
efficient	slipshod	fanatical
responsible	inept	inconsiderate
influential	uncaring	militant
self-confident	insecure	cold-blooded
pioneering	timid	rebellious
successful	vulnerable	fraudulent
venturesome	cowardly	aggressive

PURPOSE: As a person traveling along a number 8 Life Path, your purpose is to pursue success and satisfaction in the material world in a manner that incorporates honesty, good judgment, and balance. As a number 8, you must balance and weigh your desire for power, wealth, and money and channel your energies into good moral ethics, especially in business.

Since the number 8 is a karmic number, your life can be one of utter misery (bear in mind that what you sow you will reap). If your life is not lived following the straight and narrow, you can expect doom, misery, and financial disaster. Success and attainment on a dynamically large scale, however, is possible for you if you maintain balance and free yourself of abusive practices. Efficient, practical, and calmly stoical, you generally gravitate to large, powerful organizations or institutions, where your talents receive a measure of respect.

VOCATIONS: publisher, writer, banker, government worker, financier, supervisor, real estate agent, athlete, hospital administrator, character analyst, commodities broker, lawyer, archaeologist, antiques dealer.

HOW TO SPOT A NUMBER 8: It's Sunday night and you've stopped by the office to pick up something. Lo and behold, there's a light in yonder window, and someone is hard at the job. As you question what's wrong, you'll be surprised to find out that it's nothing, just some work that's got to get out. The dedicated number 8 is determined to get the job done even if it means going in on weekends. Working overtime comes natural to this type.

The number 8 Life Path is made up of two 4's, and while its masculine side is compelling and demanding, its feminine, passive side can be adaptive to suit the occasion. Whether at home or on the job, this Life Path is epitomized by the authority figure. The number 8 is the one to depend upon, especially in a crunch, when it shines the brightest of all the numbers. In fact, its compelling ambition could cause the 8 to wear out its health. This Life Path tries to be all things to all people. It is sentimentally attached to its home and the thought of land; expect the number 8 to own both, in multiples, before the music ends!

A slow, steady, determined climber, the 8's playground is linked to power, authority, materialism, and money. It knows how to succeed. If 6 A.M. arrivals at work are part of the plan to achieve, expect to see the

8 at 5:30. The number 8 is truly not emotional—ice or steel would be more descriptive of its nature. Yet calmly and cautiously the 8 will silently pull the strings of those in high places until it lands the position of leadership, responsibility, and respect.

Armed with divine awareness, the enlightened and awakened number 8 becomes the mastermind who works for the cause of humanity. Superior organizational skills often land the 8 in positions of prestige and control in the larger power structures. A true disciplinarian, practical and efficient, the number 8 knows no other way to accomplish and achieve its earthly ambitions except by exercising its balanced judgment and executive ability.

The number 8 Life Path, more somber and melancholy than the other numbers, provides the order, knowledge, supervision, and stability that can make the dreams and visions of others concrete. Stern and at times slow-moving, yet calculating every step along the way, the number 8 has a strong work ethic and a solid respect for those who have walked before it, paving the way for achievement.

Those on the number 8 Life Path should never trust to luck. Representing the number of judgment, the 8 can save itself stress and strain by filing its income taxes early and as close to honestly as possible. The 8 must beware in this realm, since one deliberately false move will not leave it laughing. More number 8's, than any other number, will face financial wipe-out at least once in their lifetimes. On the bright side, learning to manage money and property is good practice for the 8's excellent mental powers. This type learns fast. Once burnt, an 8 won't make the same mistake twice.

Unlike those on the 3, 6, and 9 Life Paths, the number 8 does not have a natural attraction to money. Nothing falls into its lap that it hasn't worked for or karmically deserved. Respectful tribute should be given, however, to the 8's tough and steady climb into the upper income brackets. Don't misjudge the slowness, either, since the 8 will never be in a subordinate role for long. With a wealth of contacts originating from some very lofty places, the 8 always knows whom to call in a pinch.

Born old and wise beyond its years, the number 8 learns early that mental strain and frustration are its primary enemy, with lust for power and money not far behind. Often subject to long bouts of depression, time to think and regroup will often place this number back on the spiritual trail and restore its missing humanitarian spirit. Armed with the God-force, the number 8 will be able to re-establish its priorities; it leads all other numbers when it comes to character analysis.

Dependable, trustworthy, and stable, no matter how many shortcuts you take on the important issues, the individual on the number 8 Life Path is one you'll want around for balance and knowledge before making important emotional decisions.

The Number 9 Life Path

An odd number, an introvert, ruled by Mars, with the possibility of Aquarius or Pisces significantly placed in the natal astrological chart.

Keywords: Selflessness, encompassing, humanitarianism, forgiveness, charity, brotherhood.

Famous saying: Hello, brother!

Famous people:

Mario Cuomo		6/15/32
Jimmy Carter		10/1/24
Clare Boothe Luce		4/10/03

POSITIVE	PASSIVE	NEGATIVE
hospitable	detached	greedy
compassionate	impersonal	unsympathetic
idealistic	superficial	prejudiced
benevolent	narrow	avaricious
broad-minded	unconcerned	uninvolved
creative	boring	restrictive
loving	uncaring	resentful
enlightened	distant	narrow-minded
understanding	unfeeling	bitter
humble	wavering	overly willful

POSITIVE	PASSIVE	NEGATIVE
sentimental	unresponsive	thick-skinned
forgiving	withdrawn	hateful

PURPOSE: Your purpose as one who has chosen a number 9 Life Path is to cultivate a sense of brotherhood, selflessness, understanding, compassion, forgiveness, and charity toward humanity in a detached and all-encompassing manner. Desirous of serving, you must engage in universal undertakings and give back to the world some measure of the knowledge, wisdom, and compassion that you've acquired in previous life cycles. As the number of completion, you must learn to incorporate and cultivate the value of forgiveness in order to maintain balance and harmony in your life.

Broad-minded, artistic, imaginative, and creative, when you are working for the good of everyone, you can dramatically and emotionally entertain or enlighten the masses as to the plight of humanity and the rewards of giving.

As a number 9, you don't like to be boxed in; you demand your freedom, preferring to live an unrestricted existence. When pushed too far, you can be shockingly indifferent. Your lesson is to convert your love of people from a personal to an impersonal status so that many can benefit.

Since 9 is the number of love, money, and philanthropy, you will thrive wherever these qualities are needed most and can attain greatness in all fields of endeavor, where your influence will enlighten the masses.

VOCATIONS: dramatist, artist, literary agent, painter, philanthropist, journalist, restaurant owner, entertainer, oil magnate, travel agent, missionary, doctor, lecturer, orator.

HOW TO SPOT THE NUMBER 9: See that character over there sauntering down the street in an outfit that could blow the socks off a fashion critic? Well, that is someone with a number 9 Life Path. Dramatic and artistic, not to mention literary, the number 9 possesses a fetish for fashion combos that can truly reduce the unenlightened to their knees. All number 9's are colorful and honest. If you're interested in one, be prepared to experience the unexpected at every bend in the road. Broad-minded and unconventional, the number 9 character is supported by the qualities of all the other numbers. They may laugh at the way you laugh at them, but will they conform or dance to another's tune? Never!

The number 9 Life Path is committed to the brother-hood of mankind. Its influence is far-reaching and all-embracing. Don't try to lasso a number 9 or tie it down to one activity at a time unless you expect to get burnt. Being pinned down to domestic duties or unwanted chores and obligations will not bring out the 9's sparkling qualities. After all, they are here to bear witness to the whispering truths of life and then serve these truths as a compassionate main course to nourish mankind. To many a 9, however, serving is not isolated from cooking: They do shine in the food business.

Despite a fixation with or innate curiosity about the lives of friends, the number 9 does not seek close attach-ments or intimate alliances. The principle of love func-tions in a more detached manner, a fact that could bruise your ego somewhat. Distance helps the number 9 to sharpen its perceptions—you did want to know how they got so objective, didn't you?

The detached emotional quality and illusiveness of the number 9 could be compared to the vague illusion of trying to catch the wind. It may sound like a delightful goal, but on a more practical note, it can be difficult. Once married and accustomed to harmony and bliss, the number 9 will belong to everyone. After reminding you that love allows freedom, it will then concentrate on doing good and lend-ing a helping hand to the rest of the world.

Take a deep breath if you're in love with a number 9 and then enjoy the ride. The 9, being a high-potency number, finds its crowning achievement in its promotion and portrayal of human understanding, compassion, and forgiveness. It marches to a drumbeat that harmonizes with the music of the spheres. Outstanding intuitive qual-ities allow it to reach top billing, where its artistic and dramatic talents can receive full appreciation. Emotionally it is drawn to the center stage of life.

The reward for this grand and universal endowment to the brotherhood of man can be seen in the ample compensation it receives. Many a 9's wallet has grown fat with fortune and money for its good service. In fact, the Life Path of the number 9 vibrates to both the words "fortune" and "money." Opportunities for the number 9 can span the whole globe. Interest in foreigners and overseas enterprises come naturally, and affairs of the world offer great achievement.

The health of the number 9 is generally topnotch, but should it be denied love and approval or be forced to experience the negative side of life, the number 9 could fall victim to severe mood swings and journeys into pits of depression. Only after a full recovery will the number 9 discover that clinging to faded illusions equates with courting disaster. On the whole, though, the number 9's life will be as colorful and unexpected as the fashions it wears.

The following Master numbers 11 and 22 have higher vibrations than the reduced numbers that they represent. As such, they symbolize the existence of a higher degree of intelligence, and their Life Paths must follow a more lofty purpose than that of the lower numbers. Because of the high frequency and powerful vibrational force of these numbers, the mannerisms of those subject to them can appear erratic, nervous, and high-strung.

These numbers represent the old souls. No person possessing a Master number as a Life Path can exist under the strain of its power and intensity for long periods of time without reducing the vibration to the less stressful and more comfortable lower vibration of the number represented. An 11 Life Path number, therefore, will also show many of the qualities and characteristics of the 2; the 22 Life Path will appear at times as a number 4. The numbers 33/6 and 44/8 are highlighted in this chapter on Life Path numbers, but not incorporated in the main body of this work.

The 11 Life Path Number

An even number, an extrovert, feminine, ruled by the Moon, there is the possibility of Virgo, Libra, or Scorpio significantly placed in the natal astrological chart.
Key words: Inspiration, revelation, and illumination.
Favorite saying: I have a dream!

Famous people: Rose Kennedy 7/22/1890
Jacqueline Onassis 7/28/29
Gloria Vanderbilt 2/20/24

POSITIVE	PASSIVE	NEGATIVE
intuitive	lethargic	misguided
clairvoyant	bumbling	uninformed
poised	high-strung	erratic
perceptive	unaware	overzealous
revealing	aloof	unequivocal
visionary	provincial	warped
inventive	lethargic	unfocused
prophetic	fearful of	vacillating
imaginative	unknown	unenthusiastic
	dull	

PURPOSE: Your purpose as an individual who has chosen a number 11 Life Path is to shed light and illumination wherever you find darkness. Inspired by the God-force, as a number 11, you must guard against being self-seeking, overly high-strung, powerful, hysterical, and more in love with your ideals than you are with people. Your movements and aims, if idealistic and not fanatical, are likely to attract public attention and influence, leaving you in a position of respect and leadership. You must be mindful of personal considerations and the sensitivities of others, however, and maintain contact with the other Life Path numbers.

VOCATIONS: theater, entertainment, voice, politics, communications, psychic, healer, aviator, television, motion pictures, minister.

HOW TO SPOT A NUMBER 11: Saint or sinner, prophet or zealot, clairvoyant revealing hidden truths to the masses, or an opinionated, hysterical fraud—which is it? The key words to describe the number 11 are "illumination" and "inspiration," and whether the number 11 is leading humanity on the largest peace march ever or being shot out of a cannon into the middle of a stadium, it's guaranteed to be the show of a lifetime.

The most idealistic and impractical of all the numbers, 11's have enough nervous tension bottled up within to create many unusual happenings. The important factor to consider in rearing the number 11 is how well members of this number respond to praise and appreciation. Encourage your number 11 to be a crusader in the interest of a good cause.

Too much criticism and lack of direction in childhood could bring out the worst in an 11 personality. The pendulum swings equally in both directions, resulting in the 11's being either very, very good or very, very bad. One minute the 11 will pepper the planet with lofty illumined thoughts and the next moment plan an A-bomb drop. (Check to see if there isn't an 11 hidden somewhere behind the number 2 who has been confusing you.)

You'll recognize the gung-ho number 11 in every walk of life. As the brilliant trial lawyer, the number 11 will treat you to the thrill and suspense of sizzling courtroom drama as it makes chop suey out of its opponent. As the eccentric surgeon, the number 11 will perform the first successful operation of anything that is unique, complicated, and formerly viewed as impossible, and it will probably be done on the wing of an airplane. As the flashy florist, the artistic number 11 will have a string of shops more creative than anything in existence. And as in the case of all 11's, when material thoughts of gain are placed aside, humanity will benefit by the splendor of it all.

The number 11's are not ignored; they're not around long enough. Unusually quick and talkative, they'll converse with themselves if they have to just to keep their thoughts going. The stream of communication that 11's generate and nurture is only one indication of the energy coursing through this Life Path.

The secret of the 11's success is that it is a dual number, with all the ambiguities that doubles denote. At first you won't know which side of the coin is up, but neither will the number 11. Don't dwell on it, though, for while you're trying to figure it out, the number 11 will be off doing two things at once, just to confuse you more.

In romance, you won't be sure on any given day if you'll be experiencing fireworks, a hurricane, or a scene from a horror movie, and despite an often selfish attitude, accompanied by spells of vanity and strong ego displays, the number 11 can develop, through practice, into one outstanding individual, not to mention an understanding mate.

The number 11's role in the development of the universe is to light the way for the benefit of others. Remember, the emphasis is on others and not the self. Material gain is usually not the motive. Frequently the number 11's will prove to be less successful when investing or handling their own money or running commercial establishments. But once this high-powered type turns its sights to acting for others, it is capable of reaching heights unattainable by almost any other number. Sad to say, however, most 11's will never even come close to utilizing half of their awesome potential.

Regardless of their faults, 11's are nonetheless special and colorful. They possess starlike qualities rarely found elsewhere. Just remember, bring your sunglasses. The number 11 is blinding.

The Number 22 Life Path

An even number, an extrovert, ruled by the Sun, there is the possibility of Leo, Taurus, or Capricorn significantly placed in the natal astrological chart.
Key words: The master builder.
Favorite saying: I'm going to build me a kingdom for mankind!

Famous people:	Sam Donaldson	3/11/34
	Hugh Hefner	4/9/26
	Katharine Graham	6/16/17

POSITIVE	PASSIVE	NEGATIVE
forceful	spiritless	pompous
masterful	amateurish	inefficient
compelling	aimless	confused
purposeful	unfocused	oppressive
dynamic	passive	overwhelming
goal-oriented	indifferent	impulsive
authoritative	submissive	domineering
progressive	apathetic	dogmatic
benevolent	negligent	abusive

PURPOSE: Your purpose as a number 22 Life Path number is to advance the plans of humanity on a huge scale. Gifted, possessing the same breath of inspiration as the number 11, you are driven to build on a larger scale and broader scope than the 11 or the 4 and you are so channeled as though you will do it realistically. As a number 22 you have tremendous power to organize and construct, which is generally accompanied by sincerity and an absolute desire for truthfulness. With your single-mindedness to benefit others, the lasting structures you build give humanity a step up to a higher state of consciousness. Positively, you are the ultimate earth-plane director. Negatively, you can become so engrossed in advancing your ego that a loss of ideals may be encountered.

VOCATIONS: founders of large institutions, executives of large organizations, international businessmen and promoters, international bankers, statesmen, diplomats, and statisticians.

HOW TO SPOT A NUMBER 22: At first the number 22 will fool you—you'll be beguiled into thinking that you're dealing with an 11, especially with all that electrical energy and nervous excitement creating sparks in the atmosphere. But look closer and you will notice the reality, an unmistakable sign of authenticity. Therein lies the difference. While the number 11 is off orbiting the earth, the number 22 has the power to combine the 11's idealistic energy with its own gift of constructive organization to create significant change.

The Life Path of the number 22 describes the master builder, an individual who consults a practical blueprint to create for humanity on a mighty, lofty scale. Possessing the characteristics of the double 2, the number 22 spends a great deal of its time harnessing the nervous tension that accompanies the great force within it. Once in control, however, the 22 has the ability to transform the most superb and spectacular visions into concrete form. Achievement- and goal-oriented, the 22 creates with an impressive scope and magnitude. You'll be in awe as you see the 22 view tomorrow through unorthodox eyes. Often the dynamic perceptions of the number 22 are not available or even understood by others.

The number 22 operates on the high-potency wavelength of the 11, but adds to this the grounded sophistication of the 4. It doesn't embellish the dream but makes it happen. The 22 has the ability to channel its superior innate wisdom concerning material problems into feats of great imagination and accomplishment. Often its commercial, business, and philanthropic endeavors are of a national and international scale. Because the panorama of the number 22 is broader and more imaginative, the potential for achievement is more far-reaching.

Charismatic and radiating a divine glow, the latent powers of the 22 are obvious to all. This number can most often be found in the throes of fundamental chaos, organizing institutions on a massive scale. Twenty-two's can masterfully accomplish anything that's never been done before.

These double 2's can also be found shining on the stage of life as actors and actresses, entertainers and agents. With the delicate sense of timing of the number 2, only greatly magnified, the 22's have been known to wow Hollywood with their talent. They're hard workers, too, and world-wide fame usually follows them.

Like the 11, this human superman will wrestle for a long time before it comes to grips with its superior powers. It will never really achieve all of which it is capable. Quite often it may appear eccentric, frantic, oppressive, or overly shy. But just give it some space and time—freedom to spread its wings and the chance to calm its nerves. Then follow the bright light of its inner fire, and allow yourself to be moved by the dynamic electrical current flowing in your direction.

The Number 33/6 Life Path

An even number, an extrovert, ruled by Venus, there is the possibility of Cancer or Pisces significantly placed in the natal chart.
Key words: service, humanitarianism, altruism, charity.
Famous saying: I will serve humanity in a grand fashion.
Famous person: Jesse Jackson 10/8/41

PURPOSE: As a person who has chosen a number 33 Life Path, your goal is to relieve human suffering, establish a higher order of justice, and show that a more responsible standard of living is attainable. Possessing this Master number, you are engulfed in a particular quest: to seek a mission on which to focus, so that humanity may benefit. Your special purpose, in any event, will require you to care for many people, at times sacrificing your free time and pleasure in order to teach, counsel, and aid others. Since this is a difficult Master number to follow, at times you will have to revert to the lower 6 vibration, where humanitarian and domestic considerations are not on a scale so large as the 33.

You must guard against your natural vulnerability: becoming a doormat for others or chasing after every cause that may seem honorable while upholding the elements of sacrifice and responsibility. A sense of self-righteousness, indulgent pride, and grating obnoxious opinions can add to your downfall. The basic descriptions of the 6's Life Path apply here.

VOCATIONS: All higher level educational, artistic, legal, medical, and healing fields of service, where tolerance of others and sacrifice for their sake may be involved.

The Number 44 Life Path:

An even number, an extrovert, ruled by Saturn, there is the possibility of Capricorn significantly placed in the natal astrological chart.

Key words: I will lead and administrate by means of Divine Guidance.

Famous person: Robert Dole 7/22/23

PURPOSE: Your purpose holding a number 44 Life Path, a Master number of recent vintage according to some numerologists, requires that you exercise and utilize a tremendous amount of physical discipline in working through high mental concepts. Common sense, logic, and advanced planning are necessary in order to attain and overcome obstacles, particularly on the material plane. Steady effort and deep concentration are necessary.

You must possess and exercise good judgment in order to achieve productivity on the earth plane, but often this requirement presents difficulty because the intuitive aspects of your higher self need developing. You are also at an important juncture in your spiritual development. Most often you are working to overcome a drastic flaw that must be corrected before new growth can occur. Examine any negative habit that has held you back (usually some excessive behavior which has gotten out of hand, or could, if you are not mindful of its destructiveness) for clues about what this flaw is. When the higher vibrations of this number become too difficult to sustain, the number 44 reverts to the lower vibration of the number 8, which is more comfortable.

VOCATIONS: The 44/8 vocations involve all high-level number 8 Life Path positions in which mental superiority, discipline, courage, and bravery are required in order to advance materially and aid others in achieving their desires.

The Life Path number can obviously offer a great deal of information. Computing it is the initial step in learning more about yourself and those around you. Any major turnoffs from the highway you have chosen to travel through life will immediately give you trouble. The old expression that you can never get rich playing another person's tune is relevant here, for you are who you are, and that's it. In a past life you chose to be this way for a reason; following your true nature will lead to your highest good.

CHAPTER 2

Birthday Power:
Your Birthday Number

The day of the month on which you were born will carry with it major significance, since the *Birthday* number is one of those that make up your Life Path number. Although the Birthday number influences your Life Path number throughout your life, it has greatest significance between the ages of 28 and 56 and has a great deal to say about the vocation you choose. This is true for all Birthday numbers except the Master numbers 11 and 22, which seem to carry full weight and force throughout the entire life of the individual. Your Birthday number points in the direction of success in one's chosen field, and so close attention should be paid to the Birthday number, and every attempt should be made to stay within the positive meaning of its vibration.

Birthday numbers run in octaves. For example, the number 10 can be viewed as a higher octave of the number 1, and the number 19 can be viewed as a higher octave of the numbers 10 and 1. Likewise, the number 28 will be the highest octave of all the number 1's. In addition, each birthday carries with it its own unique characteristics. The following list of Birthday numbers gives the characteristics of each day of birth and is designed to show how the octaves are related. More detailed descriptions follow.

The Number 1 Birthdays (1, 10, 19, and 28)

1 Great ambition, drive, logical, good mind. Apt to repress emotions and procrastinate.

10 Creative, original, willful, artistic. Must watch out for jealousy and a sense of loneliness.

19 Covers the whole range of numbers 1–9, which makes the person subject to this vibration vulnerable to extremes, reaching the highest of the highs and the lowest of the lows. Fearless, forceful, unconventional, independent, and unlimited in opportunity, the person with this birthday recovers quickly from adversity. Must watch how this native handles finances.

28 Dominant, tenacious, gregarious, and most affectionate of all the numbers, the holder of this vibration possesses an inner knowledge of the needs of others. Highly unconventional and independent, does best working in large groups. Must avoid daydreaming and laziness.

The Number 2 Birthdays (2, 11, 20, and 29)

2 Emotional, sensitive, friendly, musical, diplomatic, and analytical. Must avoid periodic moods of depression or becoming the doormat for others.

11 A Master number, psychic, intuitive, fluctuating in desires and emotions, with an electric, starlike personality, dramatic in ideas and actions. Can be highstrung, with extremist views, a dreamer instead of a doer.

20 Sympathetic, diplomatic, the peacemaker, fond of friends, family, and music. Very analytical, knowledgeable, works better on paper, where detail is required, especially in small businesses or corporate environments offering protection. Must avoid being used and abused by others or allowing deep moods to control. Must learn to stick up for self.

29 A Master number, adaptable, with creative genius

accompanying up and down mood swings. Can become prosperous working before the public, using great idealism, dramatics, and inspiration. Must learn to stick up for self and avoid erratic tendencies.

The Number 3 Birthdays (3, 12, 21, and 30)

3 Intuitive, sensitive to psychic impulses, expressive, mental, can succeed in all forms of creative ventures, such as writing, entertainment, speaking, music, and painting. Must avoid restlessness, impatience, and intolerance toward others.

12 Brilliant, imaginative, intelligent, with a magnetic flair in design, color, and speaking. Could become famous in law, acting, lecturing, or music. Must guard against mood swings and leaving too many projects incomplete.

21 Work in any art form could bring success and recognition, especially singing, publishing, textiles, advertising, music, and journalism. Affectionate and friendly, the 21 must guard against seesaw emotions, brooding, and suspicious tendencies.

30 Inspired, sociable, restless, and full of vitality, with a knack for managerial positions, the native must guard against all obsessions and excesses, as well as the desire always to be right. This vibration requires a good education in order to stay on course.

The Number 4 Birthdays (4, 13, 22, and 31)

4 Reserved, conservative, disciplined, organized, analytical, hard-working, lover of home, roots, family, and country, the native could succeed in any profession requiring methodical skills, and regulating and constructing abilities. Must guard against stubbornness, overwork, and being viewed as overly set and cold. Must learn to accept change and have fun more often.

13 Down to earth, a hard worker, adaptable, good managerial and business mind, could succeed quickly in all areas of building, advertising, and real estate

industries. Organized, the recipient of this vibration excels in areas requiring detailed statistical expertise. Must avoid appearing dominating, dictatorial, stubborn, or bellicose.

22 The great master builder, the most high-strung and nervous of all the 4 numbers, but capable of the most remarkable forms of accomplishment as well. Propelled to large undertakings and major institutions of learning and business, this vibration can transform idealistic thoughts into practical masterpieces. Great care must be exercised to live constructively, maintain balance, and avoid the black arts, such as witchcraft, in any form. The vibration requires contributing to mankind and living by higher law.

31 A higher octave of the number 13, with a great business mind. Success is possible in all avenues of business requiring loyalty, hard work, discipline, and economy. An innate knowledge of medicine and drugs is also present. Possesses a strong sense of spirituality, but usually feels uncomfortable around psychic pursuits.

The Number 5 Birthdays (5, 14, and 23)

5 Adventuresome, versatile, with great sexual attraction, life seems to bring change quite often, teaching adaptability. Gifted with words while exuding a magnetic personality, this number loves to travel and could sell anything. Success can be achieved in any field requiring good judgment and quickness, such as sales, insurance, or stocks and bonds.

14 Creativity coupled with a structured mind, the gambler of the number 5's is prepared to take a calculated risk and may be more successful than most numbers. Prophetic in nature, and in the public sphere, inherently aware of the public's needs and could succeed by following hunches constructively and not speculating blindly. Must guard against fall-

ing victim to excesses and moving on destructive tendencies.

23   Charming, popular, attracted to the opposite sex; excels in all lines of promoting, where quick, progressive decisions are required. Born with magnetic healing hands, success comes in professions requiring diagnostic talents, such as chiropractic and healing arts, psychiatry, and science. A flair for dramatics and writing, this vibration also succeeds in producing many successful actors, dancers, and performers. Must guard against ruthlessness and wide mood swings.

The Number 6 Birthdays (6, 15, and 24)

6   Devoted, sympathetic, loving, responsible. Requires appreciation and respect in order to achieve. Artistic, possessing a good voice and a penchant to mimic; could find success in radio, TV, theater, and designing or civic work with a responsible job title. Possessing strong opinions and argumentative by nature, must guard against rash emotions and alienating others through possessive tendencies.

15   Sociable, youthful, able to comprehend quickly through fast, accurate observation. Could achieve financial success if allowed to follow own impulses. Scientific, yet musical, subjects of this vibration excel in professions such as law or politics rather than business. Independent and also able to work well with others, the 15 must guard against arrogance and resentment.

24   Restless, but capable of handling successfully a number of projects at one time, learning by refined powers of observation. Builds methodically in business, combining the knowledge acquired from many talents. A practical nature combined with artistic flair, capable of working many hours in a disciplined fashion, the 24 will carry the load for those who avoid responsibilities. Must guard against repressing feelings of inferiority, worry, and becoming overly critical of others.

The Number 7 Birthdays (7, 16, and 25)

7   Technical, scientific, and must specialize. Hunches are powerful and should be followed. Logical, yet inflexible and isolated, the 7 should develop its psychic and intuitive qualities, with an emphasis on proper rest. A lover of solitude and highly intellectual, the holder of this vibration possesses fixed opinions and attitudes. Excellent at all research, investigations, and searching for wisdom. Must guard against appearing overly perfect or stubborn.

16   Strong psychic impulses and hunches, coupled with an analytical mind from time to time, causes confusion over which road to pursue. Should follow hunches first. A perfectionist, with introspective and self-centered tendencies, likely to find success in highly specialized fields that will allow far-reaching contact with others. A bit aloof and hard to understand, nevertheless, the possibility of high financial gain in this lifetime is quite strong. The 16 represses its emotions and frequently appears to be on another wavelength. The native is advised to follow the intuitive direction of its dreams and avoid procrastinating. Its logical, rational, and responsible approach can bring great recognition.

25   The most friendly and sociable of the 7's, the recipient of this vibration is also inflexible, stubborn, and often misunderstood, but more desirous than the other 7's of seeking out and enjoying new experiences. Mystical, occult, spiritual, and psychic exploration brings fascination. Must be careful to analyze all situations before jumping to conclusions or saying no to everything. Must get proper rest and take care to finish projects before starting new ones.

The Number 8 Birthdays (8, 17, and 26)

8   Highly managerial, executive in approach, and business-oriented, the 8 is often geared to working with large organizations and institutions or owning its own business. Must be in a position of power,

respect, and authority in order to reap the full measure of this vibration. Intuitively, the number 8 is a fine judge of character and the proper use of money, and if the Life Path is followed wisely, this number could bring large financial gain. The 8 must guard against domineering and overzealous tendencies. As a goal-oriented individual, large material accumulation is possible.

17   The more conservative of the 8 vibrations, this number works well alone in large organizations or in positions of power. Usually 17's are their own bosses or sit at the right hand of authority. More fixed and set in its ways, this number carries with it a shrewd yet honest response that often vacillates between extremes of thrift one minute and extravagance the next. Possessing excellent writing and analytical skills, the 17 could achieve success as an executive, accountant, or publisher. All 17's must guard against partnerships: This number should actually strive to be the boss and get others to oversee the details of the operations.

26   The responder to this vibration does well in large corporations and organizations that specialize in artistic or creative projects dealing with humanity's desire for the better, material, comforts in life. Of all the 8's, this number holds a concentration upon family and loved ones and is known to be quite generous in supplying comforts to other family members.

Making a favorable impression on others is also important to the 26. The native must guard against seesaw emotions and living too much in the past. Both of these could greatly dampen productivity.

The Number 9 Birthdays (9, 18, and 27)

9   Literary, artistic, generous, philanthropic, and a lover of travel. Universal love rather than personal love must be emphasized, or great loss, disappointment, and separation are possible. The 9 birthday is

advised to avoid marriage or live on a higher level, since this birthday is a "finishing cycle" and married life could be disappointing. Strong-willed, determined, and independent, greatness is achieved by serving others and understanding their needs, and by finishing major projects before beginning new ones.

18   Independent and driven to financial gain, achievement comes from executive, managerial, and administrative positions within large organizations, and from group work. Emotional, practical, rational, this native is friendly, helpful, and philanthropic to those in need. Eighteens are known to give wise counsel. Equally dramatic, artistic, and a lover of travel, the 18 can feel held back due to having to care for the sick or elderly, but greatness, nonetheless, is always expected. This number must beware of appearing overzealous, money-hungry, or excessively critical of others. Romance and marriage also could be disappointing unless the native learns to live for others.

27   Analytical, introspective, logical, this vibration works well with others and is considerate at the same time of their needs. Affectionate, emotional, yet forceful and determined, the personality leans toward diplomatic and persuasive tendencies rather than using force to win. Often content with less within a marriage, romance often brings loss, disappointment, and/or separation. All forms of analysis, specialization, and writing bring success.

Your birthday will also reveal how you appear to others. You may also be interested in discovering some famous people who share the same day as you. The short vignettes below may help you see yourself as others view you.

The Number 1 Birthday

If your birthday falls on the first of the month, you are independent, individualistic, driven, original, and above all *motivated*. When dedicated to a task, you are ambitious, quick, curious, and unique in outlook. You are a natural at taking charge, are idealistic, yet have good reasoning skills.

Possessing a strong ego, you generally prefer giving orders rather than taking them. This confidence stems from an innate belief in yourself and from the high level of excellence that you demand in all your undertakings. Your venturesome spirit is totally committed to the accomplishment of a full and rewarding existence. Life for you is a rewarding adventure in which your inquisitive mind can question all of its mysteries. You display executive leadership abilities and possess strong potential for financial reward.

Negatively, you are inclined to begin many projects and complete few. Moreover, although you're sensitive by nature, you may tend to display an unresponsive and cold exterior, using silence as a weapon to express yourself. Famous people born on this day are Princess Diana, William Rehnquist, Dan Aykroyd, Barry Goldwater, and Julie Andrews.

The Number 2 Birthday

If your birthday falls on the second day of the month, you are by nature tactful, cooperative, and diplomatic. A lover of companionship, peace, and harmony, you tend to enjoy working with people rather than alone. Your sensitivity to others and their opinions finds you often taking the laid-back approach, preferring to work behind the scenes of most endeavors. In essence, you are known as a background person, and your hard work and trustworthiness can land you the position of "the power behind the throne."

Because you feel that a necessary ingredient for a peaceful existence is balance, you prefer to weigh both sides of an issue before coming to a decision. This search for equanimity, coupled with the fairness and consideration that you show others, naturally places you in the position of arbitrator and peacemaker. People may look to you to smooth out rough situations.

A negative aspect of the number 2 is becoming unbalanced and paralyzed through indecision. The resultant fear can cause mood swings and periodic bouts of depression. Famous people born on this day are Edwin Meese, Alexander M. Haig, Dr. Benjamin Spock, Alec Guinness and Liz Smith.

The Number 3 Birthday

If your birthday falls on the third, you enjoy a *joie de vivre* like nobody else. Your high spirit and sparkling enthusiasm make you the life of any party. A genius at the art of self-expression, you can attract a crowd with your imaginative and lively knack for storytelling. In fact, there's a healing quality in your laughter. You really know how to have a good time.

As the perfect host or hostess, variety and uniqueness are the calling cards for a 3 birthday. With a sense of showmanship and a need to entertain, one can expect anything to occur at your gala events. When it's time to pick a lifetime partner, however, make sure that you're in agreement over where to hold the annual Lamp Shade Party. A mate unaccustomed to your antics could lead to grief down the line.

These joyous and amusing lovable 3's must be careful not to scatter their energies and resources. Moreover, their love of the good life could find them hooked on wine, women (or men!), and song, rather than on accomplishment or meeting the obligations of self or family. Famous people born on this day are Kitty Carlisle, Tom Cruise, Eddie Murphy, Marlon Brando, and Herschel Walker.

The Number 4 Birthday

If your birthday falls on the fourth day of the month, "loving," "loyal," "dependable," and "organized" are some words that describe you. As a lover of law, order, and regulation, you are the original flag waver. Life for you is built upon strong foundations; you are not afraid to work long and hard for what you believe, always laboring from the bottom up. Devoted to home and family as the cornerstone of existence, you, the quintessential lover of responsibility, can always be counted on. You are the one who answers to the proverbial whistle.

Although methodical by nature and nicknamed the "slow thinker," you, as a 4, take first prize in handing out sound, practical advice. Your literary epics can be found on the "how to" shelves of most libraries and bookstores.

All 4's value security, and money is an essential ingredient in the formula for achieving it. Naturally thrifty and prudent, clipping coupons and sleeping with your wallet is certainly not something out of the ordinary. When it comes to the tug of war, you are the one who always wins in the buck-stretching contest.

On the bleak side, you may box yourself in through your own stubbornness. Watch so that your opinions do not become fixed or your personality static and inflexible. Don't let them wonder if it's the mule or goat they're dealing with. Famous people born on this day are Dr. Joyce Brothers, Jeane Dixon, Ann Landers, Walter Cronkite, and Charlton Heston.

The Number 5 Birthday

If your birthday falls on the fifth day of the month, you're forward-looking, freethinking, adventuresome— here one moment and gone the next. Unique, unconventional, and a seeker of the up-to-date, you could easily wander off and find the answers to your many questions in some far-off land. Never mind that you started out for the library at 9 A.M., it's just that you passed the travel agent first and Burma seemed like a fine place to visit. As you very well know, you, a 5, enjoy exploration, and you never know where the experience may take you.

Quick, resourceful, and versatile, your reputation as an unconfined, dashing delight is more than offset by your feats of energy and direction: You can accomplish more in one hour than most people can in a week. A word to the wise, though: Realize that your keen wits can turn contrary with lightning speed if you're asked to follow a schedule. Control your tendency to be the original hater of routine.

Spirited experimenter and thrill seeker that you are, keep a leash on your dual nature by avoiding over-indulgence in sex, drugs, or gambling. Every so often, living on a more moderate level will work wonders. Famous people born on this day are Giorgio Di Sant'Angelo, Henry Cabot Lodge, Walter Mondale, Rex Harrison, and Arthur Hailey.

The Number 6 Birthday

If your birthday falls on the sixth day of the month, you're the cosmic parent, deeply rooted to home, family, children, and the community. Your idealism and sense of duty makes you a stable pillar of many causes. Loving, sympathetic, and compassionate, you often find people crying on your broad shoulders. The pearls of compassion that you dole out tend to have a healing quality about them.

As the fanciful idealist, you know that love conquers all. You'll scale Everest for love, beauty, and quality, and when the latter is applied to jewels, like diamonds, no risk is too overwhelming or daring to obtain them.

You must resist your negative inclinations: Exercise care not to become the universal doormat; do not allow yourself to be leaned upon excessively by every Tom, Dick, or Rhoda. Conversely, threatening situations can evoke the opposite response: Guard against irresponsibility and abrasive attitudes and speech. Famous people born on this day are Lucille Ball, Tom Brokaw, Ronald and Nancy Reagan, Ed McMahon, and Nancy Lopez.

The Number 7 Birthday

If your birthday falls on the seventh day of the month, your inquisitive and scholarly intellect definitely makes you the more studious type. Analytical and observant by nature, you could very easily find yourself a noted expert in any field of specialization. Broad-minded and alert, your interests could range from the metaphysical and occult to the mating calls of the sapsucker. Don't be surprised if you find yourself devouring twelve volumes of information on any subject, either. As you can tell, the 7's are bound by knowledge, books, truth, wisdom, and the question "why?"

On the other side of the fence, if you expect your 7 woman to serenade you with a six-course gourmet meal after the Cup-A-Soup specialty, or your 7 mate to remember where he's left anything, you're a good candidate for shock therapy. These 7's generally surface once a week, and when they do, it isn't for trivia. At times they can appear muddle-headed and backward, not to mention forgetful. But never forget the compensation: the high degree of intelligence that they possess. Famous people born on this day are Francis Ford Coppola, William Kunstler, Ivan Lendl, David Packard, and Pierre Cardin.

The Number 8 Birthday

If your birthday falls on the eighth day of the month, you love the color green, as in money and grass. This well-documented fact is proven by the comfortable balance you keep in your bank account and your ample real estate holdings. Your financial awareness and farsightedness, moreover, has situated you in high-powered executive and administrative positions.

Filled with karmic experiences and cognizant that the number 8 is the number of judgment, once burnt, you generally do not make the same mistake twice.

Your advances in life derive from executing well-thought-out business strategies, and you're respected and admired as a productive financier. In fact, you, the number 8 individual, always have a better way skinning the cat financially.

Obsessed with objects that reflect your need for power and wealth, highly conscious of the importance of appearing successful, you must guard against your possessions' power to manipulate your goals. If carried away by your innate love of competition, you may appear callous and cold-blooded, blinded by your own stark ambition and insensitive to the feelings of others. Famous people born on this day are David Bowie, Dustin Hoffman, Jack Lemmon, Sid Caesar, and Ted Koppel.

The Number 9 Birthday

If you were born on the ninth day of the month, you are truly philanthropic and humanistic at heart. Kind, understanding, reliable, and sensitive to the plight of mankind, you usually find work in occupations where the public is served. High-minded when it comes to the meanness of the human condition, you enjoy speaking out on controversial, humanitarian issues, and your opinions carry weight.

Your universal concern for people does not stop on the home front, however, but extends to distant shores. Compassionate yet drawn by the exotic, you enjoy the unique atmosphere of far-away places; not surprisingly, you may exhibit your alibilty to sustain harmony to an uncommon degree by being attracted to a foreigner as a mate.

Listening for the chord of reality will help protect you from being taken in by every sob story you hear. Remember that detachment and objectivity are not your first responses and that the lessons that love and giving have to teach may first result in bitter disappointment and even great loss. Famous people born on this day are Candice Bergen, Barbara Cartland, Roger Mudd, Billy Joel, and Kirk Douglas.

The Number 10 Birthday

If your were born on the tenth day of the month, you are not only predestined to lead, but your attainment of material goods in this life is assured. Since you are known to be in perpetual motion, people count on you to get the job done.

Because you are multifaceted and many-talented, it would not be unusual for you to promote several businesses at one time. You are excellent at starting and getting things done, but you feel the need for proper backup assistance in order to follow through on your plans.

Your *modus operandi* is such that you prefer active to quiet pursuits, along with the fundamental need to be successful. In the quest for attainment you are also courageous and bold, possessing the gift of invention. Society is often much improved because of your efforts.

On the other hand, you resist taking advice from others, tending to believe that your judgment is paramount, that you should be the giver of wisdom rather than the taker. Your insistence on independence could lead to some disasterous blunders, resulting in possibly unrecoverable crashes. Famous people born on this day are David Brinkley, James Clavell, Charles Kuralt, and Arnold Palmer.

The Number 11 Birthday

If your birthday falls on the eleventh day of the month, you're truly out to place your individualistic stamp on this world, and neither "sleet nor hail," as the motto goes, will prevent you from taking a stand on what you perceive as morally right. Generally, you'll try to carefully weigh both sides of an issue before casting your ballot.

You, the 11 individual, are outstandingly quick, creative, highly inspired—or, more accurately, charged, and like the variable chameleon, can change your mind or direction in midair and confound the closest of friends. Observers are usually in suspense until the eleventh hour.

High-strung and idealistic, you are buoyed and guided by faith, seemingly inspired by a direct pipeline to the Almighty. Creating as you go along, you usually move at lightning speed, leaving your average participant exhausted. Blessed by visions or impressions of a prophetic nature, you are often viewed as being clairvoyant or telepathic. One thing's undeniable—you always get noticed. You gravitate toward the limelight and enjoy every second of the attention.

One admiring word of warning: Be careful not to get lost in your dreams or overzealous in what you feel you can attain. Famous people born on this day are Oleg Cassini, Jerry Falwell, Rupert Murdoch, Burt Reynolds, and Irving Berlin.

The Number 12 Birthday

If your birthday falls on the twelfth day of the month, you are a master of creative expression and, concurrently, gifted with words. Whether it is in writing, speaking, singing, or playing an instrument, your artistic nature finds expression.

Your logical and practical mind, coupled with the potency and enchantment of speech, makes you adept at debating and the art of persuasion. Moreover, your powers of observation are quick and accurate.

Animated, amusing, with a fancy for drama and showmanship, you have the ability to turn an ordinary occurrence into a major event, where you're admired for your hospitality, good taste, and talent.

Regardless of the career you choose, you are able to benefit from the one flawless component of your success: your perfect sense of timing. Instinctively you know when to pull back and when to strike.

As a member of the 3 family, you must guard against scattering your energies or becoming involved in too many trivial pursuits. This lack of direction could find you beginning many projects and completing few. Mired down by too many strings, a deep depression could follow. Famous people born on this day are Andrew Young, Milton Berle, Harry Blackmun, Luciano Pavarotti, and Liza Minnelli.

The Number 13 Birthday

If your birthday falls on the thirteenth day of the month, you're nuts-and-bolts-oriented, and most likely engaged in the kind of work that produces results. Gregarious and persuasive like your number 3 sisters and yet independent and achievement-oriented like your number 1 brothers, you enjoy directing and managing the affairs of others.

As a member of the 4 family, you're more convinced than most that hard work and endurance pay off, with satisfying rewards like property, money, and the finer things of life just waiting around the bend. This certainly gives you the drive to continue long after the others have cried "Uncle."

At times overly ambitious, you must be careful not to allow your zeal to rule. When this occurs, you are often viewed by others as dictatorial and obstinate—and let's face it—limitations won't get you where you want to go. Famous people born on this day are Charles Scribner, George Shultz, Neil Sedaka, Jacqueline Bisset, and Clive Barnes.

The Number 14 Birthday

If your birthday falls on the fourteenth day of the month, you're a versatile, creative thinker, always on the go. Similar to the number 5, you're desirous of change, variety, and travel and can be found dashing off to seek out some undiscovered truth. Once found, if it becomes incorporated into your personality, all of humanity will hear your views. You, a 14 individual, insist on being heard—and that means by the world. If given the opportunity, you can truly enjoy the limelight.

Similar to the 5's in that the new and the unique intrigue you, you nevertheless uphold a strong work ethic and are capable of executing a number of tasks at the same time, all successfully. Progressive in thought and deed, you aren't afraid of plunging into new ventures or entertaining risks.

Nonetheless, this fearlessness involving speculation could get out of hand. Your venturesome spirit must take care not to get hooked on sex, drugs, gambling, or any form of overstimulation. Famous people born on this day are Ralph Lauren, Andy Rooney, Gerald Ford, Carl Bernstein, and Frank Borman.

The Number 15 Birthday

If your birthday falls on the fifteenth day of the month, you've got it all. Dedicated to family and community, blessed with the warmth of a hearty laugh, you seem to succeed in becoming king or queen of the proverbial hill. Sympathetic to mankind, concerned about the social ills of the times, you have no difficulty expounding your learned views on these issues.

A born diplomat, finely tuned for problem solving, you are recognized for your brilliant advice. Your love of mankind is based on an even stronger devotion to home and family; yet you are aware of the needs of humanity, which beckon to you from time to time. While your exploits usually do not take you far from the domestic turf—especially the kitchen, where gourmet meals are developed—if duty calls, you will follow.

On the negative side, your periodic stubbornness and argumentative streaks must be kept in check. Famous people born on this day are Arthur Schlesinger, Jr., John Kenneth Galbraith, Lee Iacocca, Julia Child, and Melissa Manchester.

The Number 16 Birthday

If your birthday falls on the sixteenth day of the month, you are among the most intuitive of the universe so always be sure to follow your hunches. Attempting to reason things out may only cloud the issues, causing you tremendous conflict and confusion. Being cognizant that your intuition is always right will save you a great deal of heartache.

Introspective and contemplative by nature, you begin pondering your life career early. Because you tend to favor perfection and are gifted in problem solving, you know that specialization is the safest road to personal fulfillment.

Certain requirements are basic to guaranteeing your cheerful existence. First and foremost is your attachment to your family. You demand that your spouse marry your family, too—mother, father, and all the trimmings—or they'd better throw in the towel. Second, you cherish money and the comforts it buys. Third, getting you to let go of your procrastinating tendencies can be a monumental feat, which others may not want even to attempt. If you realize what *they're* up against, you've gone more than half the way toward making your friendships irritant-free.

Responsible, clean living, preferring the country life, you will always be sought out for your grace, charm, and love of music. Famous people born on this day are Daniel Patrick Moynihan, Reverend Robert Schuller, John McEnroe, Katharine Graham, and Lauren Bacall.

The Number 17 Birthday

If your birthday falls on the seventeenth day of the month, you vibrate to very fortunate numbers in the business and financial world. Serious, ambitious, and very intelligent, you gravitate to those in high places. Your gift of diplomacy and strong instinctual qualities often make you an influential force behind the seat of power. Superiors admire your knowledge and work ethic and confer much praise upon you.

Because you enjoy studying, analyzing, and the satisfaction that comes from proving things, you live in your head a great deal of the time, surfacing only when you've uncovered the solution to a most pressing problem.

Possessed with a strong business acumen and an attendant desire for wealth, you must be careful that your ambitious nature does not turn to ruthlessness. Famous people born on this day are Arthur Miller, Phyllis Diller, Jimmy Breslin, Dean Martin, and Anne Bancroft.

The Number 18 Birthday

If your birthday falls on the eighteenth day of the month, you are sought out by many for your wise counsel. Trusted and respected by your friends and acquaintances, it seems that when you speak, Delphi trembles. You steady nerves by your sense of stability, and your ideas, once put into action, can change the course of history. You're considered a giant among humans.

Born with a sixth sense for profit, you can track down a successful deal from the most insignificant of tips and may manage to find yourself owning a sizable empire someday.

Knowing you're so superior, however, could go to your head. Retain your sense of perspective, and refrain from becoming argumentative and critical of those around you. Famous people born on this day are Ramsey Clark, Jesse Helms, Pope John Paul II, Sylvia Porter, and John D. Rockefeller IV.

The Number 19 Birthday

If your birthday falls on the nineteenth day of the month, your tenacity and strong will power allow you to be subservient to no one. Driven by a desire to accomplish great things, and to be fully in control of the dials and levers of your life, you 19 individuals usually remain undaunted by obstacles in your climb to the top.

Because this birthday represents the range of numbers (1–9), as a youngster you could have been governed by nervous tension and a strong emotional nature. This tentative, often irrational approach could have interfered with a need to be independent. Running headfirst into the feelings and opinions of others could have been a common stumbling block.

As an adult, learning to overcome these obstacles has resulted in an ambitious, practical thinker, whose executive abilities are accented by creative tendencies.

You must guard against appearing self-centered and becoming forgetful of others. Famous people born on this day are Malcolm Forbes, Lewis Powell, Dolly Parton, Robert MacNeil, and Lee Marvin.

The Number 20 Birthday

If your birthday falls on the twentieth day of the month, your natural grace, love and harmony, and companionship find you propelled into roles where you tactfully maintain a peaceful environment by artfully manipulating situations with a velvet glove. Your keen sense of analysis and statistical acumen can bring accomplishment and recognition on a grand scale.

Your sensitivity to the feelings of others allows you to establish close and deep friendships, both at home and in work situations. Because you are cooperative, you are able to adapt to change faster and easier than most people. Coworkers find you a blessing to associate with.

Like all 2's, you tend to enjoy a back-seat position rather than being directly in the forefront. Yet your charm and gentle persuasion, with maturity, could thrust you into the limelight.

You will benefit from a note of caution: You must make sure that people do not mistake your kindness and sincerity for stupidity and use you for a doormat. Famous people born on this day are Sophia Loren, Herbert Givenchy, Federico Fellini, Mickey Mantle, and Jascha Heifetz.

The Number 21 Birthday

If your birthday falls on the twenty-first day of the month, you're truly daring and bubbling over with imaginative energy. Your interests are wide and varied, and unafraid, you are able to handle the risks required to launch a new and challenging enterprise.

This wasn't always so. Your groundwork was often painful and slow to develop. As a youngster, even as a young adult, you may have had trouble pursuing independence; moreover, your vacillating emotions may have also taken you far off the beaten trail.

But now you've matured and cultivated the strong determination and social contacts needed to get your projects off the ground. The recognition and success, being all yours, drives you onward to create and achieve even more . . . and the rest is going to be history.

A word to the wise for our 21 birthday friends: Stay focused and attend to financial matters or your chances for success will not surface as often. Famous people born on this day are Peggy Cass, Queen Elizabeth II, Armand Hammer, Jack Nicklaus, and Jane Fonda.

The Number 22 Birthday

If your birthday falls on the twenty-second day of the month, your dedicated attitude and universal outlook should assure your success. You are the generator, the master builder, who prefers to organize and execute plans on a great and distinctive scale. Nothing is too large or too difficult to challenge your confidence.

Because you possess the double 2's, you are twice as sensitive as the average individual and feel things ever so much more deeply. Unless you regulate your frustrations, letting off steam slowly and more frequently, your everyday tensions cause you to explode in a tirade of frustration. You must be careful not to be overwhelmed by your moods.

Your pursuit of greatness, coupled with your concern for nurturing, is the kind of combination that will sweep them off their feet. You are careful to lay strong foundations in your home and family life and will go to all extremes to make sure that your needs are taken care of. In terms of your family, your emphasis on roots is important, but for yourself, it is another story. Being more global than local, you are at home anywhere in the world.

You should be aware of the physical toll that your Life Path requires: Take care of your nerves, and rest frequently due to all the energy that you expend. A love of music and comedy can help to soothe frayed nerves. Famous people born on this day are Bill Blass, Catherine Deneuve, Dianne Feinstein, and Tom Lasorda.

The Number 23 Birthday

If your birthday falls on the twenty-third of the month, you are the communicator *par excellence*. Because you maintain the attributes of the 5, you are quick, energetic, verbal, and a lover of people. The practical 2 in your number and the creative 3 often portray you as an efficiency expert in your chosen field. The energy you exude is downright awesome, and people wonder what it is that you eat for breakfast that gives you such magnetic appeal. Here's just a fraction of the secret: channeled sexual energy that gets filtered into projects. That's right, and remember you heard it here first. You and your cohorts have long staying power, and when it's directed into action, it makes you intent on achieving your goals. The rest is due to a desire to experience everything during your lifetime. One way or another, you will.

While you're out, outdoing everyone and everything imaginable, be careful not to overvolunteer. There are just so many committees and programs that a person can manage and still have time for dancing. Famous people born on this day are Johnny Carson, Chita Rivera, Gene Kelly, Bob Fosse, and Shirley Temple Black.

The Number 24 Birthday

If your birthday falls on the twenty-fourth of the month, you have a personality that attracts positions of authority. Both at home and in the work place, you're one individual who's team-oriented. Reliable, you can be called upon at any time, counted on to see that the job is done right. Success and accomplishment are essential for your well-being. You expect to be amply rewarded, financially, that is, for your taste buds require high payment.

Outside of your nine to nine workday, you, as a 24, hold your personal relationships in high esteem. As a member of the 6 family, your responsibilities extend to friends and loved ones, too: You can always be found with available ears and shoulders.

Although for the most part cooperative, you must guard against periodic moods of restlessness, tactlessness, sparring, and oversensitivity. Famous people born on this day are Shirley MacLaine, William F. Buckley, Bob Dylan, Neil Diamond, and Ernest Borgnine.

The Number 25 Birthday

If your birthday falls on the twenty-fifth, your brainy aloofness, coupled with your bouts of dynamic chattiness, leave people slightly off-kilter. Both prudent and prophetic at the same time, you are the most talkative of the family of thinkers. But like all 7's you are interested in all things that are mystical, philosophical, and hidden. An observer never knows which side of you they will encounter on any given day. Because you possess the nervous energy of the 5 and the desire to involve yourself in groups and associations, like all 2's, periodic meditation should help mellow you and prevent you from joining at least ten churches, mystical societies, and fraternities.

As a child, however, your extreme nervousness could have given you much grief; not knowing that your search stemmed from a need for perfection and desire for truth, you could have seemed quite judgmental and critical of others.

But to each his own path, as the saying suggests. Your experiences have molded you into the seeker of the keys of knowledge. Never mind that you belong to all those mystical unions . . . you're still looking for the truth. Famous people born on this day are William Brennan, Barbara Walters, Phyllis George, and Sean Connery.

The Number 26 Birthday

If your birthday falls on the twenty-sixth day of the month, you are a long-distance runner in everything you do. Known for an excellent ability to organize, coupled with the physical stamina to carry out large-scale plans, you can work for many hours without complaining. When you commit yourself to a task, you're in and that's it. Whatever it takes, you have the phenomenal staying power necessary to see it through.

Strong-willed, responsible, and always in control, you have a life that seems to revolve around the principles of power, authority, and money. The variations of the color green remind you of the different ways to make a dollar. Wherever the road leads you, your 26 number has a positive financial ring to it, and you shouldn't exit this world poor.

The 26 should be careful to maintain stability in the emotional realm. A desire for power and the need to be forever in control could subject you to brooding and mood swings. Curb your stubborn tendencies, too. These distractions could lead to financial loss. Famous people born on this day are Geraldine Ferraro, Mick Jagger, Carol Burnett, Bernard Malamud, and Jackie Gleason.

The Number 27 Birthday

If your birthday falls on the twenty-seventh day of the month, you are viewed as a practical thinker. Loving and affectionate, with your finger on the pulse of humanity, you find that people flock to you, seeking your opinion on many subjects. Because you possess great sensitivity and care about the needs of others, your positive vibration is felt immediately by those who come into contact with you. Your kindness is always the first thing noticed.

Laid back, gentle, and maintaining a strong moral fiber, you are a natural leader in that you teach by your example. You exhibit steady determination, often with a flair for the dramatic . . . as all 9's do.

Like 7's and 9's, you have the ability to be a great writer or dramatic artist. But you need time to yourself to straighten out your thoughts and ponder the condition of society. Whatever you're doing, though, those times when you are off "communing with nature," people know it is they who will be the beneficiary of your great wisdom.

On a more cautious note, try to keep your nerves in check, and recognize that a great many of your disappointments are self-inflicted because you are such a perfectionist. Famous people born on this day are William Randolph Hearst, Jr., Henry Kissinger, Nancy Friday, Jack Klugman, and Coretta Scott King.

The Number 28 Birthday

If your birthday falls on the twenty-eighth day of the month, you are the most affectionate of all the numbers—loyal, responsible, and utterly devoted to family and often animals. It is not uncommon that your loved ones are the center of your attention, especially the children.

Like all the numbers in the 1 family, you possess a strong sense of self and a need to accomplish great things. Since you prefer to associate with large numbers of people, you naturally gravitate to holding a key executive post in a large enterprise. You have broad shoulders, and the more you complain about being overburdened, the more you love it. Of all the 1's, you are the most successful at starting projects, handling the details, and following through to completion. This quality is one of your finest assets, for it usually moves you quickly up the ladder of success, but not without competition. In fact, you thrive on it.

Like most 28's, you weren't always a superachiever. When younger, you may have left projects incomplete, preferring to build castles in the sky. As an adult, you must guard against the same tendency. Famous people born on this day are Alan Alda, Ann-Margret, Jonas Salk, Jack Nicholson, and Jacqueline Onassis.

The Number 29 Birthday

If your birthday falls on the twenty-ninth day of the month, people view you, like the girl with the curl, as either very, very good or very, very bad. Possessing the strength of Samson, you enter life's arena totally expecting the unexpected. For you, the solutions to life's mysteries require flexibility: Those in your environment however, may find your methods disconcerting and a bit extreme, not being able to tolerate the way you change gears so fast and so often.

You do have psychic tendencies—you call them hunches; and even if people are confused by you, you're certainly not confused by *them*. You know their needs, and your take-charge mannerism always finds recognition; you are usually compensated in some way for your efforts. The limelight is your stomping ground.

On the negative side, overindulgence in self-absorption could boomerang, and people could accuse you of insensitivity. The result could be worry and depression on an epic level, so don't get carried away with your daydreams to the detriment of others. Famous people born on this day are Melvin Belli, Bob Hope, Michael Jackson, Chuck Mangione, and Madeline Kahn.

The Number 30 Birthday

If your birthday falls on the thirtieth day of the month, you may find focusing difficult; but making friends, having a ball, and being the life of the party should be a snap. You are to be complimented, for your gift with words and dramatic flair usually finds you commanding center stage.

A bit of a comic, with a gift for storytelling, you can perform your one-person act for long stretches, mesmerizing your listeners with your tales of woe and adventure. You have the knack for adding a dash of color and a touch of imagination to everything you say and do.

Be careful, though, not to get caught up in life by exaggerating your own stories. Remember, they were meant only to entertain others. Famous people born on this day are Arnold Schwarzenegger, Gene Hackman, Shirley Chisholm, Warren Beatty, and Paul Anka.

The Number 31 Birthday

If your birthday falls on the thirty-first day of the month, like all the 4's, you are a practical builder and a real lover of the rules and regulations of life. They make you feel secure.

Loyal and dependable, you make people feel that they can count on you. Your word is your bond. Putting your needs behind those of others, as the 1 behind the 3 in your birthday suggests, finds you surrounded by many friends and associates. It is just this tenative, selfless quality that leads to your major successes in life. You're helpful and sincere, without incurring irritation, which is one of your best assets. And you never forget a kindness.

Like the 4's, you do have a stubborn streak from time to time, but it doesn't usually get in the way. Repressing your feelings may, however; so be mindful to communicate, even when you are feeling down. Famous people born on this day are Clint Eastwood, Jane Pauley, Liz Claiborne, Richard Chamberlain, and Joe Namath.

THE BIRTHDAY CHALLENGE

In the study of numbers, there are some birthdays that carry a specific challenge or lesson, which must be addressed in order to live up to one's potential and sustain a successful, productive life. This concept is known as the *Birthday Challenge* and is in operation for most of the individual's life but more so during the productive subcycle of life (more on that soon).

The Birthday Challenge is found by isolating your Birthday number and subtracting the lower number from the higher number. With the first nine Birthday numbers there is no Challenge, because they are single digit numbers. By "no Challenge" is meant that no one particular Challenge causes a specific concern in the life, and the individual may choose or select a particular situation that needs to be addressed. With the 11 and 22 Birthday numbers, the Challenge is considered a Zero Challenge, which is considerably greater than a "no Challenge" situation. The Zero Challenge means that all the Challenges are going to cause tension and strife in the life until one learns how to deal with them effectively.

The Zero Challenge concerns itself only with the Master numbers. This challenge is given in return for the great gift of inspiration, revelation, and mastery that is their birthday gift. Since the universe is always fair and never takes without giving, one can look at the Birthday Challenge as the price one has to pay for the *Birthday Gift*, which will be discussed shortly.

The Birthday Challenges are as follows:

1st	a single digit	no Challenge
2nd	a single digit	no Challenge
3rd	a single digit	no Challenge
5th	a single digit	no Challenge
6th	a single digit	no Challenge
7th	a single digit	no Challenge
8th	a single digit	no Challenge
9th	a single digit	no Challenge
10th $(1-0=1)$	1 Challenge	to learn to individualize, to lead
11th $(1-1=0)$	Zero Challenge	all the Challenges
12th $(2-1=1)$	1 Challenge	to learn to individualize, only more so
13th $(3-1=2)$	2 Challenge	to cooperate with people
14th $(4-1=3)$	3 Challenge	to guard against scattering one's energies
15th $(5-1=4)$	4 Challenge	to organize, build, apply oneself
16th $(6-1=5)$	5 Challenge	to accept change, use freedom in a proper manner, and work through the fear of change or inertia
17th $(7-1=6)$	6 Challenge	to accept responsibilities and adjust to them
18th $(8-1=7)$	7 Challenge	to specialize, have faith in yourself
19th $(9-1=8)$	8 Challenge	to learn correct usage of money, power, and balance
20th $(2-0=2)$	2 Challenge	to cooperate with people
21st $(2-1=1)$	1 Challenge	to individuate and lead
22nd $(2-2=0)$	Zero Challenge	all the Challenges

23rd $(3-2=1)$	1 Challenge	to individuate and lead
24th $(4-2=2)$	2 Challenge	to cooperate with people
25th $(5-2=3)$	3 Challenge	to guard against scattering one's energies
26th $(6-2=4)$	4 Challenge	to organize, build, apply oneself
27th $(7-2=5)$	5 Challenge	to accept change, use freedom in a proper manner, and work through fear of change or inertia
28th $(8-2=6)$	6 Challenge	to accept responsibilities and adjust to them
29th $(9-2=7)$	7 Challenge	to specialize, have faith in yourself
30th $(3-0=3)$	3 Challenge	to guard against scattering one's energies
31st $(3-1=2)$	2 Challenge	to cooperate with people

THE BIRTHDAY GIFT

As mentioned previously, nothing is taken away or presented as a Challenge in life without returning something good, and special gifts are apparent when analyzing the Birthday number.

To find the *Birthday Gift*, subtract the number of the Challenge from the number 9. Therefore, the Birthday Gifts will appear as follows:

If the Challenge is 1 $(9-1=8)$	The Gift is 8, material success
If the Challenge is 2 $(9-2=7)$	The Gift is 7, wisdom and knowledge
If the Challenge is 3 $(9-3=6)$	The Gift is 6, success
If the Challenge is 4 $(9-4=5)$	The Gift is 5, great stability
If the Challenge is 5 $(9-5=4)$	The Gift is 4, growth and organization
If the Challenge is 6	The Gift is 3, creativity and

$(9-6=3)$ expressiveness

If the Challenge is 7
$(9-7=2)$
The Gift is 2, great intelligence and wisdom

If the Challenge is 8
$(9-8=1)$
The Gift is 1, achievement and leadership

CHAPTER 3

The Crossroads:
The Subpath Numbers

Within your Life Path number there are three *Subpath* numbers, which point the way to positive achievement, growth, and knowledge. An easy way of describing these Subpaths is to consider the Life Path number a super highway. This highway has three lanes; namely, the right, the middle, and the left lanes. During your journey, you will be required to switch lanes at some point, traveling from the left lane to the middle lane, from the middle lane into the right lane.

The individual lanes on this highway can be looked upon as routes to achievement, opportunity, and success, which you will follow for a specific number of years. They describe the good and bad influences, which you can expect to encounter in the same way, as with your Life Path number.

The three Subpaths are termed the *Formative Subpath*, the *Productive Subpath*, and the *Harvest Subpath*. The Formative Subpath has the number of your birth month; it begins at birth and lasts for approximately your first twenty-eight years of life. (To be exact, it begins at the *One Personal Year*—more soon—closest to your twenty-eighth birthday, but for our purposes, just remember that it lasts for approximately twenty-eight years.)

The Productive Subpath begins at your twenty-eighth birthday and lasts approximately until your fifty-seventh birthday is reached. It has the number of your day of birth. The Harvest Subpath has the number of your year of birth. It begins on or about your fifty-seventh birthday and lasts for the remainder of your life.

For Charles, born on October 16, 1966, the Subpaths will appear as follows:

10 (month of October) $= 1 + 0 = 1$	First (Formative) Subpath
16 (day of birth) $= 1 + 6 = 7$	Second (Productive) Subpath
1966 (year of birth) $= 1 + 9 + 6 + 6 = 22$	Third (Harvest) Subpath

At approximately twenty-eight years of age, Charles will move from the individualistic and independent aspects of the 10/1 Subpath into the specialized, introspective, and truth-seeking aspects of the 16/7 Subpath. The positive and negative meanings of the numbers will be the same as the general meanings of the Life Path numbers. The numbers of Charles's Subpaths will represent specific lessons which Charles must learn during the designated years that they cover.

The numbers represented in each Subcycle or Subpath can and often will differ in octave and potency. For example:

$2 = 2$	$11 = 1 + 1 = 2$
$20 = 2 + 0 = 2$	$29 = 2 + 9 = 11 = 1 + 1 = 2$

These four numbers ultimately equal the number 2, but they differ in range and octave. The 11 is of a higher range and octave than the 2 but lower than the 20 and 29. Likewise, the 29 is higher in range and octave than the 2, 11, and 20. As the number rises in octave or potency, therefore, it increases in power and strength.

It is important to note that as you pass from one Subpath into another, there is a definite feeling produced, depending upon the meaning of the number cycle you are leaving and the new number cycle you are beginning. If you are aware, you will begin to sense that a change is in the works. These feelings could begin to surface as much as a year before you actually enter the new Subpath.

The Formative Subpath is often looked upon as restrictive and negative. Due to the authority figures in our lives, we are not permitted to do exactly as we wish. The Productive Subpath covers the working years of life and generally brings a happier period, because we are older, wiser, and depending on our desire to achieve and our willingness to work hard, can operate our lives on a higher level and create more. The Harvest Subpath, beginning where the Productive Subpath leaves off, will span the years from before retirement into old age and can represent a reflective and introspective period, or a time when brand new activities are begun, depending upon the number designated by the period.

Some of these Subpaths will be represented by numbers which, in numerology, are called karmic. The numbers 19/1, 13/4, 14/5, and 16/7 are called karmic because they bring lessons and tests of character with them. All you need to know is that special consideration, work, and effort will have to be put forth if the Subpath is karmic, in order to learn valuable lessons that were not given attention in a past life.

The Number 1 Subpath

FORMATIVE: As a child or young adult, you will be developing the ability to individualize and express yourself in an original manner. Often you may feel repressed and restricted and unable to express yourself fully due to an environment that breeds anxiety or frowns upon individuality and independent thought. In any event, as a child you will grow up with little in the way of family support and be left to your own devices to find your way. Your family could stress independent activity and thought, and urge you to forge a path of your own. If this happens to you, consider it a lesson about learning to stand, think, and act on your own two feet. In many situations, you will find that you have an opportunity as a child and young adult to make your way by yourself, learning to lean on your own courage and independent thought. In this Subpath, there is a warning to parents neither to repress their child's ability to express himself nor allow the child too much independence.

PRODUCTIVE: In this Subpath, you will make positive strides in the realm of leading and directing others, at the same time developing and perfecting a drive for ambition, achievement, and uniqueness. While emphasizing original ideas and seeking recognition and reward for your accomplishments, you are warned not to put the self above everyone else all the time.

HARVEST: This Subpath is likely to be anything but retiring. You will find yourself involved in many activities, some new and some old. You will gain attainment from both aspects. New beginnings along different lines will take place in the latter years of your life.

The Number 2 Subpath

FORMATIVE: You may experience some difficulty as a child or young adult developing the sensitive, harmonious, and cooperative aspects of this number because of an overly domineering mother or because of the lack of the father's presence. This number suggests, in any event, that your primary influence as a child has been left to the mother or to a strong female figure, which can be due to divorce, death, or the father's job taking him away from home. You must learn to work well with others in the spirit of cooperation, exercising tact and patience as you mature within this cycle. Because you feel comfortable working in partnership rather than alone, you will probably desire to marry early in life.

PRODUCTIVE: Achievement and success will come to you by means of working with others in a harmonious environment. Partnership arrangements will be favored over working by yourself, and you will learn the value of cooperation and a pleasant environment. Marriage and family will be emphasized, as well as working in groups, organizations, and associations, in order to bring about favorable results. During this Subpath you are cautioned against pushing your ego on others or becoming overly dependent. Affairs with the opposite sex will be both positive and negative, depending on how well you handle yourself.

HARVEST: This usually indicates a very restful period, where, if desired, you can busy yourself with hobbies of a collecting nature or one in which the hands are used. Because the number 2 is a feminine vibration, you will find yourself influenced by women a great deal. For the most part, it should be a period of happy associations through close friends and loved ones.

The Number 3 Subpath

FORMATIVE: This is an enjoyable Subpath, where as a youngster and young adult you can find expression through pleasurable friends and artistic pursuits. You should strive, and your parents should encourage you, to take part in school plays, music recitals, writing, or arts and crafts hobbies. Although emotions may be a bit overstrained at times, since you feel timid and shy, you should push yourself to take part in creative activities. Care must be taken to emphasize the lighter aspects of life. Opportunities to sing, write, act, and engage in dramatic and artistic pursuits should not be missed. As a young adult, the main emphasis of your life will revolve around warm, loving friends and festive social activities.

PRODUCTIVE: During this period as an adult, you will benefit by pursuing activities of a highly creative nature. Business and pleasure will generally mix well, and the all-around environment should be most carefree, gay, enjoyable, and free from financial burdens. You may be swept away with the joy of living, possessing a warm and caring group of family and friends. This is a period of great self-expression, but you must still exercise your will to remain focused on activities. Hopping from one project to the next without completing tasks can limit accomplishment. Scattering your energies could also lead to frustration, lack of accomplishment, and physical depletion.

HARVEST: This period should be one of the most pleasant for you, with plenty of time for socializing and reflection. Creative pursuits never attempted before will find their fullest expression with a great degree of self-satisfaction and confidence. At retirement, you will have an opportunity to pursue many activities previously unattainable during the other Subpaths. This is probably one of the most pleasant Subpaths to live through.

The Number 4 Subpath

FORMATIVE: This Subpath may find you as a child or young adult in a restrictive environment or one that places a heavy emphasis on work. You will benefit by working hard and setting a proper foundation for your future. Not much time will be spent on pleasurable hobbies or creative pursuits. For whatever reason, be it the lack of money or a harsh and restrictive family setting, you will usually labor long and hard with constant effort, developing an orderly and systematic approach to life. Emphasis will be on work, persistent effort, and practicality, sometimes but not always accompanied by little feeling of appreciation or recognition. Not much time will be spent on flights of fancy or idealistic pursuits, but you will develop an appreciation for the importance of work and the value of saving money. As a young adult, your main emphasis will remain on working hard and maintaining an orderly existence, while accomplishment remains slow and steady. You may still feel somewhat boxed in, but more balance and structure will be evident.

PRODUCTIVE: During this period you are likely to make major and positive strides toward building a strong and dependable foundation for life. While hard work, economy, and conscientious effort are emphasized, you will make great progress toward slow and steady growth, always upward, taking a realistic approach to life. Money may not be overabundant or finances may have to be budgeted, but a practical viewpoint will stress saving and investing conservatively and slowly. Over the long haul you can accumulate a great many assets.

HARVEST: During this harvesting period, hard work and a determined effort will be emphasized, with little time for rest and relaxation. Caution must be exercised to avoid resentment and aggravation over what you view as restrictive and relentless hard work. More particularly, service during this period is emphasized, accompanied by a constant effort. If you enjoy working, these latter years will bring rewards based on consistent effort. A boxed-in feeling may exist, since you have little time for pleasure or reflection. Retirement is usually not forecasted, and financial concern may, but not always, exist.

The Number 5 Subpath

FORMATIVE: This cycle will bring you a great deal of variety, change, and freedom, coupled with not much responsibility. As a child or young adult, you will reap the rewards of venturing out, and discovering and promoting your talents, generally preferring to avoid the duties, drudgery, and responsibilities of everyday life. Since energy will be high, a sense of frustration and restlessness can be felt if you are not always on the go. During the early years money can fluctuate, and parents must be mindful of teaching its correct usage. Moreover, they should observe their children carefully, since the number 5 also vibrates to the negative aspects of abusing freedom by engaging in drinking, drugs, gambling, careless sex, stealing, and lying. As a young adult, you can live in a more balanced atmosphere, but the feelings of restlessness, coupled with sudden changes, will be more pronounced. Excessive living can cause serious trouble if you have not been taught the correct use of personal freedom.

PRODUCTIVE: As this cycle unfolds, the positive use of freedom and change will enhance your individual level of attainment and accomplishment. Romantic love affairs will be plentiful, accentuating a release from the cares and responsibilities of life. While travel brings excitement and forward progress, the cares of home and family can cause problems. Personal, business, and career changes can and will occur frequently as you learn the value and lesson of change accompanied by adaptability. Money will fluctuate sharply from being plentiful to just getting by, so care must be taken to dispense with it wisely. Since change will occur frequently, you are advised to establish some form of permanent roots and cautioned to handle domestic responsibility when the need arises.

HARVEST: This cycle will bring a great deal of travel, adventure, and pleasure in the latter years of life. Although life will change greatly with each passing year and sometimes dramatically within each year itself, heavy responsibility will not be shouldered, and burdens will be light. Finances will still have the tendency to fluctuate, but a sense of movement and advancement will bring more satisfaction.

The Number 6 Subpath

FORMATIVE: During this childhood and early-adult period, you may feel restricted by an overpowering sense of duty and obligation toward others, usually within the family. Lessons of responsibility will be taught, coupled with caring for the needs and welfare of others; parents must try to lessen the burdens shouldered by their child. They would be well advised to refrain from overly involving their children in their own personal problems. As a child you may feel that your ability to promote your own projects and desires is stifled because of obligations to others within the family. Early adulthood may afford a release from some of the weight of previous years, but domestic responsibilities will remain, especially if you marry early, as many will. Cultivation of artistic pursuits, coupled with a strong emphasis on education, will be a valuable asset in later years.

PRODUCTIVE: This cycle will bring with it strides toward a happy family life, but not without the problems, obligations, and sacrifices that accompany domestic duties. Promoting harmony, teaching, counseling, and shouldering heavy responsibility in your chosen profession will bring steady advancement, coupled with financial protection.

HARVEST: The love of family and friends will combine with a sense of duty and responsibility. Having to adjust to the needs of others could bring frustration, and you may prefer to be more reflective or follow a different path. Generally, taking care of others, possibly even elderly parents and relatives, will bring feelings of warmth, love, and self-satisfaction. Security within the family and career will bring rich rewards.

The Number 7 Subpath

FORMATIVE: As a child, you may feel repressed, moody, withdrawn, and misunderstood by those in your immediate environment. Moreover, you may desire to be alone. Parents should make every attempt to draw these youngsters into the mainstream of life, where a few close friendships can be developed. Advancement is possible along the lines of study, religion, and scientific and technical skills. Avocations promoting spirituality, deep reflection, and specialization will lessen the tensions of this period. As a young adult, marriage may be difficult for you, since the number 7 often desires to follow his own path in order to develop inner peace. Individual pursuits will be accented. A good education along the lines of a specialization will bring rich rewards later in life.

PRODUCTIVE: This cycle will bring much inner peace and growth along the lines of religion, spirituality, study, and specialization. Marriage still may not be emphasized, since you prefer to be alone or to proceed independently. Opportunities will be presented for advancement so long as you do not strive too hard for material gain alone but wait patiently for projects to develop at their own pace. Success will come through writing, teaching, researching, investigation, specialized knowledge, or expertise in difficult areas. Practical affairs will not be of much interest, as inner growth will be emphasized.

HARVEST: This cycle will bring time for restful reflection. As an adult, you can look forward to a peaceful retirement or semiretirement. Unburdened by social and family restrictions and obligations, you will have plenty of time to study metaphysical, religious, or philosophical and specialized pursuits.

The Number 8 Subpath

FORMATIVE: As a child, you can learn a great deal about handling and balancing business, material, and monetary aspects of living. Parents are cautioned not to overindulge these children with an excessive amount of spending money, since economy must be learned at an early age. Your family atmosphere may fluctuate between status and power or be one in which material and financial matters are severely strained. Both situations can cause you some confusion as a youngster when deciding the correct form of management. As you progress through this cycle, you will find yourself in a more balanced environment, where material accomplishments and comforts can be gained.

PRODUCTIVE: If handled properly, your adult years will allow you to make huge advancements through powerful commercial and financial organizations. Although little time will exist for rest, relaxation, and avocations, you will discover that much accumulation of power and wealth will result from pushing hard and maintaining a steady pressure for accomplishment. Business advancement on a large scale is possible with continued effort; however, not without the accompanying tensions. Health must be watched, since unrestricted strain can wear out your body.

HARVEST: Forget about retirement or even semiretirement during this cycle, since the chance to accomplish on a large scale will continue to present itself. Opportunities to make money and achieve power and prestige will bring rich rewards, but a practical and pragmatic management style will be required. Material gain will be uppermost.

The Number 9 Subpath

FORMATIVE: As a child, this cycle is likely to be a difficult one, since it requires that you learn selflessness, compassion, and giving at an early age. These are tough lessons even for the adult to accept, no less for the young child. Being unable to sort out or understand your own feelings and needs can result in much theatrics and strong emotional outbursts, coupled with complaints of dissatisfaction. While this may be a trying cycle for parents, much love, compassion, and understanding must be shown in order to create a positive environment in which lessons can be learned. Artistic, dramatic, and humanistic pursuits, coupled with emphasis on education, will aid you in future endeavors.

PRODUCTIVE: A truly dramatic cycle. Significant progress will be made along humanitarian, artistic, or philanthropic lines, coupled with a great deal of individual freedom. Personal attachments and nagging responsibilities, such as those which exist in marriage or locked-in relationships, can cause you problems unless universal love and brotherhood are accented and displayed toward others. You will reach peak performance in your chosen field by understanding and attending to the needs and concerns of others. Emotions and imagination must be kept in check, since this cycle of endings can cause physical problems.

HARVEST: A period of humanitarian concerns, philanthropic endeavors, and much freedom will allow you to explore and grow within a less restrictive environment. Freedom will exist both on a personal and financial basis due to universal concern, compassion, and love shown to others. Artistic and dramatic pursuits will also bring a feeling of satisfaction and accomplishment. Negative emotions can cause physical problems if you don't cultivate the ability to "let go."

The Number 11 Subpath

FORMATIVE: As a young child, this Subpath most always will reduce to a 2, since the 11 vibration may be too difficult for you to handle. As you grow into your early teens, you are likely to acquire inspiration from studies such as metaphysics, philosophy, art, music, and religious pursuits. Parents are encouraged to emphasize the beauty of cooperation, friendship, and association with others. As with the 2 vibration, your mother or close female relative will have a great influence over you.

PRODUCTIVE: This can truly be a wonderful period of illumination in all aspects of life except speculative ventures in the business world. Greatness can be attained in fields in which you are able to illuminate the ideas of interest to you. There is a tendency to involve yourself on the stage of life and an accompanying desire to act upon your dreams and aspirations. Since you have starlike qualities, it is more advisable to work before the public than in commercial operations.

HARVEST: This will be a period of quiet retirement. You will benefit from attending classes, and from reading and writing on topics of interest. Great inspiration will drive you to learn more and reveal this knowledge to others. If you prefer not to retire but to place yourself before the public, therefore, attainment is possible on a large scale. Activities with women and female relatives will go well.

The Number 22 Subpath

FORMATIVE: No 22 first cycle is possible, since there are not twenty-two months in the year. It is a good thing, too, as this cycle would bring with it an enormous amount of nervous strain and tension, impossible for any youngster to handle.

PRODUCTIVE: Despite the fact that the tension of this period is likely to drive you to distraction, it is, nevertheless, a period in which the individual is capable of masterful achievements, leading to greatness and leadership on an impressive scale. Business with influential corporations, organizations, and institutions will take up a significant amount of your time and offer advancement. While ideals will come quickly, you are advised to build upon a strong, firm foundation and to keep all business plans on a practical footing.

HARVEST: If you are planning to retire, you might as well forget it if your last Subpath is a 22. Large-scale projects are likely to be successful but in need of continuous attention. The tendency to be high-strung and nervous will exist, but a practical, firm foundation in business ventures will do wonders to ease the tension. Accomplishment on a huge scale can also bring you a great deal of self-satisfaction and rich rewards.

CHAPTER 4

Timing Is Everything: The Pinnacles

Success knocks at our door many times throughout the course of our lives. Being aware of changing circumstances and potentials for growth during a specific period in life can be vital in opening the doors to success. These moments are preordained. They are highly prophetic. We can look ahead, see what is coming at the bend in the road, and prepare for it in advance. These periods of change and opportunity are called *Pinnacles*.

There are four Pinnacles in our lives, with the first and the fourth being the longest. Each pinnacle represents a specific time in our life, a time when major growth can occur along the lines of the designated number.

Locating the Length of Each Pinnacle

Finding the Pinnacle numbers is easy. Using the number 9, as the cycle of humanity, and multiplying that number by 4, since there are four Pinnacles, we arrive at a starting number of 36 for calculation purposes. To determine the First Pinnacle subtract the Life Path number from the number 36, and that will be the length in years of the First Pinnacle. For the Second Pinnacle, add 9 years to the age arrived at for the First Pinnacle. For the Third Pinnacle, add nine years to the age obtained for the Second Pinnacle. The Fourth Pinnacle will cover the remainder of the life. Now you can see how we arrive at the fact that the First and the Fourth Pinnacles are the longest in length.

Computing the Numbers for the Pinnacles

To compute the numbers that influence your Pinnacles, first take your month, day, and year of birth, and reduce each number to a single digit. At this step in the procedure, even the Master numbers should be reduced. Let us use the birthday of Elton John, born Reginald Kenneth Dwight, on March 25, 1947.

3 /	25 /	1947
3 /	2+5=7 /	1+9+4+7=21=2+1=3
3 /	7 /	3

Now just follow the formula below.

The First Pinnacle Number: Add together the digit for the month and day of birth and reduce your answer to a single digit. *Do not reduce your answer if it is a Master number.*

Elton's number for the First Pinnacle is 3+7=10, or 1.

The Second Pinnacle Number: Add together the digit for the day of birth and the year of birth, and reduce your answer to a single digit. *Do not reduce your answer if it is a Master number.*

Elton's number for the Second Pinnacle is 7+3=10, or 1.

The Third Pinnacle Number: Add together the digits for the First and Second Pinnacles, and reduce your answer to a single digit. *Do not reduce your answer if it is a Master number.*

Elton's number for the Third Pinnacle is 1+1=2.

The Fourth Pinnacle Number: Add together the digits for the month of birth and the year of birth, and reduce your answer to a single digit. *Do not reduce your answer if it is a Master number.*

Elton's number for the Fourth Pinnacle is 3 + 3 = 6.

Important changes will take place as you move from one Pinnacle into the next, especially around the twenty-eighth birthday, when you are moving from one cycle, or Subpath, into another (same as crossing from living in the month of birth into living in the day of birth). At this time major destiny changes will take place in your life. Likewise, changes will take place around the One Personal Year closest to your fifty-sixth birthday, when a shift takes place from living in the second (Productive) Subpath to living in the last (Harvest) Subpath (also known as moving from living in the day of birth into the year of birth).

Things to Remember:

1. If one of your Pinnacle numbers matches your Life Path number, consider yourself lucky, since not only will the experiences that you encounter forward the purpose of your existence, but there will also be an ease in your life, a reduction in strain and tension, that will help you in learning valuable lessons. Necessary opportunities will come your way to further your goals.

2. If one of your Pinnacle numbers matches your *Soul Urge* number (explained later), then the opportunities that are necessary to further your desires will be realized and will come with ease.

3. If one of your Pinnacle numbers matches your *Expression* (explained later) number, you can expect a great deal of help along the way from others if you reach out for it.

4. If one of your Pinnacle numbers matches your *Reality* number (explained later), then success likewise can be expected around the middle years. Opportunities will move in the direction you've planned for.

5. If one of your Pinnacle numbers matches your karmic

lesson, there is going to be great difficulty if you haven't already focused on mastering the lesson as outlined by the karmic lesson number. If you have sought to fulfill your destiny in this regard, there will be no great difficulties to overcome.

It is also important to note that with the Pinnacles, oftentimes the numbers representing them seem to carry heavier weight than even the Life Path number. Your attainments in life may represent or more closely resemble the Pinnacle number than the Life Path number.

Another important consideration is that the Pinnacles coincide with what is happening to us during major periods of our lives. The First Pinnacle is always very personal, since it emphasizes the experiences of the early years, when we are not overly concerned with what is happening in our outer world, but just with what is happening to us.

As we move into the Second Pinnacle, we become more worldly and group-oriented. Relationships in personal and business affairs become relevant, and we become more aware that there are outside forces that also must be reckoned with in order to be successful. It is at this Second Pinnacle that we begin to acquire obligations, such as starting a business or beginning a family.

As the Third Pinnacle is begun, most of us will make major commitments. Some may turn to national and international pursuits, having the free time in which to pursue these interests and avocations. Most importantly, however, we must make sure that we have a firm foundation laid for the future. This Third Pinnacle is the most important if we are to be comfortable for the remainder of the life.

The Fourth Pinnacle is often called the Pinnacle of Reflection. It takes place in the winter of our lives. Having developed many of our skills, we can reflect on the meaning of our lives and our accomplishments, not just for ourselves but for the welfare of mankind as well.

Now let us uncover the meaning of the Pinnacle numbers.

The Number 1 in a One

A number 1 Pinnacle can be difficult going especially in a First Pinnacle, but in many ways it is a blessing in disguise. Since it is a number of leadership and individuality, not to mention executive abilities, during your First Pinnacle you may find life disordered and perplexing, because there is no one in your home environment to give you any definite direction. You will have to go it alone, so to speak; slowly you will orient your life and goals toward leadership and individuation.

As a Second or a Third Pinnacle, you will have new beginnings. With determination and the courage to stand by your convictions, you will be able to venture into new undertakings, and to individualize and execute talents by forging forward with the ideas that have been maturing for a long time.

As a Last Pinnacle, the 1 can be difficult, since it represents a major chance to do outstanding work, coupled with much activity. A possible move of home is not unlikely. The 1 as a Last Pinnacle does not leave much room for quiet retirement, since there is still much responsibility required, but often it will release you from a certain type of obligation that has lasted for a long time. If you are not prepared to forge new territory, much frustration and anxiety can be expected.

With number 1 in any Pinnacle, especially if it is in the First Pinnacle, the chance to wake up and exercise leadership and executive skills can sometimes appear suddenly. The number 1 in a Pinnacle at any time demands that courage be exercised, which, because of circumstance, can be trying and difficult. But the period always forces you to think, act, and stand on your own.

Two

The number 2 Pinnacle is the number of partnerships,

associations, and relationships, in which the basic goal is learning to get along with others in a cooperative spirit. It represents a period of time when you must cultivate the skills of persuasion, cooperation, and diplomacy, instead of being forceful and pushy. A 2 in a First Pinnacle usually indicates that you have been raised or greatly influenced by a female vibration, either the mother, grandmother, favorite aunt, or a woman who was familiar or intimately involved with your upbringing, and that a male parental figure was not in attendance much of the time. It also points to the fact that the female vibration in charge of raising you could have displayed domineering tendencies, a trait that you may have picked up and tend to emulate. In any event, this strong female is going to be a major influence in your life.

During the First Pinnacle, oversensitivity could exist. You are advised not to rush into marriage, since early divorce is possible. During a Second and Third Pinnacle, great accomplishment can result from cultivating good friends, partnerships, and associations. Working harmoniously within large public and cultural organizations in analytical and statistical positions could also bring recognition. Difficulties in marriage and business partnerships must be kept in check, since problems can result from a susceptibility to criticism. Rewards will come from patience and diligence.

During a Final Pinnacle, retirement is quite possible and also pleasant. While sensitivity may still exist, a more receptive attitude should result in peace and joy. Joining with others in group activities will cultivate many warm and close friendships.

Three

You can expect this Pinnacle number to be basically a positive one during any period of life. During a First Pinnacle, an active social life can be expected, with plenty of romance, friends, and entertaining. The 3 in a First Pinnacle is usually one of pleasure, and as a youngster or young adult, you may have to be pushed and cncouraged more by your parents to put forth your full effort in developing artistic and creative tendencies. It is important that education be furthered along creative and artistic lines of expression.

During a second and third Pinnacle, tremendous growth can take place along the lines of verbal, artistic, and creative endeavors. You must take responsibility for your own actions and conserve, not scatter, your energies. The emotional life under any 3 in a Pinnacle can be difficult, due to careless speaking, extravagance, or taking others and things at face value, especially regarding affairs of the heart.

During a Fourth Pinnacle, much enjoyment can come from expressing your talents and mixing business with pleasure. Good friendships can be established. During any Pinnacle, it should not be forgotten that the 3 brings the blessings of attraction and luck in matters of money.

Four

During a Pinnacle influenced by the number 4, it is always important to lay a good foundation for the future. Since this is basically a slow moving period, you will feel limited or restricted in some way because of the heavy load. A 4 Pinnacle during any time does not indicate a leisurely period; it requires work, order, solid endeavor, and a concentrated application of systematic energy in order to build for the future. During a 4-influenced First Pinnacle, going to work at an early age may be of interest or a necessity, with not much free time left for enjoyment and play. Usually there is a strong work ethic established within the family, whereby you are encouraged to plan, pursue, and struggle for what you want. In any event, you will learn early in life that long-held dreams can be realized only if you are practical and serious.

During a Second and Third Pinnacle, four presages a lack of economy, resulting in failing finances, which can lead to feelings of restriction and fiscal impotence, until a more practical outlook is developed. Extravagance cannot be sustained for long during any Pinnacle under a 4, but if you harness your energy and make use of the ambition that you possess, a strong and solid foundation can be established and built upon in every aspect of living.

During a Last Pinnacle, much hard work is still ahead and retirement will not be considered practical, although you still may plan for it. For many, it is not until the Last Pinnacle that long-held desires are attainable, coupled still with much work.

Five

Under a 5 Pinnacle, change in any form and at any time can be expected. This very progressive period involving great freedom will let you feel unrestricted. Although this is a somewhat restless and uncertain period, great strides can take place in the human arena, where new and different ideas are introduced. Marketing, selling, promoting, as well as civic, administrative, and legal pursuits, can bring you great success. During any Pinnacle when the 5 is in control, the ability to travel and experience life will be presented.

The 5 is not a domestic number, and those under its influence must be careful not to ignore family responsibilities totally. While a liberal environment will still exist, however, establishment of some form of permanent roots is advisable. While great freedom and progress are possible, care must be maintained in financial areas, in order to avoid the pitfalls of overspending or impulsive shopping. Finances often fluctuate, but fortunately the money is there just when you need it most.

During a First Pinnacle, 5 will find you restless and uncertain as to which direction to follow. Many projects may be left incomplete, resulting in lack of accomplishment. A desire for movement could cause you to explore new territory abruptly. In a Second and Third Pinnacle, especially if followed by a Pinnacle influenced by the restrictive 4 or responsible 6, the 5 will bring years of freedom from restriction, variety, and change enhanced by new friends, travel, and versatility. During this period, you must be careful to read the fine print before signing documents, since haste and impulsive actions could cause loss later on.

With a 5 during a Final Pinnacle, change and variety will dominate the remaining years of your life, bringing interesting friends, as well as fluctuating finances. Some form of roots must be cultivated and maintained within an aura of challenging progressiveness. Retirement is definitely not part of the picture with a 5 in a Final Pinnacle, but learning to adjust and be prepared for change can make the final years of your life very rewarding and exciting.

Six

The 6 Pinnacle brings responsibilities, adjustments, and duty in the form of humanitarian and family pursuits. The joys and problems that accompany love, marriage, children, family, inheritances, and trust funds, as well as operating and managing your own or someone else's business, are generally addressed. A great deal of happiness and satisfaction, as well as financial reward, comes from attending to the needs of others unselfishly, as well as giving wise counsel when requested. If your Pinnacle is influenced by this number, you will be moved to settle down and be responsible for others, which at times can cause a feeling of restriction and being overburdened. Also present will be a teaching and healing aspect, in which money may be spent caring for the sick and needy, and providing an education for younger children. Attending to your duties and responsibilities in a gracious and loving manner will bring ample financial reward later on, as well as improved financial conditions.

During a First Pinnacle, 6 demands that obligations of home and family must be met, such as being the responsible big sister or brother. It also brings great love and protection, with enough money when needed. As a young adult, you should avoid jumping into an early marriage, especially if not sufficiently matured, for the responsibilities involved could last a lifetime.

Under a 6 during a Second and Third Pinnacle much

can be gained and accomplished from settling down, cultivating family love, and serving the public in a useful and willing manner. By helping others, financial reward and protection are possible. Marriage, counseling, teaching, and the arts are all favorable avenues leading to recognition, harmony, and success.

With 6 in a Final Pinnacle, the warmth of a comfortable retirement and home life can be expected, with many loving friends and relatives gathered around, coupled with financial protection. Since the teaching and counseling element is still present, the artistic individual might venture into these areas as favorable avocations.

Seven

To insure success during a Pinnacle influenced by the number 7, knowledge, education, and a sense of specialization are demanded. The number 7 in a Pinnacle, being the number of perfection, indicates a time of study and applying the skills learned. Outstanding use of acquired knowledge can bring great reward and recognition but in a quiet, poised, and patient way. The number 7 has a special attraction for money, and while at times money may seem lacking, a careful application of one's talents can bring forth sufficient finances when needed. For those in a 7-influenced Pinnacle who have success, there is usually less interest in the material aspects of life than there is in the deeper hidden and specialized forms of knowledge.

Under 7 in a Pinnacle you must guard against covetousness. The grass may seem greener on the other side of the fence, but concentrating on this approach to life will only make you feel miserable, causing depression, repression, and a lack of accomplishment. An interest in metaphysics and philosophical and occult studies, coupled with a search for wisdom and specialization, will bring recognition, along with financial rewards and success.

During a First Pinnacle, you frequently may show signs of repressing your emotions. This denial can cause poor health. Emotional upsets and outbursts can filter into the academic environment, resulting in learning problems and deep feelings of inferiority. Parents of such children are advised to use encouragement and a reward system rather than being overly strict or disciplined. By doing so an interest in educational pursuits will be awakened, and the negative habit of repression will be lessened.

With 7 in a Second and Third Pinnacle, research, writing, and investigative skills will bring recognition along specialized lines of employment. The material and practical interests of life will not be of major concern to you as much as acquiring knowledge and the truth about the deeper hidden aspects of life or specialized subjects. You will be more of a separatist and a loner, and as such, marriage can often be troublesome and irritating unless your partner is aware of your desire to pursue singular interests.

If 7 influences your Fourth Pinnacle, unless specialization has been obtained in some field, you will have financial problems; therefore, it is important to acquire some form of education before the Final Pinnacle is reached. An appearance of aloofness and introspection may be preferred in a Final Pinnacle, but so, too, will the elements of quiet, scholarly repose, with friends of the more intellectual type.

Eight

The 8 in a Pinnacle is a powerful indicator that much can be acquired in the area of prestige and finances, but it demands constant effort and an ambitious nature. During a Pinnacle guided by the number 8, you will have the stamina to get down to work and establish yourself in a profession or business enterprise by exercising good judgment and management skills especially in terms of finances. Expenses may be high at times, and budgeting may be necessary to place fiscal affairs in good operating order, but the rewards of this period are outstanding. Often property and possessions will be acquired through hard work and executive skills. Significant groups and influential organizations will bring recognition and positions of authority, demanding the exercise of sound business judgment. Eight being the number of karma, it carries the warning never to trust to luck alone. Misplaced trust and confidence in others can bring disappointment and defeat. An intellectual rather than an emotional approach to problem solving must be adhered to.

With an 8 in the First Pinnacle, you will be interested in going to work at an early age or engaging in a profession that demands constant effort in order to achieve. Expenses may be high in order to secure your goals, but the outcome will be rapid success and accomplishment. Parents whose child possesses an 8 in the First Pinnacle must teach the proper use of money, as well as the positive aspects of utilizing one's personal power. Balance will be called for in every aspect of living.

During a Second and Third Pinnacle, an 8 can make you a V.I.P. or a superstar in your chosen profession—if you devote lots of work to it. Lack of ambition or laziness in any form will only frustrate your ambitions. Success, status, and financial gain are just a few of the rewards possible, during an 8-influenced Pinnacle, for maintaining a persevering and efficient outlook.

If you have an 8 as your Final Pinnacle number, you must forget about early retirement. At best, partial retirement is possible but generally not lasting too long, since there is still constant care and attention needed in operating a large successful commercial, business, or professional enterprise.

Nine

Learning to love without expecting anything in return can be difficult, emotionally charged, and dramatic, but that is exactly what the number 9 in a Pinnacle demands of you during its passage. The lessons of compassion, universal understanding, and tolerance for others, with less concern for your own personal needs, can be

enhanced by humanistic, artistic, and philanthropic endeavors, with the chance of attracting fame and fortune.

The number 9 is not personal in nature; therefore,
during a Pinnacle governed by it, selfishness of any kind
will bring disappointment until tolerance and compassion
for others is developed. You must not dwell on yourself
too often but aim high and attend to the needs of others
with an attitude of brotherhood. Only in this manner will
the lessons of the 9 be learned and success achieved.

Nine is the number of completion, and during any Pinnacle subject to it, major endeavors and responsibilities
and relationships will end, sometimes emotionally, but
they will free you for the future. Success and attainment
are possible once you have learned to let go and pursue
other activities. Sometimes these completions are not at
all desired and become emotionally charged and upsetting, but in the end the completion will be seen as beneficial in nature.

During the First Pinnacle, the lessons that number 9
require of you may not be easy for you to accept. Tolerance, compassion, selflessness, as well as sharing, can be
difficult even for the adult to learn, but if acquired early
in life, they will lead you to greatness later on. During
the First Pinnacle the importance of the father is also
accentuated, a condition that may cause you some confusion or distress, resulting in an unrealistic attitude. Either
the father is considered a superman possessing suprahu-
man characteristics that you view as unattainable in yourself, or he is part of the problem, having caused some
feelings of disappointment through death, absenteeism,
or not having been there when you needed him. Additionally, by the end of the First Pinnacle, some form of
romantic attachment, marriage, or line of work may be
left behind or demand completion. While initially viewed
as disappointing, it usually frees you of a burden, becoming ultimately a blessing in disguise.

During the Second and Third Pinnacles, accomplishment and great attainment are possible by tending to the
needs of others. Achieving your goals will bring success
and great financial reward, as long as you demand less

for yourself. Money can be lost and just as quickly can flow back again. Therefore, you should not dwell too much on losses. Human drama and emotions will run high, adding beauty and color to your life, coupled with much warmth and appreciation from others, as long as narrow-mindedness is not maintained.

As for the Final Pinnacle, retirement is possible, bringing an interest in philanthropic pursuits, which uplift one's spirits. An interest in art and drama may likewise be pursued.

Eleven

The 11 in a Pinnacle, being a higher octave of the 2 and a Master number, brings the opportunity for expansion along the lines of inventiveness, spiritual and religious understanding, and outright fame, as long as you stick to your ideals. Partnerships, associations, and marriage, also emphasized, bring great rewards coupled with problems, due to nervous tension and strain sometimes caused by immaturity.

The Pinnacle governed by an 11 is an electrically charged period in which you expend much talent, often gaining the opportunity to be in the limelight and to appear before the public through TV, dramatic performance, or by illuminating one's personal beliefs.

During a First Pinnacle, the conditions required and imposed by the 11 can be quite difficult. Some form of religious, philosophic, or metaphysical training will work wonders to add inspiration, illumination, courage, and confidence to your personality and help out during tense periods. It will also train your mind in the proper method of thinking in order to achieve success. During this period, you will not be practical or materially minded. Often parents find teaching their child good values a struggle, since the child can be difficult, yet sensitive, at the same time. As in a Pinnacle governed by 2, the mother or important female figurehead carries much of the weight and responsibility for your early years.

During a Second and Third Pinnacle, 11 brings great

inventiveness, leadership, and inspiration, which, if cultivated, can pivot you right into the limelight, bringing
electrical excitement and applause for work well done.
Nervous tension will be a problem, but spiritual expansion, a philosophical attitude, and metaphysical training
will shed light and aid living the good life.

During the Final Pinnacle, retirement or at least partial
retirement can be expected and enjoyed, during which
you will be brought into the limelight and will receive
recognition due to participation in groups, associations,
TV, radio, metaphysical and religious pursuits, or speaking out on your expertise.

Twenty-two

Any Pinnacle influenced by 22 or 11, is a Master Pinnacle, since 22 is a higher octave of the number 4. As
with a Pinnacle governed by the Master number 11, an
expanded consciousness is required in order to be successful. You must *Think Big*. A Pinnacle under 22
requires the full use of your inventiveness and illumina-
tive qualities in order to bring about material accomplishment on an impressively huge scale. This Pinnacle covers
a wide arena of endeavors, bringing the very highest
achievement possible for mankind.

As one can expect, there are very few individuals who
are capable of carrying the heavy vibration of the 22
coupled with such weighty demands for the benefit of
others; yet it is possible. Just look around you and immediately you can name the influential corporate and international concerns involved in promoting national and
international affairs, all being mobilized by individuals
who possess Pinnacles under the Master 22.

As with the 11-governed Pinnacle, a great deal will be
demanded of you in order to receive the large material
reward that accompanies the 22. Often the drive to
accomplish on a grand scale will leave little time for
yourself.

During a First Pinnacle, the force of the 22 is so great
that the average person usually converts this energy to

the lower vibration of the 4, which is more manageable. Yet there are some youngsters and young adults, however few, who can create masterfully. These individuals usually find themselves working and acquiring knowledge through large national and international concerns before embarking out on their own. Many actors, actresses, real estate developers, and business people involved in national and international activities carry the 22 vibration.

During a Second, Third, and Final pinnacle, idealistic approaches that bring about practical results on a large and universal scale are possible, carrying with them tremendous responsibility. Don't expect retirement, since the requirements of this number are awesome, and much energy and directed force must be applied to keep big projects moving. Wherever mankind benefits, you will see great projects moving forward. The more highly evolved you are, the more you thrive on this type of energy, and you won't be too interested in retirement, anyway.

CHAPTER 5

Stumbling Blocks:
The Challenges

No great accomplishment during the Pinnacles can take place without your first overcoming some obstacles along the way. These weak traits in the personality must be tackled directly, for they carry with them a red flag announcing *Danger, Roadblock Ahead, Look Out.* If you are to advance in life, you must know which difficulties may be encountered so that you are prepared to meet these problems with the application of positive will power and energy.

The best approach in tackling the *Challenge* numbers is to be willing to admit that you're not perfect and that there are weak traits to your character. Even the most brilliant of scientists, teachers, healers, politicians, numerologists—you name it—are well aware that they have personality flaws. Life would be awfully dull and boring if we were all born perfect. There would exist very little reason to change and improve one's existence.

It is easy to say, No, not me, I don't have that problem or that fault. Facing ourselves and looking our frailties straight in the eye takes courage. At times such honesty can be difficult. But if you lighten your attitude and add a bit of humor while you learn, you may even have a laugh or two along the way.

Determining your Challenges is a form of self-discovery and can be an enriching experience. Awareness is the key and the first step to progress. We've all heard people say, If I only knew then what I know now, I could have overcome this or that difficult period. By discovering your Challenge numbers, you can take a great deal of action so that the same mistake is not made twice. The key is to incorporate into your life the positive elements of your Challenge number, while at the same time guarding against falling into the temptations and pitfalls that the negative aspect of the Challenge number implies.

By using your Challenges as a tool for growth, you can look to the future, become aware that this or that aspect of living may present a difficulty, and slowly improve yourself so that when you reach a specific Challenge, it is no longer a problem but instead has become an asset.

It is our weaknesses that transform us into great human beings, not our strengths. Often our strengths make us lazy, because we can always fall back on them. But our weaknesses call for extra effort and hard work, and once they're overcome, the doors to success seem to open and the rewards of right living fall into our laps.

Basically throughout one's life there will be four Challenges, with the third Challenge being considered of major importance, since it will have an overall effect throughout the life. Its presence will also be felt in all other Challenge periods.

The Challenges shift into position at the same time as the Pinnacles and are active for the same number of years. Like the Pinnacles, the Challenges also cross over into the three Subpaths, or subcycles, as represented by the month, day, and year of your birth. A new Pinnacle and Challenge number always begin technically in the One Personal Year. When this happens, you will become aware of the newness of opportunities and obstacles. You may not know exactly where you are going, and some letting go of the past may still be needed, but you will fccl the forcc of thc ncw vibrations by the use of your intuitive human antenna.

Like the Pinnacles, your Challenges are found from your Life Path number. If the numbers making up your Life Path contain a Master number, such as 11 or 22, it is best, for computing purposes, first to reduce the Master number to a single digit.

You will remember that you employed the rule of addition in locating the Pinnacles. In computing your Challenges you will employ the rule of subtraction. This means that a zero will sometimes be your answer. Let us again use the birthday of our friend Elton John and compute his Challenge numbers. First, we will reduce the numbers of the month, day, and year of birth each to a single digit.

MONTH	DAY	YEAR
3	25	1947
3	$2+5=7$	$1+9+4+7=21=2+1=3$

Computing the Challenge Numbers

The First Challenge Number: Using the numbers representing the month and day of birth, *subtract* the lower number from the higher number.

Elton John's first challenge number: $7\text{-}3=4$

The Second Challenge Number: Using the numbers representing the day and year of birth, *subtract* the lower number from the higher number.

Elton John's Second Challenge number: $7\text{-}3=4$

The Third Challenge Number: Using the numbers representing the First and Second Challenges, *subtract* the lower number from the higher number. This is considered the *Major Challenge* and will be active throughout the life.

Elton John's Third Challenge number: $4\text{-}4=0$

The Fourth Challenge Number: Using the number representing the month and year of birth, *subtract* the lower number from the higher number.

Elton John's Fourth Challenge number: 3−3 = 0

Now, using the birthdate of William H. Rehnquist, Chief Justice of the United States Supreme Court, we can quickly locate his four Challenges. As we did with Elton John's birthday, we will reduce the three major Subpath numbers to single digits for convenience. Birthdate: 10/1/1924

Birthdate: 10 = 1 + 0 = 1   / 1 /   1924 = 1 + 9 + 2 + 4 = 16 = 1 + 6 = 7

$$1 - 1 = 0 \qquad\qquad\qquad 7 - 1 = 6$$
(First Challenge number)   (Second Challenge number)

$$6 - 0 = 6$$
(Third Challenge number)
Major Challenge number

$$7 - 1 = 6$$
(Fourth Challenge number)

At a glance it is obvious that Chief Justice Rehnquist's Major Challenge throughout his lifetime will be the number 6. However, let us first look at the number connected with his First Challenge, the 0, or Cipher. We can see that Elton John also had a 0, or Cipher, Challenge, as it is called.

The Zero Challenge

A Cipher, or Zero, as a Challenge number is the sign of a test and can be the most difficult, puzzling, and troublesome of all the Challenges depending on where it is located.

A Challenge ruled by a Cipher can mean either of two things: (1) You may face all the Challenges; or (2) you're in luck, since you have no Challenges at all and can choose whichever areas of your life you desire to work on. In both cases the Challenge governed by the Cipher represents *choice.* It means that you can choose your own direction, the way in which you desire to go, either for good or bad, coupled with many tests along the way. Your life can be smooth, or it can be frustrated by the roadblocks as represented by all the numbers and not highlighting any one Challenge in particular. The zero in connection with a Challenge means that the situation is totally within your hands. It also indicates that you may be an old soul.

As a First Challenge, the Cipher can indicate that as an old soul, you have reached a point in your evolution where you can choose for yourself what you want, regardless of the fact that there is not much indication as to which way to go. It is not a Challenge in which you can or should rely on others. You already possess the knowledge and the talents to be successful, but refinement is necessary. You will have to use your present knowledge to make life better.

The "Cipher Challenge," as a representative of all the Challenges, can be very difficult. It signifies that you must choose wisely or you will constantly be bombarded by the obstacles and hindrances of life, represented by the negative aspects of all the numbers, until you place yourself on the proper path to correct living.

The number 9 can never appear as a Challenge number, since it is the highest number. Any number when subtracted from 9 will always yield a number lower than 9. So don't look for the number 9 to appear in a Challenge anywhere. If it does, you've made a mistake.

Some Challenge numbers are more popular than others. For example, 1, 2, 3, and 0 crop up most often in connection with Challenges, followed by 4 and 5. Six and 7 don't show up nearly as often as the other numbers. Eight often appears with a 0 or Cipher as a First Challenge, which indicates that the individual will be a self-made person. Once again, 9 in connection with a Challenge never appears. Now, let us look at the meaning of the other Challenge numbers.

One

When a 1 appears as a Challenge, you can feel restricted or held down by circumstances or by those around you, whether family or otherwise, who have stronger wills. Because you may often try to please everyone, the more you try, the less satisfied and more frustrated and confused you become, until you don't know which way to turn. Little will be gained if you become resentful or revert to brooding as a way out. What must be cultivated and developed is strong determination and will power, which will increase a feeling of self-respect.

In order to promote yourself and those magnificent creative ideas that lie hidden within the number 1 ruling a Challenge, you must first try to satisfy yourself. If time and energy are consistently focused or channeled into attempting to please others, you may end up pleasing no one, especially yourself. First determine where your goals and aspirations lie and then set out to accomplish them with as little fanfare as possible. Caution must be exercised not to push headfirst into the feelings of others or attempt to demand that they accept your views. These negative qualities represent a major hindrance of the 1 in a Challenge. Just decide if the path is correct for you. If it is, move ahead with courage. Be careful not to vacillate, become pigheaded, or appear to know all the answers.

Two

The number 2 Challenge is a very *sensitive* one, in which you may be constantly making yourself miserable by allowing yourself to feel hurt over every issue you face. By doing so, you place yourself in a constant state of sensitivity, where these hurts can seem insurmountable. The resulting anger or pain can hinder your ability to let go and forgive.

With a number 2 even little things can transform themselves into major problems. You can be totally inconsiderate of the feelings of others, forgetting social graces taught earlier in life. During the 2-influenced Challenge, you will desire to be liked by everyone and should guard against being used as a doormat.

In order to overcome the Challenge put forth by the

number 2, a conscious effort must be made to develop a broader viewpoint concerning life. Energy must be exerted in cultivating self-confidence and being your own person, with less time spent dwelling on feelings of insecurity and inadequacy. By doing so, feelings of usefulness and self-respect will develop, along with the strong psychic powers hidden in all Challenges governed by the number 2.

Three

A major problem encountered with a 3 Challenge is that of *scattering* your energies in too many directions, thereby accomplishing nothing or less than initially anticipated. Latent in all 3's in connection with Challenges is a brilliantly creative mind gifted in writing, speaking, artistic pursuits, music, and dance. By cultivating these artistic talents, you can open doors.

Another aspect of the 3 Challenge can be seen by the vacillation that occurs between desiring to be alone, on the one hand, and appearing as a social butterfly on the other. While it is important to strengthen social contacts and enjoy one's friends and acquaintances, it is imperative not to scatter funds, time, or energy, indulging your every whim. By trying to strike a balance, you will allow new people to come into your life with more than enough time available to improve your artistic talents. Lastly, moods must be kept in check, idle gossiping eliminated, and care exercised in not taking others at face value.

Four

The 4 carries with it the need to bring more order and discipline into the life, while not neglecting the need for playtime. Difficulty can be encountered if you live in a rut, maintain narrow-minded or straight-laced views, or remain intolerant and inflexible to the ideas of others. A more realistic set of values, views, and opinions must be adhered to along the lines of work, order, and organization. Laziness, procrastination and inattention to the details of living will thwart your success.

While living within the period of a Challenge influenced by a 4, you must become more aware of when to make major changes. You may be inclined to force issues instead of waiting patiently until a more appropriate time presents itself. Moreover, you must guard against appearing stubborn, opinionated, and hard-headed to those around you. Developing a sense of routine and order will help you to let go of the worry and frustration that can accompany this number. Patience must be cultivated.

Five

Anything is possible while you live within the period of a Challenge connected with the number 5, and the whole world may be your playpen, but you must be mindful of a rebellious nature and periods of restlessness that have a tendency to surface. The 5 carries with it a twofold problem. The first deals with the abuse of personal freedom that accompanies all experiences involving a misuse of the senses, such as drugs, gambling, drinking, illicit sex, and overeating. The second aspect of the Challenge connected with the 5 deals with learning what to hold on to and what to discard—those people, places, and things that you must let go of in order to move on with your life.

In many ways the number 5 in a Challenge speaks for itself. All number 5's indicate the need to seek freedom, but often it is only freedom to escape from responsibilities, and change just for the sake of change. This can lead to disaster later on. You must set your sights on becoming more progressive in thought. Seeking new avenues to promote your talents and mingling with new people can bring rich rewards. While you are actively involved with change and progress, cultivate some roots.

The sexual dangers of the number 5 in a Challenge lie in acting on one's sexual and sensual impulses irresponsibly. A desire to try any new drug or odd and unusual forms of sex in today's day and age can lead to woeful consequences and even death. All natives operating under the number 5 in a Challenge must ask themselves, "Am

I overdoing it?" If so, they must correct the situation immediately.

Six

The number 6 connected with a Challenge relates to expressing strong opinions and ideas (especially those which apply to domestic issues) that may not be valid or correct. You may try to set down the law as you see it and expect others to follow obediently, showing little tolerance for their opinions.

Within a Challenge governed by the number 6, you may insist upon being right and may not admit when you're wrong or mistaken. The inability to determine right from wrong or allow your views to be changed can become a major hindrance. To be successful, you must not expect everyone to conform to your rules, since this will lead only to resentment, bad feelings, and possibly bad judgments.

You must cultivate the power to view all sides of an issue with an air of tolerance, compassion, and understanding. Failure to do so could lead to disharmony in family or marital relationships. You could end up arguing with *everyone*. You naturally like to be right and enjoy the atmosphere created by debate, but you should avoid participating in arguments. Energy must go into improving yourself by acquiring a good education and utilizing your personal magnetism to make life better for others, as well as for yourself. Only in this manner will you acquire the appreciation that you so rightly long for.

Seven

The number 7 can present a difficult Challenge. It brings both a rebellious nature and an element of destructive repression. If you possess a 7 Challenge, you must guard against allowing anger and false pride to dominate your personality. You must also refrain from appearing aloof, reserved, or superior.

The 7 can bring depression, melancholia, and feelings of resentment caused by some hidden episode in your family life, often related to the mother. Beware using alcohol as an escape.

Living through a Challenge influenced by the number 7 will require an advanced education, or technical or analytical skills in some specialization, in order to change what you view as intolerable conditions. Do not dwell on your limitations. Instead, take action to promote positive change in your life by specializing. Failure to move out of a rut or make a shift in your life, coupled with an indifferent attitude, could be tragic. You must learn to forgive and forget, to let go of past embarrassments, and to cultivate brain power. Moreover, you must learn to have more faith in yourself and in your self-worth.

Eight

A Challenge ruled by number 8 brings an excellent chance for success and recognition as long as you don't get carried away with a desire for power and money. Some form of philosophical attitude and balance must be developed in order not to swing to extremes.

Often the 8 is coupled with a Cipher, or Zero, as a First Challenge. When the Zero is connected to the First Challenge, it often signifies that you are an old soul and possess the ability to be a self-made individual but you must be mindful not to strain after power and money for fear of being poor or limited. A Challenge under the 8 must learn to balance the material side of life with the spiritual aspects by eliminating false values. By focusing on a good job and living an ethical life, great monetary and spiritual rewards will justly follow.

Nine

There is none.

CHAPTER 6

The Universe is Alive: Discovering the Universal Vibrations

The entire universe and everything in it is alive and moving in a specific vibratory cycle known as the *Universal Vibration*. This Universal Vibration refers to the experiences and events that the world in general attracts during any given year. These vibrations have an effect upon all of us. Additionally, while being affected by the Universal Vibration, each individual moves through *Personal Year* vibrations, which will be discussed in the next chapter.

The *Universal Years* 1–9, 11, and 22 disclose important information. They point to certain ideas and feelings that will force the world to think and act in a specific way, thereby creating major events. These incidents affect each of us and have an impact on our lives, so it is important to know what each Universal Year vibration means and how it can influence our thinking.

Computing the Numbers for the Universal Year

Computing the Universal Year is not difficult. Just take the current calendar year, and reduce it to a single digit or Master number. Let us use the year 1991 as an example. By adding all the numbers across $(1+9+9+1=20=2+0=2)$, we can determine that the Universal Year is 2. It's that easy. Now discover the thought patterns and events that will influence the world around you.

The 1 Universal Year

The 1 Universal Year brings advancement on a worldwide basis. The new, the bizarre, the different, will be experienced as countries decide to follow a new and different path. Taking the initiative and expressing more positive attitudes will bring achievement and reconciliation between formerly hostile nations, and new techniques will be implemented to resolve international and global disagreements. Nevertheless, new discoveries and sudden breaks in relationships could cause rupture. New methods will be employed to attempt to resolve such global issues. Domestically, individual cities and states will seek to establish new ideas and embark on new plans that place operations on a more productive level. Inventions in aviation and engineering will be particularly plentiful. New ground will be broken and progress made by pioneering new ideas. Exploration of new places will likewise be encouraged as the world embraces and welcomes change.

The 2 Universal Year

The 2 Universal year will find national and international governments of the world making a serious effort to come together and unite in order to establish global harmony and peace. New peace treaties will be signed and friendships formed in a spirit of cooperation. Conversely, if care is not taken, many alliances will likewise be broken.

Since the number 2 represents manual dexterity, inventions of machinery made by hand will come into existence. Statistical work will be plentiful, and governments may formulate new tax codes or attempt to perfect or simplify old ones.

The number of marriages, in general, will be higher

than in prior years, and a great deal will be said and heard from the women of the world. Many new companies and alliances will be formed, and some older ones may go bankrupt or be broken. Countries already in financial trouble can expect more problems, with severe measures being taken to end inflation and balance budgets.

Movements involving groups and associations will demand being heard, and conflicts could erupt suddenly if care isn't taken to bring about a peaceful settlement revolving around domestic and international issues of an explosive nature. More pronounced will be all forms of group, partnership, and association work in which tact and diplomacy are required.

Interest in religions, spiritualism, and psychic phenomena will also receive a greater share of the public's attention. Since the number 2 is associated with water, projects and problems connected with water, such as floods and droughts, will be more pronounced. Moreover, major events will have a tendency to occur suddenly and without warning.

The 3 Universal Year

The 3 Universal Year will bring an overflow of interest in the creative arts, movies, music, ballet, and the theater. Attitudes will be hopeful, and an attempt will be made to bring joy and optimism to the world again. Countries will be friendlier toward one another, and people will be encouraged to travel extensively and experience different cultures. New forms of global communications will be instituted, with fewer restrictions existing between countries. Recreational activities and creative hobbies will be highlighted, and for those who cannot afford to indulge in travel, expect to find the local beaches and public facilities more crowded than usual.

The world will seek to express its joy for living in a variety of ways. Socializing in business and with friends and neighbors will be more popular, with a simultaneous undercurrent of restlessness. As countries and individuals express themselves by means of their possessions, improvements will be made that bring more fun and creativity into our lives, and consumer spending will increase. Since the number 3 pertains to procreation and children, much attention will be given to the plight of children. Spending will increase for children's clothing, toys, and educational programs.

The 4 Universal Year

The 4 Universal Year will find the world settling down to hard work, with an eye to living in a more economical fashion. The extravagant spending of the 3 Universal Year will take its toll and demand payment in the 4 Universal Year. After last year's fun and extravagance, it is now time to budget wisely and live within a sound structured environment. For many cities, states, and countries, pay cuts and layoffs can be expected in order to keep expenses in check. The world will look to implement practical ways to solve the hunger crisis, feed the homeless, and clothe the underprivileged. Countries will be expected to cooperate financially in order to fight drugs, crime, and the war on global poverty. More conservative measures will be taken to improve the global climate and ecology. At home and abroad new measures will be implemented in the area of affordable and economical housing. While jobs may not be plentiful, progress will be made at a slower place. The world will attempt to lay stronger and firmer foundations upon which to build.

The 5 Universal Year

The 5 Universal Year will be one of great change, coupled with a renewed interest in all aspects of psychological, metaphysical, and occult sciences. The world will feel a pull toward expansiveness and progressive thought, allowing for greater expression. Global economics may be unstable, but basically some improvements will be seen. International trade and personal spending will increase also as past restrictions will lessen or disappear.

Sales will experience an upswing, and the public will show an eagerness to purchase the new, the nonsensical, and the different.

Space exploration can be expected to make outstanding progress, with research and scientific advances expanding our present knowledge of the universe. Major corporate and industrial leaders will be eager to risk and speculate, with new discoveries geared to improving global communications, but not all plans implemented will be successful. Peace on a national and international level will be greatly endangered if states and countries act out impulsively without exercising thought on the consequences of their actions.

The 6 Universal Year

The 6 Universal Year will require that adjustments be made based on the changes instituted the previous year. Governments will take on a more conciliatory approach with their citizenry in an effort to reduce civil unrest. They will be more responsive in accommodating the needs of the people by providing better care and services. On an international level, negotiations will be pursued to adjust foreign treaties, with an emphasis on avoiding warfare. More time, energy, and money will be devoted to improvements in the educational and health systems on both a national and international level; governments and citizens will experience a heightened sense of being responsible for each other. On a domestic level, individuals will be pulled into the mainstream and become more interested in establishing and maintaining domestic and global harmony. Expect the marriage rate to rise.

The 7 Universal Year

The 7 Universal Year will be more of a spiritual year, with less interest in materialism. All forms of religious, metaphysical, and occult interests will receive a greater share of attention as the world looks inward for wisdom and truth. Outwardly things will appear more restful and meditative, but beneath the surface the seeds of dissatisfaction will be encountered. It is said that the 7 Universal Year is indicative of what will end, or have to be let go of, in the 9 Universal Year. Much will happen in the realm of the unexpected, with scandal developing in the most surprising places, especially in the religious sector. Efforts may be made to revise and reform various religious doctrines and procedures in an effort to by-pass problems later on. As the world attempts to awaken to the universal spirit of the God-force, there will be less of an emphasis on business expansion, but all forms of international and national water-related industries should prosper, since the number 7, like the number 2, carries with it an emphasis on water. The cruise industry should flourish as people plan their days in the sun and contemplate the decisions, revisions, and preparations for the following year.

The 8 Universal Year

The 8 Universal Year will be one of power, big business expansion, and trade on a national and international level resulting from the plans that were developed in the previous year. All forms of money exchange will flourish as relations with foreign countries experience a boom in trade and industry. Many big businesses will execute plans to expand by implementing business strategies. The real estate and building trades should see a profit, with no great bargains in purchases or sales, with top dollar being paid and received for all transactions. More money, however, will exist by which to purchase goods.

The world, in general, will plan, think, and execute on a large scale, since prosperity is in the air. The potential for conflict among the world powers via nuclear force and unusual forms of warfare will be more pronounced, and sudden friction could rupture existing international relationships. Natural catastrophies, such as earthquakes, hurricanes, and large-scale fires, will be on the rise and will make headlines. Additionally, food and grain shortages will be more pronounced in the Third World countries, as well as some larger nations.

The 9 Universal Year

The 9 Universal Year will be one of global cleansing, as nations make an effort to end past differences and accent the rewards of peaceful coexistence. The peoples of the world will reach out to one another in a spirit of brotherhood, and of understanding and sharing their joys and sorrows. The public will demand that their leaders do something to end oppression and hunger. The major world powers will be pushed to send more aid to less fortunate nations, accepting kindness as its own reward for right action. Policies and strategies that no longer yield results or have not been successful will be let go, with a realization that some ground has been lost. A year of global housecleaning, nations will complete much unfinished business, and some major world projects could come to an end. New projects will not be successful or will have numerous problems in the start-up phase. Aspects of publishing dealing with human issues should meet with success. Attendance in houses of worship, as well as the theater, should also show an increase. A year in which tolerance and compassion can pay off, countries will attempt to end conflicts on a positive note.

The 11 Universal Year

The 11 Universal Year will find the world more receptive to spiritual and occult thought as a pronounced interest surfaces in psychic phenomena. Seminars on personal growth, inner peace, the occult, and meditational practices will be plentiful. People will turn to unconventional methods in order to establish harmony. Religious and metaphysical philosophies will be more popular than in previous years. Mass movements, conventions, and association meetings will increase, with the aim of exposing existing problems and implementing new methods. All specializations of the mind, such as psychology and psychiatry, will also receive attention. Many new issues, concepts, and ideas will receive increased attention in the media. Movements will click in and catch the public's eye. Big business will introduce and promote unique concepts, with less of a concentration on financial gain and more on improving existing conditions.

The 22 Universal Year

The 22 Universal Year will see projects launched on a vast national and international scale, many of which will involve the building of comprehensive and lasting structures. A strong humanitarian force will be present, with pronounced effort taking the form of improving the condition of not only mankind but of local communities as well. Money will be spent expanding hospitals and institutions of learning. While much idealism will exist, there will also be those who can build strong bridges between spiritualism and materialism, laying the foundation for programs in humanistic endeavors. Building for the future will be substantial, but much emphasis will be placed on order, system, practicality, and economy. Some monumental projects will most definitely be launched.

The influence of the Universal Year should not be overlooked. While its vibrational force may be more subtle, nevertheless, its effects and nuances will be felt. For example, if the Universal Year is a 1, bringing forth newness, leadership, and innovation, and your Personal Year is a 4, which emphasizes work, order, and practicality, you may just find yourself picking up a new and unique form of work along the lines of your career or profession. Likewise, if the Universal Year is a 2, stressing cooperation, partnerships, and companionship, and your personal year is a 6, which stresses home, family, harmony, and adjustments, you could very well find yourself getting married, having a baby, forming a partnership with a friend, or attending more to domestic situations throughout the year. To a greater or lesser extent, your life will be pulled in some manner along the lines of the Universal Year vibration.

THE UNIVERSAL MONTH

Each month and day of the year also carries a Universal vibration that will be felt by each individual. If these vibrations are recognized and worked with, excellent guidance and assistance can be received in planning and conducting your daily life. The meanings of the *Universal Months* and *Days* are the same as the meanings of the Universal Years.

Locating The Universal Month

Each month of the calendar year can be reduced to a number based upon its position within the calendar year. The value of each month of the year will always follow the calendar. Therefore:

January = 1	May = 5	September = 9
February = 2	June = 6	October = 10 or 1
March = 3	July = 7	November = 11 or 2
April = 4	August = 8	December = 12 or 3

To find the Universal Month, first reduce the number of the Universal Year to a single digit or Master number, and then add it to the number representing the calendar month. Then reduce your answer to a single digit or Master number. For example, if today's date were November 11, 1989, you would find the Universal Year by taking 1989 and reducing it to a single digit. $1+9+8+9 = 27 = 2+7 = 9$, so 9 would be the Universal Year. Then you would use the number 11 for the month of November and add that number to the 9 Universal Year to arrive at a 20, or 2, Universal Month vibration for November of 1989.

When months appear as Master numbers, such as the month of November, and can be computed as an 11 or as a 2, often your answer will have Master overtones and will also appear as 11/2. We can see this relationship if we compute the Universal Month as follows:

1989 = 1+9+8+9 = 27 = 2+7 = 9 Universal Year for 1989

November = 11 = 1+1=2 Calendar month for November

11/2 Universal Month for November of 1989

Because the Universal Month of November is represented by the number 11, a Master number, one can expect more exciting and sudden happenings during the month.

MEANING OF THE UNIVERSAL MONTH

1. Newness, planning for the future, originality, progress along both new and older lines, and leadership will be in evidence. Action taken to sell, promote, or lead will meet with success.

2. Cooperation, attention to detail, diplomatic and harmonious work with others, collecting facts, figures, statistics; and attending to group activities will be forthcoming and significant. Action taken to promote peace, harmony, and tactfulness will meet with success.

3. Creative ideas, socializing, expressive activities, and entertainment will bring joy and fun. Action taken to promote self-expression and beauty will meet with success.

4. Hard work, organization, economy, and discipline in personal and business activities are indicated. Action taken to budget, schedule, systematize, and build a solid foundation will meet with success.

5. Travel, change, and speculation in new and unique projects are indicated. Action taken to promote or increase sales and advance domestic and international ventures will meet with success.

6. Attention to family and community affairs, health, births, beauty, and artistic ventures are indicated. Action taken to care for children and loved ones, and involvement in human welfare will meet with success.

7. Concentration, study, and analysis involving future endeavors are indicated. Reflection on inner awareness and spiritual development will stimulate growth at a

future time. Actions taken to invent, study, and develop intuitive faculties will meet with success.

8. Domestic and international business advancement and expansion along the lines of big business are indicated. Financial progress and growth in personal and business-related matters will require good judgment. Action taken to incorporate sound business judgment with a less materialistic philosophy will meet with success.

9. World peace, love, compassion, understanding, and kindness are indicated. Major projects will reach the completion stage. Action taken to discard old and outmoded attitudes and philosophies and practices will foster progress.

11. Idealistic philosophies, religion, metaphysics, and spiritualism are indicated. Aviation and electrical inventions will become more pronounced. Action taken to illuminate and develop ideas for the advancement of humanity will meet with success.

22. Large-scale national and international projects that emphasize improving the condition of mankind are indicated. Organization, practicality, and the implementation of master plans will receive public attention and recognition.

THE UNIVERSAL DAY

To find the *Universal Day*, you need only add the number of the current day to the Universal Month vibration. To find the Universal Day vibration for November 11, 1989, you would proceed as follows:

11	/	11	/	1989
11/2	+	11/2	+	27/9
2	+	2	+	$9 = 13 = 1 + 3 = 4$

or:

$$\begin{array}{r} 11 \\ 11 \\ \underline{1989} \\ 2011 \end{array} = 2 + 0 + 1 + 1 = 4 \text{ Universal Day vibration}$$

The next step is to follow the basic meanings of the number 4 and to discover what the world is pulled to create on a 4 Universal Day. The general meaning of the numbers will apply.

While the meaning of the Universal Day vibrations lasts for a mere twenty-four hours, as opposed to thirty days for the Universal Month meaning, a key understanding to their meanings is that the "forecasts" dependent on the vibrations of the Universal Day will be the same as those that are subject to the Universal Month vibrations. Refer to the Universal Month meanings in order to discover the Universal Day.

CHAPTER 7

What to Do and When: Your Personal years, Months, and Days

The Universal Year gives an indication of the general direction in which the universe, and our world, in general, is moving. It is a major indicator of what overall influences will be directly affecting each of us through our environment.

The *Personal Year* vibration is a highly important indicator in our personal lives and reveals the activities, conditions, duties, and obligations that must be attended to during each particular year of life in order that our lives may flow with ease and harmony. Knowing what can be expected each year can make planning for the future easier and more rewarding.

Computing Your Personal Year

In order to compute your Personal Year number, first the Universal Year must be computed. If the calendar year is 1991, and we are computing the Personal Year for Shirley MacLaine, born on April 24, 1934, in determining the Universal Year, first we must add together the digits of 1991.

$1+9+9+1=20=2+0=2$

Therefore, 1991 would be a 2 Universal Year number.

To find Shirley's Personal Year, we add this Universal Year number 2 to her month and day of birth. It is always advisable, if you are adding the numbers across, to reduce all double digits in the month and day of birth to single digits before you do your computations. The addition would appear as follows:.

$$\begin{array}{ccc} 4 & / & 24 \\ 4 & / & 2+4=6 \end{array}$$

$$2 + 4 + 6 = 12 = 1 + 2 = 3 \text{ Personal Year}$$

You can also compute your addition in a downward direction and achieve the same results. Your addition would appear as follows:

$$\begin{array}{l} 4 \\ 24 \\ \underline{1991} \\ 2019 = 2 + 0 + 1 + 9 = 12 = 1 + 2 = 3 \text{ Personal Year} \end{array}$$

For the year 1991, therefore, Shirley MacLaine's Personal year is 3.

A study of the Personal Years will answer many questions. It will answer why during one year you feel perky and are up and eager to create new situations, and why during another year you feel loss as you let go of people and existing situations, and allow elements to flow out of your life. By following the advice of your Personal Years, you will know when to initiate, cultivate, and conclude projects in your life. There will be less guessing and more order and predictability in your year-to-year activities.

There are nine Personal Years, 1 through 9, with the Master years 11 and 22 substituting in certain individual charts as a higher octave of the 2 and 4 Personal Years. If your Personal Year computes to a Master number, do not reduce the number to a single digit. First read the meaning of the Personal Year as it applies to the Master number and then read the meaning for the *Reduced* number. The chances are that you will probably be living a good deal of your Personal Year in the Master number, with added overtones of the Reduced number when situations start to get hectic.

THE MEANINGS OF THE PERSONAL YEAR

The 1 Personal Year

Of all the Personal Years, the 1 Personal Year is the most important. During this year you will begin a new nine-year cycle. Whatever you cultivate during the 1 Personal Year will have the potential of remaining vibrant and bringing rewards for the entire nine-year cycle.

The 1 Personal Year is a year of advancement and progress. It requires courage and a willingness to allow for change. It is a year to stand alone, lead, individuate; for more than any other year, your destiny is placed in your own hands. Anything begun of a new nature in the 1 Personal Year is almost guaranteed to be successful, so don't be afraid to take that brave first step.

Don't stand still or remain idle during the 1 Personal Year. It's the best time to go after opportunities and broaden your horizons. If you are contemplating a change in position or career, or are planning to make any kind of advancement, make the move after you have organized your thoughts and mapped out your moves.

Unlike other Personal Years, a fair amount of letting go will still exist during your 1 Personal Year. The cleansing effect of the 9 Personal Year may still be felt up until about August and may account for some of the unruly emotions felt during the early and middle part of the year.

During the 1 Personal Year you will be called upon to make decisions for yourself. Do not expect opportunities to fall into your lap, since they must be sought after, investigated, and researched. While you should avoid being impulsive, don't be afraid to take a chance, either.

Most important, *do not allow anyone to talk you out of your plans*. Keep pushing toward your goals, follow your own intuition, and do what your instincts tell you is the correct action.

Your masculine Yang energy is most pronounced during the 1 Personal Year due to all the strength that is necessary to begin and promote new projects. Because of this forceful vibration, you can expect to be associating with many more males rather than females. This masculine vibration prefers to remain independent to do things alone rather than dealing in partnerships. If you are interested in a partnership, therefore, it is better to put it off to the 2 Personal Year or at least wait until you are getting closer to the latter part of the year.

The 2 Personal Year

The 2 Personal Year can be confusing and difficult to understand because of its dualities. You will need to exercise a great deal of patience in order to maintain balance and harmony in your life. Nothing will move as quickly as it did in the 1 Personal Year. Pushing projects too hard or attempting to force issues will only cause stress, disappointment, and loss.

The 2 Personal Year calls for cooperation, friendliness, and peaceful associations. It is best to remain in the background while you cultivate, improve, and perfect the new path or changes made during the 1 Personal Year. The 2 Personal Year is a waiting period, and a great deal of patience must be exercised if you want the seeds of your 1 Personal Year planting to grow.

During the 2 Personal Year contact with females will be more pronounced. The 2 Personal Year, being a wonderful love vibration, may find you romantically involved, but you will have to remain emotionally balanced as much as possible. You must be willing to give and take in the relationship or a breakup is just as much indicated as a marriage. Moreover, the 2 Personal Year may also bring the birth of a child as the physical manifestation of your love.

Since cooperation is favored, the 2 Personal Year is the time to be alert to a favorable partnership, association, or agreement with another. Here again, discretion must be used in the early part of the year to iron out all the details, or a rupture in your relationship could occur. Don't try too hard at anything in particular, but continue to move slowly and patiently, accumulating, assorting, and collecting all the necessary knowledge and data for your projects. Practice the art of graciously receiving from others any assistance that they may be able to pass your way. Only then will you be pleasantly surprised by the opportunities that come to you.

The 2 Personal Year calls for improvement in all aspects of your life. It is a good year to buy new clothes and redecorate your house, always keeping an eye on the budget so as not to overspend. Gambling, speculating, or investing in commercial ventures should be looked at carefully, since a real loss could occur in these areas. You may also experience a loss in not receiving something expected. Should anyone owe you money from the past, however, the 2 Personal Year is the perfect time to collect the debts. There is more of a chance of unexpected income from the past than there is from trying to drum up new business. Additionally, all forms of metaphysical, philosophical, and religious activities will bring rewards. If you want to write or take up a particular hobby using your hands, there is no better time to begin such projects than in the 2 Personal Year.

Part of the duality of the 2 Personal Year comes in the form of delays with and disappointments in making valuable contacts, in both friendships and love relationships. All delays in career should be graciously accepted, since usually something better lies ahead. Misunderstandings with loved ones can be averted by not pushing your ego on others and remaining more deferential. Remember, this is your year to cooperate.

Refrain from engaging in gossip and slander during the 2 Personal Year, for it is also a year of personal betrayal. Be particular in choosing new friends, and exercise good judgment in choosing whom you wish to share your secrets.

The 2 Personal Year is not the year to make major changes. It is best to stay put and cultivate the plans you already have in progress. Maintain a firm faith that things are working out underneath the surface. Keep your feet firmly on the ground, and check every once in a while that your associations and friendships are on a solid footing. Understand that although the pace is slow, you are moving forward.

The 3 Personal Year

The 3 Personal Year is a year to get out and enjoy life. It's your year to have fun and socialize, both with old friends as well as with new ones. All forms of creative expression will bring joy and possible rewards. If you wish to decorate, write a book, lecture, promote yourself on radio or TV, or involve yourself with another form of communication, by all means go out and do it.

The 3 Personal Year will give you the opportunity to improve upon the plans you've been cultivating since the 1 Personal Year. Don't be afraid to cut your hair, change your wardrobe, or take a few courses here and there in subjects that interest you or will improve your career. Make new friends, since your associations and friendships will contribute greatly to promoting you this year.

Cultivate the dreams and aspirations of your 2 Personal Year. Start creative projects that interest you, but be sure to list your priorities. You won't be able to accomplish all of your dreams at once, so work only on the few important ones.

Scattering your energies can be disastrous and can lead to emotional loss during the 3 Personal Year. It is important to complete existing projects before beginning new ones. Fear of failure and nonattainment of dreams can really put a damper on this year of fun. Also be careful of how you spend your money. Extravagance and waste could catch up with you fast.

During the 3 Personal Year try not to converse much about the projects you are working on, and avoid being talked out of the recent plans you've made. The year carries with it much luck, but you'll have to preserve secrecy as much as possible. More friendships are ruined in the 3 Personal Year due to careless speech and slips of the tongue than in any other year. It's important, therefore, to guard against gossiping as well.

The 3 Personal Year can bring romantic love affairs that are colorful and quite emotional. Love affairs begun in the 3 Personal Year often cement fast and furiously. If not handled correctly, they fall apart just as quickly, leaving the individual in a shambles emotionally. If the love affair was begun in the 2 Personal Year, however, the next year, 3, will usually find the relationship cementing nicely into a permanent commitment.

Most individuals desire to be foot-loose and fancy-free during the 3 Personal Year. Therefore, you should not overcommit yourself. Keep a close watch on your money, and if possible, save some for a rainy day. It may prove difficult, since increased socializing could cause you to spend more and scatter your funds, but try your best to put some money aside.

Sell, sell, sell—anything that no longer has value to you. The 3 Personal Year has a great deal of luck attached to it. A sale could bring in a surprisingly nice price.

Work to strengthen existing business and love relationships, since they are likely to bring opportunity and pleasure. Take advantage of the ability to promote and sell yourself and those creative ideas you've been working on, but be sure to finish one venture before beginning another.

The "down" side of the 3 Personal Year can take place in the area of one's emotions. Avoid giving in to gloomy, negative thoughts or to becoming fearful. Bleak or uncontrollable emotions can truly ruin the playful atmosphere of this pleasurable year.

The 4 Personal Year

Now that the 3 Personal Year is over, it is time to get down to some practical work. The 4 Personal Year will require an organized and more systematic approach at home and on the job, with an emphasis on building a firm and solid foundation underneath all undertakings. This is your work year, not a time to neglect financial, physical, or emotional affairs, since matters can easily backfire.

The 4 Personal Year requires attention to detail and tests your ability to get down to hard work. Your free time may be limited, and you could feel boxed in or restricted. You will gain much, however, if you put your nose to the grindstone and establish routine and order at home as well as at the work place. While romance is not emphasized, a love relationship begun in the 4 Personal Year has a good chance of surviving for a long time. Moreover, any new friendships made during the year could last indefinitely.

The 4 Personal Year carries with it an element of karma. Be prepared to pay for past physical, emotional, and financial debts incurred from previous years. You are cautioned not to be lazy and to avoid escapism in significant areas of living. It is time to place family relationships and business activities in proper order and maintain a budget in all financial matters. The 5 Personal Year will bring much freedom, but for now it is best to resist taking the easy road.

While some individuals will feel utterly limited and restrained by the work requirements of the 4 Personal Year, much can be accomplished, so it is best to rise to the challenge. Many ideas, thoughts, and creative inspirations have been known to take shape and bloom in the 4 Personal Year. While your personal magnetism will be somewhat lower than in previous years, much good is being accomplished beneath the surface to further your ambitions.

Petty arguments, disputes, and misunderstandings could put the brakes on your happiness during a 4 Personal

Year. Make every attempt to understand the opinions of others, but don't overlook your own intuitive messages, either. Concentrate on establishing order in all areas of work; save money, and budget with an eye to being economical and practical.

The 4 Personal Year is a good year to handle property, real estate, merchandising, and legal matters. Be sure to get wise counsel before signing all documents, and resist overextending yourself.

The 4 Personal Year is not the year to make a major change in position or career, but do cultivate the seeds that you have previously planted. If you must change jobs, do so after very careful deliberation. To be without a job in a 4 Personal Year could find you in financial misery. Exercise self-discipline, watch your diet, and get plenty of rest, since a heavy workload could bring on physical and emotional exhaustion.

On a positive note, enough strength and will power will exist to break old habits that have inhibited your past performance. With a little determination, all aspects of your life can be placed on a better footing. If your ideas of the past three years have been positive, you can expect some nice rewards this year.

The 5 Personal Year

After the hard work and organization required of you during the 4 Personal Year, be ready to enjoy more freedom and a less restrictive pace during your 5 Personal Year. Earlier in the year, however, be on guard for hasty and impulsive actions, since these two elements alone can lead to problems and sour your year.

The 5 Personal Year by its very nature is fast and tricky. On the one hand, it brings more excitement and an adventuresome spirit, coupled with a desire to change some of the existing conditions. On the other hand, it also brings a hectic pace, with a mood of uncertainty pervading the whole year. Avoid resentment toward those who you feel have impeded your progress. If you must make changes, do so in a constructive way without quarreling.

Major pitfalls of the 5 Personal Year lie in scattering your energies in many directions without planning in advance, jumping to false conclusions, acting impulsively without forethought, and overindulging in food, drugs, sex, gambling, drinking, or abuses of the senses. You should, therefore, exercise caution in making all decisions.

The 5 Personal Year is one of great change. Existing conditions can be made better or worse if things are not thought out carefully. One way or another, all changes that occur in the 5 Personal Year will act to free you from restrictive conditions. In the end the changes are always for the better.

In many ways the 5 Personal Year is a vacation from past limitations. You may begin new projects out of a feeling of restlessness, but these enterprises may bring only short-term benefits and may not be long-lasting. It is better to expand and improve existing projects. Speculation could go either way, although there usually are better prospects for profit, since there is an element of luck in the 5 Personal Year.

In romantic situations, the 5 Personal Year brings exciting new relationships. Your personal magnetism and sex appeal will run high. The possibility of pregnancy is also very strong, so exercise caution in all sexual matters. Moreover, Don't marry in haste, since you may repent in leisure. If a love relationship remains strong throughout the year, plans to marry can be made for the 6 Personal Year, in which more spiritual protection exists.

As the "5 Year" emphasizes freedom from restriction and change, major commitments should be avoided as much as possible, especially in romantic and financial matters. Finances in the 5 Personal Year can fluctuate. While you may tend to overspend, still, more funds will exist than in the 4 Personal Year.

The best way to take advantage of the 5 Personal Year is to keep an open mind. If a creative opportunity presents itself, by all means jump at it, for the 5 Personal Year is positive for all forms of the arts, writing, lecturing, sales, advertising, and communications. If you want to speculate, be sure to make sure it is of a short-term nature. Long-term projects will not bring long-term rewards. It's a year for business promotion and expansion. The end of the year may even bring a new offer of employment that is more to your liking.

The good-luck factor that runs through the 5 Personal Year is similar to the one that exists during the 3 Personal Year. If you're a gambler, the chances are that you may come out a winner but not all the time.

The "5 Year" is positive for all forms of travel and exploration to near and far-off places, offering you the opportunity to meet unusual people and make some unique contacts. There will be more fun and entertainment in the air, with an accent on variety and change.

Feelings of restlessness during the 5 Personal Year could make you nervous and tense, but every attempt should be made to flow with the change. If you move with the tide and don't act out of impulse, the year should end on a positive note. Remember, do not make any major changes of residence or business, or sign long-range agreements unless you have no desire of reversing yourself in the future. Changes made without proper thought may require adjustments later on.

The 6 Personal Year

After the quick pace of the 5 Personal Year, things will settle down, and the 6 Personal Year will be filled with peace and harmony, as well as with a bit more regularity. It is often considered the most pleasant of all years.

Responsibilities and obligations will be more domestically oriented and must be met and attended to unselfishly, with charity and compassion toward others. The 6 Personal Year has a settling effect. It calls for an emphasis on duty and attention to matters previously overlooked or avoided. It is a year to patch up past difficulties and let go of past resentments. More importantly, all domestic matters should be placed on a better footing.

The "6 Year" calls for adjustments on all projects begun previously. Sympathy and concern for others could find you carrying more responsibility at home and on the job. Appreciation of good work will bring financial remuneration.

The 6 Personal Year is the best year to marry, move your home or business, or engage in community projects. This year provides ample spiritual protection, and taking the feelings of others into consideration will bring more harmony into the home. It's a year to make necessary improvements of a domestic nature and to enjoy the beauty of your personal surroundings, for it is in this area that some major accomplishments will be made.

The 6 Personal Year will basically be a harmonious one, but some family members may still lock horns or require attention. A major pitfall of the "6 Year" is failing to mind your own business, finding fault, maintaining a self-righteous attitude, or voicing an opinion where none is called for. Not exercising tact could bring major problems. Beware of sloppiness and of neglecting personal responsibilities as well.

The 6 Personal Year carries with it a marriage vibration. For those who are single and desirous of finding the perfect mate, the year is blessed with a luck factor. For those already in marriage, the adjustments called for will bring ease and smoothness into the marriage, with the added benefit of strengthening the bonds of love, devotion, and friendship. It is only if the marriage has been in a great deal of trouble that a split could come in the 6 Personal Year.

Home, family, and attention to the mate are going to dominate the 6 Personal Year. Domestic concerns, painting and improving existing structures, or moving into a better home are all favored. Care and concern for children, as well as for the elderly, are likely to dominate and require your attention, and it's probable that new additions to the family group are possible. A loved one may also do something unsettling, but since it is a year to patch up all disputes, forgiveness and understanding will have to be tactfully exercised.

There are separations and divorces that take place in the 6 Personal Year, but these happen only in negative relationships in which selfishness and ego are deemed more important than love and consideration. Then, the "6 Year" is a blessing in disguise, since it puts an end, once and for all, to long-term disputes.

The 6 Personal Year usually brings freedom from financial worries. If a business or partnership has been in trouble for some time and breaks up in the 5 Personal Year, it is not unusual that more money will now be available in the "6 Year," but it will also have to be shared with family members and others who are close. Somehow problems with indebtedness have a tendency of clearing themselves up. By accepting more responsibility or taking on extra work, the financial situation usually increases nicely. Contracts and agreements also work out well.

The 6 Personal Year favors creative ventures and educational pursuits. All forms of schooling are emphasized and will bring rewards later on.

The 7 Personal Year

The 7 Personal Year is one of rest, retreat, meditation, and reflection. It is also a year when many individuals make the most blunders because they do not slow down and analyze their next move.

The 7 Personal Year brings with it an inner desire to be alone and rest the weary soul. For the most part, it is time-locked and slow-moving. The year requires patience and a great deal of physical rest. Overwork and strain will usually cause the body to break down. Worry, resentment, and brooding can cause melancholia and bad temper, resulting in a general overall feeling of utter loss and repression.

Most people make their worst mistakes in the 7 Personal Year, due to an overriding thirst for materialism. Refusal to take life at a slower pace causes karmic repercussions, resulting in loss of money or love, delay, frustratration, bad health, and all forms of unforeseen obstacles.

Yet, of all the Personal Years, if used wisely, this year brings with it a great deal of spiritual protection. Marriages commenced in a 7 Personal Year, especially for women, frequently bring a special gift, as well as the feeling that this is the love of a lifetime. Although romance is often down-played, it is more clandestine and secretive in nature during the early part of the year. As the forceful vibration of the 8 Personal Year draws near, the relationship usually surfaces into public view.

If any advice can be given on how best to handle this confusing year, it would be *not to push anything* beyond the day-to-day workings of ordinary living. It is better to take a laid-back approach in all areas of life and for the most part coast with existing situations. The 7 Personal Year belongs to God. It is a year to rest one's soul and reflect upon the past and more or less analyze and outline any changes that one desires to make in the future concerning career or relationships. It's a year to engage in inner growth and attempt to make improvements. Schooling, as well as meditation of all kinds, can have a positive influence, especially since most individuals do not feel like socializing or entertaining much, within this time period, anyway.

In a 7 Personal Year, investing, speculating, or beginning any new form of business that requires a financial investment or great physical stamina can lead to disaster. Think carefully, and don't take risks, since your tide of life is way out to engage in these activities. It is much safer to plan during the 7 and execute action in the 8 Personal Year. Never trust your luck in the 7 Personal Year. Any form of illegality will definitely bounce back and cause grief. If you wait to employ the gifts of the 7, however, which are analytical in nature, coupled with meditation, rest, and reflection, the rewards in the 8 Personal Year will surface and be more beneficial than previously believed.

The 7 Personal Year is positive for taking that long-awaited trip to an out-of-the-ordinary place. Often during this type of year the "trip of a lifetime" occurs, bringing exciting travel and a much-needed rest. Trips over water are generally most enjoyable.

The 7 Personal Year is a time to perfect the inner self. The research and study of metaphysical, spiritual, or religious pursuits of any kind generally bring satisfaction and a soothing of bad nerves.

The 7 Personal Year can also bring inner turmoil created by broken relationships or even the rekindling of a past love and/or the reappearance of relatives previously out of communication, who suddenly play an instrumental part in the future.

The 7 Personal Year is mental in nature. No major moves should be undertaken without careful planning and forethought. Feelings of repression or of being restricted and boxed in by circumstances are not uncommon in the 7 Personal Year. Close friends, relatives, and business associates will tend to do strange things, but it is all part of the year, forcing you to slow down, to live less critically, and to invest in improving yourself and your life. Plans will be made in the 7 Personal Year that will have a major impact later on, so use the time wisely.

The 8 Personal Year

After the rest and relaxation of the 7 Personal Year, along with thinking, worrying, and planning, it is now time to *execute* your business plans in a decisive and tactful manner. The 8 Personal Year is one of increased power, and as the months pass, you will find yourself organizing and reorganizing in order to be successful.

Advancement is in the works this year, but absolutely nothing is going to be handed to you. Expect to work hard for what you want. No promotions will be received that you haven't rightly earned. Mental strain may accompany the hard work, good judgment, and efficiency that must be exercised in all decisions, but right action and well-thought-out plans will bring improvements in finances, business, and career.

The 8 Personal Year is a time to reap the harvest. Go after what you want in a most businesslike manner. Buy-

ing and selling property or personal goods and services
take precedence. More strength and ambition will exist
than in the previous year, but once again, do not wear
your body out by overdoing the work schedule, straining
after money, or trampling bullishly over others. Contracts and business agreements can be signed, but don't
overestimate your abilities. Seek professional advice
when you are in doubt or you feel your judgment is not
solid.

The 8 Personal Year is karmic, like the 4 Personal
Year (being comprised of 2 fours). Whatever you have
sown in the past eight years you will now reap, especially
if you have lived well. Overzealousness in personal relationships, greed and unscrupulous behavior, will only lay
the foundation for the loss that will take place in the 9
Personal Year. It is preferable, therefore, to practice tact
and diplomacy in personal relationships. Be mindful that
around mid-November, personal and business relationships may be explosive and could rupture friendships. If
a rift does occur, it is at this time that the seeds of regret
may be planted for what must be let go of in the 9 Personal Year.

The 8 Personal Year completes the cycle of man, with
the cleansing and letting go taking place in the following
year. Be sure to keep arrogant tendencies in check, and
avoid appearing power-hungry, selfish, and impatient.
Make sure that all transactions are legal, aboveboard,
and proper.

Romantically the 8 Personal Year does not carry the
protection of the 7 Personal Year, or the peace and harmony that the 6 Personal Year offers. Romance can be
ambivalent or unemotional, but women who marry in
this year marry well, with little or no financial strain
existing. More apparent, however, are the powerful emotional forces that toward the latter part of the year can
result in ruptured relationships as most individuals feel
feisty, stronger, and more rebellious.

The greater emphasis of the 8 Personal Year is in the
direction of material gain, of advancement and improving
your financial status. Real estate transactions and part-

nership formations are more pronounced. Top dollar will
be paid to purchase properties and to buy and sell businesses, with more interaction with lawyers and courts
than in previous years. Papers signed in haste can lead
to litigation, so be sure to consult professional help when
necessary.

If you are planning any type of venture, especially one
that was born from your thoughts during the 7 Personal
Year, the "8 Year" is a good time to launch your plans.
You may feel more comfortable taking a gamble on
something new, but make sure that you are economical
in your plans. If you are expecting a refund on any monies due and owed to you from individuals or major institutions of any kind, such as an income tax refund, the
chances are that you will be successful in your attempts
to collect. The 8 Personal Year brings with it a desire to
get all financial transactions on a sound footing. It is
better not to invest past the month of September. Be
mindful of shaky investments made later in the year.

Use the dynamic qualities of this year to your best
advantage. Energy and personal magnetism will run high,
bringing exciting opportunities, but you must not hold
back and wait. Success won't fall from the sky.

The 8 Personal Year usually begins at a slower pace,
but by the early spring job and career opportunities could
begin to surface, along with more competition and an
arena in which to exercise sound judgment. Make all
decisions without emotional or sentimental interference.
Try to see things the way they actually are. Social
engagements should also not be overlooked, since important contacts can be made leading to advancement in
your career. It is best to be forceful but not arrogant.
Free yourself of minor details by delegating the work to
others.

Often during the 8 Personal Year we change living
conditions or move our home. Sometimes in order to do
so, a break must be made with worn-out or disagreeable
relationships. Be mindful that as the end of the year
approaches, you will be pulled into the vibration of the
9 Personal Year, which will cause you to let go of the

older and nonproductive aspects and associations in your life. Emotions may be tense and heavy unless you realize that letting go of the old will make room for the new. Learning to move with the flow and change of life will cause less resistance and pain in the 9 Personal Year, the year of completion and cleansing.

The 9 Personal Year

The 9 Personal Year is often the most misunderstood of all the Personal Years. It is a year of endings and completions pertaining to people, places, things, jobs, and relationships that are no longer useful or bring meaning into your life. Great love and understanding must be shown toward others. The number 9, being the number of brotherhood, requires you to give a little extra to those around you who may be in need. Sometimes it may be a good friend, who is troubled or having difficulty in a love relationship. At other times it may be sickness in your family or a situation that is not working out the way you had hoped. It will be time to let go of a number of situations or relationships.

The 9 Personal Year may find you entertaining thoughts pertaining to a change in career or ending a relationship that no longer is fulfilling. Feelings of loneliness may exist as your children leave to get married, go off to college, or move into their own homes. Uncontrollable emotions and feelings of exhaustion can be expected. Proper attention to your health—getting proper rest and replenishing the physical body—can often put an end to nagging, debilitating conditions.

The secret of the 9 Personal Year is that it will be as good or as bad as you make it. For some, it will bring feelings of loss and suffering. For others, the burdens may not seem so damaging. If you have worked hard and have lived a good life, it can culminate in satisfying ways that may bring recognition and fame.

Do not make binding commitments in the 9 Personal Year, since your tide is *way out*. A trick to surviving the "9 Year" is to refrain from beginning anything of a new nature. Such a restriction does not preclude you from investigating new forms of employment that may interest you, enrolling in a class (metaphysical classes are especially helpful), or embarking on a refreshing, long trip overseas to some exotic place.

Romantic opportunities frequently present themselves in the 9 Personal Year but may not be long-lasting. Love affairs begun in this year often wash out by August or September of the 1 Personal Year. It would be to your advantage, therefore, to go out and have fun and concentrate more on a universal type of love and friendship.

The 9 Personal Year can bring sickness brought on by emotional stress and strain. Overwork can cause accidents, so be mindful of getting proper rest and keeping your body in good physical shape. Visit the doctor and dentist, and don't avoid getting a general checkup.

In the area of finances, keep a watchful eye on spending. Money has a tendency to come in and go out just as quickly, and in large sums. The 9 Personal Year is famous for the breakdown of large appliances, so put some money aside just in case the occasion arises. Don't take speculative risks or gamble on purchasing anything new like a stove or a car. You could buy a lemon. A good suggestion is to fix whatever is broken for now and to put off new purchases until the 1 Personal Year when the vibration is more favorable.

In an attempt to get rid of the old and make way for the new, the thought may cross your mind to sell a few items that no longer have meaning or are no longer useful. The vibrations of the 9 Personal Year favor sales. Large sums of money can be received from the sale of a home or business, but you should not gamble with the profits in any speculative ventures. It is best to place them in a safe place and begin making investments in the 1 Personal Year.

By the time September rolls around, you may begin to see your way clearer. It may be a particularly emotional month, especially around the Personal Days that total 9, such as the 9th, 18th, and the 27th. Maintain your personal power by remaining in charge of your life, and let go of all things that request their freedom . . . don't hold on!

For those who have lived well during the past nine years, this is a favorable year to travel to far-off places that you've always longed to see. Vacations can be particularly restful during the months of July and September.

A 9 Personal Year can also bring the limelight, and you may receive the recognition that you have worked so hard for. It is one of the rewards for having lived well and having been considerate of others. Accept all promotions and honors with humility, and continue to show compassion to others. Try to be as helpful as possible to those in need.

Don't be surprised during this finishing year if you finally complete that manuscript, publish that book you've been slaving over, or engage in the arts either directly or indirectly. All are positive activities for the 9 Personal Year, so go out and enjoy yourself.

The 11 Personal Year

The 11 Personal Year is a higher octave of the 2 Personal Year. The 11, being a Master number, will demand that you rise above the more passive vibrations of peace and harmony, cooperation and diplomacy, of the 2, and seek illumination and recognition of a higher nature, which could lead to stardom, fame, or the limelight. Be advised, however, that if the vibrations are too heavy or difficult to carry, you can always naturally revert to the 2.

In many ways the 11 Personal Year resembles the 7 Personal Year, since it is also one of inner spiritual growth and personal development, some of which you may be guided to pass on to others.

The 11 Personal Year brings with it an interest in psychic phenomena and metaphysics, and the urge to study the hidden sciences. Such an investigation into these fields will heighten intuitive qualities, and if followed, could lead to a great deal of recognition. It is important to remember all the requirements of the 2 Personal Year.

Tact, diplomacy, and cooperation will be called for in your dealings with others, especially women. Be careful not to step on people's toes as you climb the ladder of success. In many areas, it will still be a slower-moving year than the 1 Personal Year, and you will have to attend to many details. If you maintain a positive attitude, follow your psychic ideas and hunches, and honor your ideals, you can reach for the stars.

The 22 Personal Year

The 22 Personal Year is a higher octave of the 4 Personal Year and will find you organizing and executing plans on a major scale for the benefit of mankind, the world, or at the very least your community. In any event, it will not be for just yourself alone that you will be working. Anything is possible, and some involved and far-reaching projects may find themselves getting off the ground.

In a 22 Personal Year, do not concentrate on endeavors that involve just you personally. If you cannot handle the intensity of the vibration, at the very least, you can revert back to the 4, and much can be accomplished through hard work, concentration, and being practical and efficient. If you wish to go for the challenges of the "22 Year," be mindful that the practical aspects will still remain. Great insight, drive, and inspiration, however, will bring far-reaching possibilities and attainment, coupled with long-distance travel.

YOUR PERSONAL MONTHS

As with the Personal Years, much valuable information can be obtained from your *Personal Months*, but the opportunity and vibrations last for only thirty or so days. To compute your Personal Month, just add the number of your Personal Year to the number representing the actual calendar month. The number values for the calen-

dar months follow their same calendar placement and are
as follows:

January	1	July	7
February	2	August	8
March	3	September	9
April	4	October	10 or 1
May	5	November	11 or 2
June	6	December	12 or 3

In computing the Personal Month, add the number
value of the calendar month to your Personal Year
number. For example, using Walter Mathau's birthday,
October 1, 1920, the first thing you would do is compute his Personal Year by adding together the month
and day of his birth to the Universal Year number, or
the current year. If 1991 is a 2 Universal Year,
$(1+9+9+1=20=2+0=2)$, your addition would appear
as follows:

```
  10    (the number value for October)
   1    (the day of birth)
1991    (the present year)
2002 = 2+0+0+2 = 4 Personal Year
```

In order to compute the Personal Month, add the number value of the actual calendar month to your Personal
Year number. If you are desirous of knowing the Personal Month for the month of October, your addition
would be as follows:
4 (Personal Year) +1 (the month number for October)=5 Personal Month. The month of October, therefore, would be a 5 Personal Month for Mr. Mathau.

You may have figured out for yourself by now that the
number 9 added to any number will always result in the
same number. The month of September during any Personal Year will be the same vibration as the Personal
Year itself, only *intensified*. If you are in an 11 Personal
Year, the month of September will be an 11 Personal
Month. The vibrations of the Personal Year will be the

greatest in September of any year. This is an important principle to remember. The number 9 added to anything will result in the same number. During September of a 9 Personal Year, it will be especially apparent that situations are going to change. People, places, things, and relationships will go out of your life as you make way for the new to unfold.

The chart below may help you quickly determine at a glance the Personal Months for any nine-year cycle.

MONTHS		PERSONAL YEARS								
		1	2	3	4	5	6	7	8	9
January	(1)	2	3	4	5	6	7	8	9	1
February	(2)	3	4	5	6	7	8	9	1	2
March	(3)	4	5	6	7	8	9	1	2	3
April	(4)	5	6	7	8	9	1	2	3	4
May	(5)	6	7	8	9	1	2	3	4	5
June	(6)	7	8	9	1	2	3	4	5	6
July	(7)	8	9	1	2	3	4	5	6	7
August	(8)	9	1	2	3	4	5	6	7	8
September	(9)	1	2	3	4	5	6	7	8	9
October	(10/1)	2	3	4	5	6	7	8	9	1
November	(11/2)	3	4	5	6	7	8	9	1	2
December	(12/3)	4	5	6	7	8	9	1	2	3

While the vibration and intensity of the Personal Years can be felt throughout the entire year, the mood or vibration of each Personal Month will be restricted to that specific month. The effects of the Personal Month may feel stronger during the latter two weeks of the month when the vibration is more in place than in the beginning of the month, when the new vibration is first entering.

THE MEANING OF THE PERSONAL MONTHS

Read the meaning below for your Personal Months. If you follow their advice, you will find that making decisions is much easier in your life.

1. Take action, be original, and don't be afraid to take

a chance on beginning something new. Focus your energy on creating or inventing along a different line or unique approach. Strike out and meet new people; learn a new profession; take up a creative hobby. Avoid laziness, and refrain from appearing overly pushy, domineering, or bossy.
2. It is a time to cooperate and associate with others on common projects. Concentrate on intricate details, and improve upon the old. Patience, understanding, and tact should be considered and cultivated. Do not begin anything new, but work harmoniously and quietly on forwarding all activities. Opportunity for advancement will follow along the lines of writing, metaphysics, music, art, and statistical work and education.
3. A lighter, more creative, and enjoyable month, in which business can mix well with pleasure. Strike out on vacation, or socialize with friends. Put off heavy responsibilities, if possible, for a later date. A time to develop artistic, creative, literary, and expressive pursuits. An enthusiastic and optimistic attitude should be cultivated.
4. A heavy work month, all projects should be built upon a solid and practical foundation. Details at home and work must not be avoided or overlooked. Feelings of restriction or overwork should not be dwelled upon. Get the job done. In financial matters, adhere to a budget, and curb overspending. Save money for the future. Work at a consistent pace, and build a solid foundation under future projects. Hard work will bring rewards later. Take time to strengthen the weak spots relating to physical health and work-related situations.
5. A busy, adventurous month, loaded with activities relative to expansion and change. A month to take a calculated risk to promote a new and unusual idea. Initiate change if the odds look favorable. Refrain from overindulging in food, gambling, drink, sex, or drugs. Take advantage of socializing with different kinds of people, visiting different places, and partaking in various activities. Guard against taking long shots, acting on impulse, or remaining in a rut.
6. Responsibilities relating to home and family will take precedence. Attend to the needs of spouse, home, chil-

dren, and parents. The more love and attention given, the more harmonious a life will be led. Financial protection will exist in matters of the heart. Avoid selfishness, and strive to share what you have with those close to you. Activities related to beautifying the home or work place and making your surroundings more pleasant will bring happiness. Great imagination and creativity can be enhanced by developing artistic projects along the lines of the written and spoken word, art, and music. Inspiration coupled with imagination and action can bring successful pursuits.

7. A month in which some time should be spent alone contemplating, planning, and analyzing future goals. Great strides can be made in the areas of writing, teaching, research, and study in one's area of concentration. Metaphysical and spiritual development, coupled with deep self-examination or education, will aid you in all forms of inner growth. A slow month, the element of waiting might exist, and patience must be exercised in order to perfect the goals at hand. An overconcentration on material pursuits or brooding over past mistakes can cause confusion, emotional loss, and possibly bad health.

8. Courage, force, energy, and power are at your command this month. Exercise good judgment in all business and financial matters. Expansion of business enterprises is favored as long as overstretching and impulsive speculation are kept in check. Opportunities to expand your vision and improve your reputation and finances will be present, but beware of being intolerant or arrogant toward others. Set your pace, and focus on which direction you wish to follow, but use discretion in pushing your weight around. Nothing will be gotten that has not been worked for, so don't be lazy.

9. All self-seeking must be cast aside, as you will be called to serve others. People will make demands or seek guidance. Love, compassion, and understanding must be exercised toward those in need. It is a time when service-related jobs go well, but the individual must seek to serve as many people as possible in an impersonal fashion. Philanthropic work can bring recognition. Give help to

others, and ask for little in return. Push artistic creations in areas of art, music, drama, or writing. Expect to complete or end some projects and relationships.

11. A month for inner growth and development, coupled with nervous tension and heightened sensitivity. Much can be accomplished in expressing your ideas to launch unique inventions; seek the help of associates. Religious and psychic studies can bring interest and illumination, along with the opportunity to gain public recognition. TV, radio, and all work dealing with the public domain bring rewards. Work with women will be more pronounced.

22. Extensive recognition is possible from the launching of significant projects. International pursuits, either business or personal, or projects dealing with material mastery on a large scope may bring success and accomplishment. While engaging in the structuring of worldly projects, you can combine the idealism of the 11 with the practical, physical mastery of the 22 to bring about enormous results.

YOUR PERSONAL DAYS

Like the Personal Year and Month, each day within that month will have a personal vibration that you can take advantage of. Each vibration changes in just twenty-four hours. Nevertheless, you will feel the push and thrust of each day. If you work with your daily vibrations, much can be achieved.

To compute your *Personal Day* vibration, add the actual calendar day number to your Personal Month number, and reduce the answer to a single digit or Master number.

For example, if you are in a 6 Personal Month, and today is the 11th day of the month, your computation would appear as follows:

           6   Personal Month
          <u>11</u>   calendar day
          17 or 8 Personal Day

The meanings for each Personal Day are going to be basically the same as the meanings for the Personal Month. Locate your Personal Day number below, and apply its meaning to your daily life.

THE MEANING OF THE PERSONAL DAYS

1. Begin something, take charge, lead, invent, be original, trust your own instincts and intuition, be self-reliant, and go after what you want.

2. Cooperate, use balance, act receptively, peacefully coexist, analyze and collect important data, write, remain poised, harmonize, bite your tongue.

3. Entertain friends, be sociable, work on creative projects, improve your speech, try to shed brightness and bring happiness into the lives of others, put on a smile, and do your best to express the joy of living. Create through singing, dancing, art, music, and the written word. Let the sunshine in.

4. Be practical, economical, employ order and a system in all work projects, stick to a timetable, and keep your nose to the grindstone. Work hard toward your goals, rise early, and plan your schedule. Lay a firm foundation under projects, build for tomorrow, and rest.

5. Buy, sell, or trade anything, promote yourself or a new project, network with people, travel, promote new ideas, exercise versatility, advertise, communicate, make contacts, meet new people, and expand your horizons.

6. Act responsibly toward spouse, children, family, friends, parents; and avoid being overly opinionated. Assume responsibility for others. Do your best to serve, make necessary adjustments, curb judgments, make necessary phone calls, and maintain the role of interested parent, counselor, or host. Make sure that all matters are running smoothly.

7. Meditate, reflect, study, focus, and concentrate on self, ideals, writing, and specialties. Follow your hunches, research topics of interest, remain introspective, listen to the inner voice, pause, smell the flowers,

go to the country, avoid self-seeking, perfect steadily, and think about your future. Refrain from allowing despair or melancholy to enter.

8. Engage in big business, real estate, securities; sign documents and exercise good judgment. Demand organization and efficiency in all work-related projects, and don't doubt your abilities. Harness your power, and zero in on your master plan. Get a good grip on how well things are operating. Be careful not to act tyrannical, domineering, or greedy.

9. Serve humanity in a selfless manner; be kind, considerate, and compassionate for the plight of others without holding onto their problems as your own. Promote artistic and dramatic talents, and be generous, understanding, and loving to others. Tie up loose ends, and discard old and outmoded clothes, attitudes, ideas. Let go of people who have caused you pain.

11. Lead, illuminate, and reveal the truth to the public, engage in psychic and metaphysical pursuits, follow your hunches, invent, analyze, write, express your ideas, keep the peace, and avoid commercialism. Dream, but don't miss necessary appointments.

22. Work on developing a project that will have broad appeal and that will benefit mankind. Get involved in meaningful pursuits on a wide scale, possibly national or international projects, and try to cooperate as much as possible. Be concerned about improving community affairs. Utilize all your powers to organize, develop, and execute your master plans.

PART II

THE LETTERS

CHAPTER 8

The Moving Picture of Your Life: The Alphabet

1	2	3	4	5	6	7	8	9
A	B	C	D	E	F	G	H	I
J	K	L	M	N	O	P	Q	R
S	T	U	V	W	X	Y	Z	

Important experiences that shape your life can be discovered by studying the letters in the first, middle, and last name given you at birth. The letters constituting your name at birth carry vibrations that move you to experience life in a particular way. By analyzing these letters you can uncover your likes, dislikes, hopes, dreams, desires, as well as the opportunities and experiences you will encounter during each year that you live.

The letters of your name form a moving picture of your life, indicating and foreshadowing important happenings. Each letter of our alphabet, symbolized by a number, carries a particular number vibration that causes you to act, react, and experience life in a certain fashion. Since there are 9 basic number vibrations, each letter of the alphabet is represented by a number from 1 to 9 and is placed under that specific number as seen in the chart on the previous page. As we complete the first nine letters of the alphabet and reach the letter *I*, we return to the letter *J* and place it under the 1 vibration. As the letter *J* is the tenth letter of the alphabet, it is also the higher octave of the number 1.

The letter *A* is the first letter of the alphabet and has a number equivalent of 1. The letter *J* is the tenth letter of the alphabet and also has an equivalent of 1 but is of an octave higher. As we learned in the chapter on Birthday numbers, the *Letter* numbers run in octaves. While for computation purposes the letter *U* carries the number 3 vibration, it is important to remember that it is the highest octave of the number 3. As such, it carries a unique vibration that encourages creativity in a certain manner.

Note also that although the letter *K* has a vibration of 2, it carries a Master vibration, the higher octave of 11, and as such is a Master number. Similarly, the letter *V* carries the vibration of 22 and is a Master number.

All the letters of the alphabet can be reduced to single numbers. What these numbers actually are, however, are vibrational forces. We give a number to each letter of the alphabet, but what we are actually doing is assigning a number to the *vibrational sound* of each letter. Each letter in our name vibrates to a specific sound, and these vibrations lead and influence us to experience certain conditions.

While many American and Western names can be computed by using our alphabet, foreign names, such as Far Eastern names, must be converted to our alphabet before the name can be accurately computed.

Each letter of the alphabet carries an overall general meaning and a specific meaning, depending upon whether it falls in the first, middle, or last name. The name that you use to compute the transit of the letters is the entire full name given to you at birth. Generally speaking, baptismal and Confirmation names *do not count* and should not be used for computation purposes.

Each name you are given at birth pertains to a certain aspect of living. If you were given three names at birth, the meanings cover the mental/physical, emotional, and spiritual aspects of life. If you were given four names at birth, the meanings cover the mental, physical, emotional, and spiritual aspects of life.

If you have 3 names at birth:	**If you have 4 names at birth:**
First name: mental/physical	First name: mental
Middle name: emotional	Middle name: physical
Last name: spiritual	Middle name: emotional
	Last name: spiritual

Your first name and the first of your middle names, if you were given two at birth, have a profound effect on your physical life and mental life. The letters forming these two names affect where you work, live, what you enjoy doing, your reasoning powers, how you analyze situations, and make mental deductions. The letters in your middle name have control over your emotional life, meaning your likes, loves, emotions, marriage, and hobbies. The letters in your last name have control over your spiritual life, the inward and subconscious growth that takes place within you during the course of your life.

Some letters of the alphabet are more conducive to radiating favorable living conditions in the first name than when found in the middle or last names. Other letters are more spiritual by nature. As time goes by, you will see that some letters carry more force than others.

The letters R, S, T, U, V, W, X, Y, and Z are known as testing letters, because they are the highest octave of their respective numbers. These letters will carry certain problems and tests that you must experience on all levels in order to awaken spiritually.

You will discover that many of the letters will influence or vibrate over the entire line, affecting the physical, mental, emotional, and intuitive aspects of your life. Therefore, always understand the general meaning, as well as the specific meaning, of each letter regardless of where it falls in your name.

The number vibration that each letter carries will dictate how many years it takes to transit or live through that letter of the alphabet. For example, the letters *I* and *R*, which carry the number 9 vibration, take nine years to transit, regardless of the fact that the letter *R* is a higher vibration of the letter *I*. The letters *B*, *K*, and *T*, which carry the number 2 vibration, each take two years to transit.

Following are the general and specific meanings of each letter of the alphabet. In the next chapter when you compute the essence of the letters in your name that you are now transiting, you will discover both the letter experiences and number meanings that you may encounter along the way.

The Letter A (A 1-Year Transit)

GENERAL MEANING

No matter where the letter *A* appears in your name, there is going to be dynamic change taking place. It will be a year of new activities and possibly a move of home of some sort. There will be an opportunity to charge forward on a goal or career previously thought about but not pursued. New people will come into the life, offering new associations and important contacts.

Depending on the essence or final numeric total of the letters for any particular year, frequently travel can be expected. If the essence of the letters is 5, the letter *A* will allow for short trips, usually over land. If the total of the letters is 7, there will be travel, usually over water or on trips that are water-connected. If the total of the letters is 22 or 9, very long-distance or foreign travel is indicated. Advancement is possible, but good judgment must be used.

Under the *A* vibration important decisions will be made, often without notice or preparation. This condition could account for sudden and unusual happenings. At any rate, success and attainment will be made through taking action in a positive direction.

The Letter A When Found in the First Name

In this position, the letter A denotes a change of domicile, an unusual trip, or a major move of some kind. Financially, conditions are going to change either up or down. Financial concern may also be present.

The Letter A When Found in the Middle Name

As a child, there could be a sudden move or upset in the family. As you move more toward adulthood, positive changes and new beginnings can be expected, either positive or negative, depending on the judgment that is used. You could suddenly marry, divorce, or give birth to a child. At any rate, emotional affairs or relationships are going to change.

The Letter A When Found in the Last Name

Much growth will take place spiritually within you, coupled with new and exciting beginnings.

The Letter B (A 2-Year Transit)

GENERAL MEANING

The letter B denotes a personality that is quiet, shy, and often retiring, that enjoys working in conjunction with others. It signifies an excellent ability for undertaking projects that require working with details in scientific and artistic pursuits as well as interaction with groups and associations. The letter B signifies a highly strung nature and a vibration that can bring rupture if issues are forced. Health matters should be attended to immediately, since constant emotional upset could cause illness.

From time to time, the letter B will signify a change of home or business location in regard to professional or career advancement. The change can usually be expected to be a happy one that may lead to better things. Since the letter B requires a more passive approach, one way or another you may be called upon either to submerge your greater desires for others, or to work for their benefit.

The *B* transit could bring trouble, difficulty, frustration, or hesitancy in making decisions, with vacillation or procrastination more the norm than otherwise. Since the 2 vibration is feminine in nature, periodically women will cause or experience romantic problems. More often than not, however, the letter *B* will find you being proposed to or involved in deep and satisfying love relationships.

The Letter *B* When Found in the First Name

When you are a child, the letter *B* will have a tendency to make you high-strung and nervous. As an adult, keep your nerves in check, since overstraining could precipitate the manifestation of negative health conditions. From time to time finances will have to be watched closely.

The Letter *B* When Found in the Middle Name

For children, the letter *B* could bring bad nerves and emotional upsets, which leave lasting scars. It is important that speech be maintained as much as possible in a quiet and calm tone so as not to cause emotional upset. After the age of eleven or twelve, and more particularly during the years sixteen through twenty-three, bad nerves could be caused by the termination of a close love relationship or a love affair.

The Letter *B* When Found in the Last Name

When found in the last name, the letter *B* does not indicate any significant growth on a spiritual level. It usually finds you dashing and darting around in an attempt to take advantage of any opportunity that comes your way. Such overactivity could cause minor problems but is nothing much to worry about.

The Letter C (A 3-Year Transit)

GENERAL MEANING

The letter C in any name can bring achievement and success on a large scale as a result of creative endeavors. When the C transits, regardless of the name, you will possess a strong desire to improve your life both creatively and financially. Often there is a need to change old living and working conditions in favor of branching out in new directions.

The letter C indicates a very social tendency, and you can expect to engage in interesting life styles during its transit. Caution must be taken, however, not to involve yourself in triangle or unwise love affairs. To do so will result in deep involvements of a negative nature that have a tendency of bouncing back on you. Positive love relationships begun in the C will bring a lovely home life, coupled with romance and much success.

During the C transit, all of the negative aspects of the letter must be guarded. One major pitfall is the scattering aspect, which can cause overspending, gossip, overspeculation, taking others at face value, and an overexpenditure of your energies, leading to no beneficial result. Involvement in the negative placement of energy can lead to loss of position, loss of money, and loss of your good name. The highest form of success can be attained when creative inspiration is applied to all projects at hand, especially if they benefit others.

At times, the product of love will bring the birth of a special child, one who fills the hearts and minds of other members of the family with great love, joy, and inspiration.

The Letter C When Found in the First Name

Basically, the C transit will bring happiness and enjoyment into your life. Self-confidence will be present and can be applied to all talents, both at home and in your profession. You can find pleasure in any number of creative modalities, such as writing, acting, public speaking, and art.

The Letter C When Found in the Middle Name

In the middle name, the letter C will bring a more relaxed and laid-back life style, with nothing much affecting you of a negative fashion. In this position, the vibration of the letter C is positive. Love affairs of a triangle nature or those not based on honesty will have a tendency to be short-lived.

The Letter C When Found in the Last Name

In the last name, the letter C brings a beneficial vibration on the spiritual level, coupled with much inner peace and growth. A great deal of insight, inspiration, and satisfaction will be present, and you will gain much from the higher knowledge received.

The Letter D (A 4-Year Transit)

GENERAL MEANING

The letter D in any name is going to require that you apply your energies in a concrete manner in order to achieve results. The affairs of business and home life will have to be regularly attended to in order to keep things moving on a proper footing. This steady application of work and energy will bring satisfying results.

The D transit brings an interest in property, land, and contracts, often having to do with family interests. You will be called upon to live responsibly. Financial adjustments and budgeting may be necessary. A firm foundation must be laid in business and family matters, with nothing left to chance. Contracts and agreements should be signed only after all conditions are fully understood.

The letter D can bring lowered health conditions caused when nagging health problems are overlooked or disregarded. It is best to attend to all health matters immediately and not procrastinate.

In day-to-day living, many problems and situations previously overlooked or unattended may surface and require attention. Disagreements and quarrels between friends, lovers, and family members could lead to rupture and separation. Every effort must be made to maintain positive relationships.

The Letter D When Found in the First Name

During the early formative years, your physical resistance to illness and disease may be lowered. Attention should be given to all health matters immediately. Often the D involves travel or a move of home due to sick or dying relatives.

The Letter D When Found in the Middle Name

Care must be taken not to involve yourself in unwise love affairs of a negative nature. During this transit, you may find yourself in situations in which you must seek protection from emotional or physical violence. Law enforcement agencies may be encountered or an interest in the law developed. Marriage, if undertaken, must be based on truth, love, and honesty, and not engaged in to escape difficult situations. At times, the D transit will be difficult and not the easiest to cope with. Discretion should be used in all major decisions.

The Letter D When Found in the Last Name

There will not be much growth of a spiritual nature, since practical matters will require more of your time and attention.

The Letter E (A 5-Year Transit)

GENERAL MEANING

The letter E will involve you in five years of activity and change, bringing new and interesting contacts from different walks of life. Before the age of thirteen, you will encounter a great deal of change, along with feelings of insecurity. A few moves of home are possible. Communications will bring legal, media, and public involvement of both a positive and negative nature. Your health on the whole will be good, coupled with periods of temporary upset and minor ailments. Governmental agencies will be encountered. Love affairs will be fast and furious. Marriage should be given great thought before being entered into. Sudden marriage should be avoided, if possible. You will be more prone to accidents caused by maintaining a fast pace or not taking proper safety precautions.

Financial matters under the *E* transit can fluctuate both up and down, with an emphasis on the side of increased profits.

The Letter *E* When Found in the First Name

Before the age of fourteen, you could encounter some form of instability and perhaps even insecurity within the family. On the whole, your health should be good, with only occasional upsets. Expect financial success. Changing your home is possible somewhere during the transit and maybe more than once.

The Letter *E* When Found in the Middle Name

The letter *E* found in this middle position can bring mood swings, along with an intense desire to be independent. As a child, your nerves may be high-strung. On the whole, there is going to be more than enough variety in your life. After the age of fourteen, love affairs of an emotional nature are emphasized. Although positive in nature, these love affairs will not generally end in marriage, and some endings will be unpleasant.

The Letter *E* When Found in the Last Name

This position is not a bad placement for the *E*. After some reflection, spiritual changes of a positive nature will take place. At times, the actions of others will seem strange, creating inner confusion, but on the whole, this placement will bring positive experiences.

The Letter F (A 6-Year Transit)

GENERAL MEANING

The letter F in any name is going to bring responsibility and a concentration on domestic and family living. At times, you will feel restricted because of the duty, care, and attention that must be shown to family members and elder relatives. Cultivate the proper emotional attitude, one that willingly gives of yourself to loved ones and family members. Giving ungrudgingly and with compassion will create positive vibrations, thereby increasing your tendency for success and abundance. A negative attitude can cause strife and arguments, as well as separations and divorce among family members.

The letter F demands an unselfish nature, with less self-absorption and more concentration on concerns outside yourself. This period can be burdensome at times, with all the needs of family members pulling in different directions. The secret to success is to unburden yourself of any unnecessary responsibility, but at the same time to maintain a giving attitude.

The letter F also brings artistic tendencies, and you may become interested in a variety of art forms, some for the benefit of the public. Involvement in institutions such as schools, community service centers, and big business will bring success on a broad scale. Work with large corporations will go well, as long as you attend to responsibilities.

Under the F transit you must avoid worrying over insignificant matters that seem to pile up. Excessive concern with the responsibilities and burdens of spouse, children, and parents should be kept to a minimum. While obligations will be present, all needs will be met.

There are no major disasters under the F transit that you cannot handle. Affairs should progress steadily, with arguments and separations patched up quickly.

The Letter F When Found in the First Name

Within the home, you will have a great deal of domestic responsibility. From time to time, upsetting relations between parents and other family members can be expected, due to the death of a family member, separation, or divorce. In adulthood, around the center of the transit, some form of sickness in the family could occur, and then you may be called upon to care for others. In any event, family responsibility will exist.

The Letter F When Found in the Middle Name

Some emotional upset will exist in the family, but generally most of the transit will go smoothly. While your time and energy will have to be sacrificed for others, all of your needs will be met.

The Letter F When Found in the Last Name

Expect divine protection with the letter *F* in this placement. While responsibility will still exist for others, a great amount of protection will also be present. This period may be the smoothest and may present the most growth of all the *F* transits.

The Letter G (A 7-Year Transit)

GENERAL MEANING

The transit of the letter *G* brings the opportunity for prominence and influence when dealing in big business. The start may be slow, but the climb will be steady. Large-scale business projects will be carried out for the betterment of society as a whole. At times, you may not possess an abundance of confidence as a result of periodic opposition from unexpected sources. Nonetheless, you are warned to keep a firm grasp on plans to see that they remain intact. Living conditions will improve as more money is channeled into your life. In addition, travel is quite common during the transit. While socializing can be expected, the *G* transit will also bring a more reserved demeanor. More often your interactions will be with a select group of friends.

While the letter *G* is being transitted, you can benefit by a good education and the development of technical and mathematical skills pertaining to a specialty. A position of influence and authority accompanies the *G*, if you live up to the challenge.

Secrecy, swindles, and love affairs of an emotional nature are also more pronounced during the *G* transit and must be avoided. Moreover, you may be called upon to face up to problems that you have previously run away from. A loved one could become ill, requiring your time and assistance, but great love within the family will also be present.

The Letter G When Found in the First Name

As a child, you will have the tendency to be quiet, shy, probably secretive and withdrawn. Parents can expect an occasional fib but should not be overly harsh with punishment. Family finances will be abundant. After the age of thirty-three, financial gain will again appear in your life.

The Letter G When Found in the Middle Name

Emotions may run high in this placement, with occasional outbursts of temper. A desire to engage in a meaningful love relationship will exist, but you may have some difficulty in finding one.

The Letter G When Found in the Last Name

The main characteristics of the *G* will be present, but not much spiritual growth will take place.

The Letter H (An 8-Year Transit)

GENERAL MEANING

The letter *H* during any transit will create an inner drive to attain a greater financial base—more money—

and more power. The possibility for gain is just as prevalent as that for loss.

The 8-year *H* transit brings a quickened pace, coupled with the opportunity for advancement. Good judgment must be used when assessing the character and intent of others. A constant effort may be needed in order to build and maintain a solid foundation for all undertakings. Business activities will take the form of buying and selling, particularly of land.

An interest will exist in associations, groups, and secret organizations. Much effort will have to be exerted if success is to be lasting. A strong financial base will be laid during the first and second years of the transit, with great care exercised not to exhaust savings by the last year. Constant attention must be shown in business affairs. Family matters and romantic relationships may take on a business overtone or revolve around work. Emotional problems could exist if proper attention is not given to loved ones. Attempts to control all aspects of your individual relationships will only result in stress and frustration. It is best to let go and delegate authority as much as possible.

Achievement, status, and a financial base can be attained or strengthened during the *H* transit. You can grow in prominence if the *H* vibration is lived up to.

The Letter *H* When Found in the First Name

Vacillation in your love life and fluctuation in finances can be expected. This lack of equilibrium can cause problems in love relationships; marriage, therefore, should be entered cautiously.

The Letter *H* When Found in the Middle Name

Of all the placements, the middle name holds the greatest possibility for financial advancement. Your desire for recognition will usually be fulfilled, but your love life may still vacillate.

The Letter H When Found In the Last Name

With the letter *H* in the last name, you may not seek much spiritual growth unless you see a reason for it. At times, your large ego may need bolstering. You are cautioned not to allow an inflated opinion of yourself to run away with your reason.

The Letter I (A 9-Year Transit)

GENERAL MEANING

The letter *I* is a very dramatic, artistic, and impressionable letter that can attract prominence through creative endeavors. Great sensitivity and emotionalism will exist, causing you to think that you have lost control. The key is to avoid getting hooked into the emotional states of others. Jealousy and resentment directed at, and received by, those close to you may be present and may cause upset.

While constant effort may be required during the *I* transit to keep on an even keel, help can be attracted, and asked for, to get projects off the ground and running smoothly.

Great human compassion is required under the *I* transit, along with a desire to improve both the home environment and family relationships. While problems will be caused by other people, you are cautioned not to exacerbate existing conditions. Country life is usually more desirable than city life, because of its more relaxed and less hectic environment. It will also do much to soothe your delicate nervous system.

High artistic and creative expression belongs to the letter *I* when the ideals are lived up to. Help will always exist when needed, and financial success can be expected. A jealous nature is to be avoided, if possible.

Negatively, the *I* is divorce-prone, especially when selfishness, intolerance, and a lack of compassion are allowed to control your relationship with your spouse. Unless this tendency is checked, you will find yourself traveling along a self-destructive course.

The Letter I When Found In the First Name

During the *I* transit, you should refrain from outbursts of temper that could lead to ill health, especially during the middle fourth, fifth, and sixth years of the transit. Problems that existed within the family during childhood can transform themselves into emotional upsets in adulthood. While your financial status increases during the transit, it will be negative during the fifth year.

The Letter I When Found In the Middle Name

The letter *I* when found in this placement can bring negative emotions if you do not curb selfish behavior. Such conduct will only enhance the possibilities of separation and divorce. Emotional changes occurring during the fifth year of transit can bring significant upset. You are advised to refrain from wasting time brooding.

The Letter I When Found In the Last Name

The letter *I* in this position denotes that spiritual growth will take place, not by choice, but rather through circumstance or the surfacing of issues that will force such action. You should not allow your ego to become dominant. If you keep selfish actions in check, emotional suffering will be minimized.

The Letter J (A 1-Year Transit)

GENERAL MEANING

Usually during the *J* transit health will be excellent and opportunities plentiful. In all activities, you should take the initiative. Much growth and promotion will follow, along with more responsibility and travel. Long-held desires will be awakened, and you will make a major thrust to effectuate change, possibly to a new location. While will power will be necessary to get affairs off the ground, others will be surprised by the force of your desire and effort to advance.

The Letter *J* When Found in the First Name

In your first name, the letter *J* will bring increased responsibility and more recognition. You will possess a quick, alert personality, which makes learning faster and easier. Important business contacts will be made and will be of great assistance in your advancement.

The Letter *J* When Found in the Middle Name

As a child, you could experience a chaotic domestic atmosphere due to the desertion of a loved one or their absence through death. As an adult, increased responsibilities in the home will have to be attended to. Relationships will have a tendency to rupture, leading to separations and divorce between loved ones.

The Letter *J* When Found in the Last Name

Not much growth will be seen when the *J* is in this position, and the general aspects of the letter will usually apply.

The Letter *K* (A 2-Year Transit)

GENERAL MEANING

During the 2-year transit of the *K*, you will usually step into some form of prominence. Emotional changes are possible, with renown in associations and unusual love affairs manifesting themselves. You can expect to change your home or locality due to a windfall of some kind.

In addition to the increase that can be expected in finances, strange occurrences will take place, bringing about emotional upset and even illness, but all sickness will eventually result in recovery.

The letter *K*, denoting a vibration of increased activity, is a good indicator of success in business, but caution must be exercised to avoid becoming overly optimistic or trusting others too much. The possibility of being cheated is great. The tendency to be extravagant must also be curbed.

The Letter *K* When Found In the First Name

Great caution must be exercised in the emotional realm, since you will tend to be high-strung. Hidden fears may also surface and require attention.

The Letter *K* When Found In the Middle Name

In this position, the *K* signifies that you may appear high-strung and possess less confidence. You will also tend to be more secretive and inward.

The Letter *K* When Found In the Last Name

Expect prominence and a possible windfall in this position. Many positive changes will occur, coupled with inner spiritual growth.

The Letter *L* (A 3-Year Transit)

GENERAL MEANING

The letter *L* in any placement will bring a desire to travel, socialize, and attain status. It is not a negative letter in any position, since it brings more inner happiness. Still, some sacrifice for loved ones can be expected, though not of a restrictive nature. Self-improvement is the key to advancement, and positive contacts can assist you by offering valuable opportunities. A lazy attitude or one that is overly dependent on others should be avoided.

Travel and romance are part of the *L* transit. Much pleasure and enjoyment can be attained through friends and favorable associations. You should not strive only for pleasure but spend time developing your creative and expressive talents.

The Letter *L* When Found In the First Name

Good health can be expected, coupled with romantic involvements and a good deal of travel. You are prone to minor accidents and tripping, so extra care should be exercised. Happiness can be expected, along with financial gain. The *L* in the first name is a positive position, bringing favorable conditions in transit.

The Letter *L* When Found in the Middle Name

The letter *L* in this placement brings emotional contentment, and you may never be happier than during its transit. In this position, marriage is not only possible but successful.

The Letter *L* When Found in the Last Name

In the last name, the letter *L* brings spiritual growth and inner illumination. As a result, major decisions will be made somewhere around the middle of the transit.

The Letter *M* (A 4-Year Transit)

GENERAL MEANING

The *M* transit will bring a 4-year period of mental activity. You must work hard and plan for the future. At times, you may feel held down or restricted. It is best to just keep going. This transit is good for the accumulation of money and property, but a constant effort must be maintained, whether the project is building a business, establishing a love relationship, or maintaining domestic harmony. Occasionally a quarrelsome nature will cause problems, especially in the realm of understanding your in-laws, who may seem like "out-laws" during this transit.

Basically the *M* transit in any position will bring out the need for responsibility in home and property matters, together with carrying out a structured plan for the future. Strong business ties will be made, requiring that contracts be drawn or attended to. Overwork could cause health problems; a good checkup, therefore, is advisable at the beginning of the transit.

The *M* transit is not as limiting as the *D* transit but does require a sharp lookout for business opportunities that bring advancement. Building a good reputation will require constant attention. A large accumulation of money is also possible.

In the area of health, although your body may periodically become run down, a quick recovery can be expected.

The letter *M*, with a 4 vibration, emphasizes home, family, and marriage. Travel for these purposes can also be expected.

The Letter *M* When Found In the First Name

As a child, health problems are possible, along with changing your home. As an adult, you can expect to move your home around the middle of the transit, more particularly, in the second or third year. It is advisable that you not incur unnecessary financial obligations that can lead to strain.

The Letter *M* When Found In the Middle Name

The letter *M* in the middle name brings a more outwardly stable home life, although some inner instability will exist from time to time. An emotionally stable marriage will be sought after and will probably take place during the middle of the transit. Secret love affairs should be avoided, especially during the middle year of the transit when they seem to crop up the most. Much financial gain can be expected in this position, together with travel.

The Letter *M* When Found In the Last Name

The letter *M* in the last name will bring a feeling of inner confusion, along with some vacillation. At times, you may not be too happy with your present life but may not know how to bring about an improvement.

The Letter *N* (A 5-Year Transit)

GENERAL MEANING

The letter *N* in any position will bring a concentration on progressive activities that have to do with governing the world. More inner and mental control will exist than with the *E* vibration. Still, you must work conscientiously, and accept the routine nature of life in order to be successful. The key in this position is for you to accept the personal and business responsibilities that accompany day-to-day living.

The *N* transit can bring about improved marital and love relationships if husband and wife take an honest and sincere interest in the activities of the other party. Financial conditions generally improve.

Under the *N* transit, plans can change overnight; you should remain flexible enough, therefore, to move with the flow of life and accept constant change and activity. A move of residence is possible.

The Letter *N* When Found in the First Name

The letter *N* in this position can trigger changes that occur suddenly, in your life both as a child and an adult. Changes in the love life, residence, and home life can happen at any given moment. Finances can go up or down, and some discontent or emotional turmoil could exist in relationships.

The Letter *N* When Found in the Middle Name

As a child, you may show signs of being misunderstood or difficult to deal with. Later on as an adult, this vibration will have an effect on love affairs. With the letter *N* in the middle name, the ability to judge between sex and love must be developed in order for you to attain happiness.

The Letter *N* When Found in the Last Name

In the last position, the letter *N* brings a period of change in some major aspects of life. You may experience a fluctuation and vacillation in personal affairs and should guard against the development of a brooding nature that will result in little or no growth. If attention is paid to responsibilities while maintaining a progressive outlook, this transit will bring positive experiences. If you neglect those people and concerns close to you, including business matters, loss of important ground could take place.

The Letter *O* (A 6-Year Transit)

GENERAL MEANING

The letter *O* brings protection in all positions of your name, as long as you are not selfish and maintain peace and harmony within the home. Failure to bring domestic harmony could cause serious health matters.

The *O* transit, in any name position, can denote a beautiful period of love and harmony, as well as a time when a significant financial gain is possible. Generally speaking, emotional stability will exist, with few or no major disasters occurring within the home. A great deal of family responsibility and care will be required. You can expect to concentrate on legal matters and banking, and to attend to the accumulation of material wealth.

During the *O* transit there is always the concern that money should be invested wisely and safely. Do not lend, borrow, or speculate, since losses could be attracted. On the whole, a great deal of financial and emotional security can be established during this transit.

Love and marriage are spiritually blessed during the six years of the *O* transit, as long as you are not overly self-centered or neglectful of other family members. A strong love of home and family will exist but with less responsibility required than during the *F* transit. Banking, legal activities, artistic pursuits, and community service will take precedence. A desire to help humanity brings rich reward and financial gain.

The Letter *O* When Found in the First Name

As a child, family stability will exist. You can expect good or improved health. As an adult, responsibility will be present, along with financial gain during the middle third, fourth, and fifth years of the transit. No major disasters of any kind will take place.

The Letter O When Found in the Middle Name

The letter *O* in the middle name carries a sound emotional vibration. As a child, emotional security will exist within the family. As an adult, this stability will continue, with responsibility increasing in domestic areas due to marriage or the birth of children in the middle of the transit.

The Letter O When Found in the Last Name

In the last name, the letter *O* will bring emotional security and great inner peace and harmony. You may be interested in and attracted to spiritual and mystical experiences.

The Letter P (A 7-Year Transit)

GENERAL MEANING

During the *P* transit, you will desire solitude in order to think and reflect. You may be more secretive in regard to what is happening or has occurred in your life. Great recognition and advancement is possible through a proper education. Expect to be working for the benefit of others. All changes that are contemplated must be examined carefully, since many of them will not work out as planned.

All forms of speculation and gambling can lead to a damaging loss under the *P* transit, resulting in strained, high-strung, and upset emotions. If possible, partnerships should be avoided or carefully scrutinized.

Care must be exercised in order to maintain a stable family life. Although things may look better on the other side of the fence, in actuality you will find that they are not. Others possess the same problems as you.

A good education will always bring rewards if determination and will power are applied to the subject at hand. Occult and mystical studies can do much to improve negative and depressed moods and maintain positive thinking.

The Letter P When Found in the First Name

In your youth, you may show the tendency to become depressed or possess an inability to differentiate between true love and sex. As a child and adult, moreover, there is the tendency to be secretive and withdrawn.

The Letter P When Found in the Middle Name

As a child, early sexual experiences could be encountered. As an adult, you should avoid leading a promiscuous life, especially during the middle period of the 7-year transit. If love affairs don't work out, and they generally do not, bitterness can result and leave lasting negative scars, especially if you expect others to bring you happiness, as opposed to finding it for yourself.

The Letter P When Found in the Last Name

The letter P in the last name brings great spiritual and inner growth, along with a desire to spend more time alone reflecting.

The Letter Q (An 8-Year Transit)

GENERAL MEANING

The letter Q is powerful during its 8-year transit. You can expect to make a major push to improve your life in more than one direction. Ambition will be heightened to increase your financial base and gain recognition. Prestige and power are attainable through unusual business interests and activities. You may also combine two different interests at one time, such as religious or philosophical pursuits coupled with business. Unusual associations may be formed, such as political and diplomatic liaisons.

In any event, new and unusual lines of work and thought are likely. Moving your home to one much larger and finer is also possible. Educational pursuits for the self and/or family members will also be of interest. Personal advancement can be achieved along the lines of publishing, writing, public speaking, or travel.

It is important to scrutinize carefully, for legality and fairness, any financial relationships that may be entered into during the Q transit. Partnerships can bring prominence and power, as well as favorable publicity. Illegal and imprudent liaisons and financial arrangements could bring adverse publicity and lawsuits, as well as criminal charges and imprisonment.

One way or another your financial status is going to come to the forefront. Money should be carefully budgeted and some saved for a rainy day under this vibration.

The Letter Q When Found In the First Name

In the first name, the letter Q is a vibration favorable to good health and financial success. During the transit, you will probably move to a larger, more impressive home, one that will reflect your financial and social standing; along with the elevation in finances will come an increase in prestige, power, and position. Moves into unusual businesses and forms of endeavor are common.

The Letter Q When Found In the Middle Name

Not necessarily a favorable vibration emotionally, the letter Q in the middle name will neither add nor detract from the overall general meaning of the letter. As a child, you will experience emotional ups and downs, with little or no lasting emotional scarring. There should be no fear of permanent damage done to the personality.

As an adult, you can expect to encounter some fluctuation and movement, either up or down, in your finances. Marriage should be commenced cautiously because of it.

The Letter Q When Found In the Last Name

In the last name, because of the Q's position and the vibrations it carries, you will be concerned with financial

gain, and with seeking prestige, power, and influence.
All partnerships and financial arrangements must be
scrutinized as to their legality and fairness. While dishonest practices can lead to heavy losses, dealing with integrity can lead to extensive profit.

The Letter *R* (A 9-Year Transit)

GENERAL MEANING

The vibrations connected to the letter *R* bring an interest in humanitarian pursuits. For children, the requirements of the letter *R* can be difficult to understand
because the joy and rewards that accompany an interest
in humanistic pursuits require compassion and generos-
ity, qualities which may not have been experienced or
developed yet. A concern for humanity will bring prestige and prominence later in life, coupled with delays,
accidents, endings, sorrow, and loss. The more humanistic and universal an approach to living, with little or no
self-seeking, the greater and more fulfilling will be your
reward.

The letter *R*, along with its vibrations, is a difficult
letter to sustain, since it brings endings and experiences
that tend to tug and pull on the emotions. Everything
gained during an *R* transit must be earned; nothing
generally will fall in your lap. Unlike the letter *I*, however, you are able to effect more self-control under its
influence.

Opportunities to serve mankind are unlimited under
the *R* transit, and high ideals must be maintained. Any
slippage from this lofty position, especially in love relationships, will bring a backslide, emotionally accompanied by heavy losses. As a testing letter, the *R* brings
experiences that challenge your character to live for others and to be less self-seeking. Business pursuits dealing
with the arts, writing, creative and practical methods for
improved living conditions, as well as all lines of the food
business and human services, will bring success.

Under the *R* transit there can be legal agreements and difficulties. It is important to set your priorities, double-check them for fairness, and then move on. Unfairness could result in protracted legal problems; it is important, therefore, to get expert advice, especially of a legal nature before signing contracts.

With the heightened sensitivity that accompanies the letter *R*, you could self-destruct emotionally. Love relationships, such as marriage, must be carefully scrutinized, since they can bring emotional loss.

The *R* transit is a difficult one. During the middle of the transit accidents and misfortune are possible if you do not keep safety in mind.

The Letter *R* When Found In the First Name

In the first name, the letter *R* is not the most fortunate of influences to be under. Accidents and destructive behavior must be avoided, especially during the middle year of its transit when nervous tension is more elevated. You may become interested in abstract thinking, as well as philanthropy and humanistic concerns.

The Letter *R* When Found In the Middle Name

The letter *R* in the middle name brings misfortune. Marriage and love relationships can be problematic. A termination of a close relationship can be expected during the fifth year of its transit.

As a child, emotional problems may be present in the home. As an adult, you may experience unhappiness, loss, and sorrow.

The Letter *R* When Found In the Last Name

Perhaps this last placement is the best for the letter, but you may not learn life's lessons through your own initiative. Many experiences and situations will come to a head and force you to make decisions or take a stand on some issues. You will grow spiritually.

The Letter S (A 1-Year Transit)

GENERAL MEANING

The letter *S* during any 1-year transit will present a new and better way to advance, but some upheaval or dramatic change can be expected. Often a sudden and unexpected home move is necessary in order to push forward in life.

Additionally, you may encounter an unexpected adjustment that is both emotionally charged and thrilling in nature. Unusual love affairs and experiences may occur that must be handled if an improvement is to come about.

The letter *S*, as a winding letter, is shifting, vacillating, and emotional by nature. Deep emotional and sensual affairs can result in stress, breakup, and betrayal. Participation in unusual, secretive, and unwise love affairs should be avoided, since they can shake and disrupt your outer and inner life. Moreover, you may experience a sense of loneliness, resulting in a lack of socializing.

In any event, the *S* transit is apt to bring quite an eventful year. As a karmic testing letter, the *S* will bring unusual experiences that challenge your ideals.

On the positive side, real estate transactions can bring wonderful opportunities and substantial financial gain.

The Letter S When Found in the First Name

In the first name, the letter *S* frequently indicates a move into a new home, possibly even a new job. The change may be both sudden and may represent an upheaval of some type, *but it will be a good move!* Unusual, sudden love affairs of a sexual nature could cause emotional turmoil and conflict; you should, therefore, avoid them if possible.

The Letter S When Found in the Middle Name

As a child, disruptions within the family could cause problems. As an adult, you should guard against emotional upsets and breaks in love relationships, although they are usually temporary in nature.

The Letter S When Found in the Last Name

When the letter S is found in the last name, a sudden spiritual awakening is possible, coupled with turmoil. Your health should be closely guarded, especially lung problems, which have a tendency of developing into chronic conditions. In this placement, the letter S is generally a troublesome vibration.

The Letter T (A 2-Year Transit)

GENERAL MEANING

During its 2-year transit, the letter T is going to bring progress in business and love relationships, but it will also require more self-control. Others may try to interfere and cause problems in your life. Separation is usually caused by the untruthfulness of one party or a loved one. Love affairs can be fast and furious, bringing emotional upheaval and scandal. Unwise liaisons may cloud your ability to judge important matters correctly. Relationships can falter due to suspicion and lack of trust on the part of one or all parties involved. Prolonged emotional strain can cause health problems.

The letter T brings activity and progress along the lines of business, career, and finance. One of the challenges to be faced will be dealing with those who wish to disrupt your activity or private happiness. Disruptions by family members or loved ones as a result of jealousy can cause some form of emotional stress or upset.

Work related to business and social associations generally goes well, and a great deal can be learned about human nature if you remain observant during the T transit. Self-control must be exercised. It is also important to think things out as calmly as possible, to avoid making emotional decisions.

Marriage during a T transit can bring positive benefits if both parties are fair and honest. In any event, all situations should be checked out carefully before making a final decision.

The Letter *T* When Found in the First Name

The letter *T* is at its best in the first name. Money can be made through partnerships, and generally some acquisition of property can be expected. Romance and travel bring additional benefits.

The Letter *T* When Found in the Middle Name

As a child, this vibration will have little effect. As an adult, marriage is possible, usually during the second year.

In the middle-name position, the *T* is going to bring about a search for true love, as well as the establishment of a meaningful love or marriage relationship, sometimes against all odds.

The Letter *T* When Found in the Last Name

In the last name, periodic upset and strained emotions can be expected but not of a serious nature.

The Letter *U* (A 3-Year Transit)

GENERAL MEANING

Although creative, the vibrations of the letter *U*, depending on its placement, will indicate the presence of some emotional problems, as well as financial strain. You should build business and love relationships upon a solid, honest foundation.

The influence of the letter *U*, being sensual by nature, may push you in the direction of sexual affairs and sometimes unwise love triangles. You should exercise discretion and care, since problems closely associated with the sex organs are usually encountered. While love affairs may be different and sexually satisfying, they generally do not end up in marriage.

The letter *U* can bring you prominence before the public, especially through the written word. Financially, you must be careful to create a strong financial base and not harm yourself through your own stupidity by scattering funds, unwisely speculating, or relying totally on the judgment of others.

The Letter *U* When Found in the First Name

In the first name, the letter *U* does not necessarily denote a happy home life before the age of fourteen. There may be sickness, death, or friction in the family, which causes concern or emotional pain. After the age of fourteen, you should not try to begin new projects under its transit, since money may be slow in materializing. You may encounter loss instead of gain.

The Letter *U* When Found in the Middle Name

In this placement the influence of the letter *U* may facilitate emotional endings in certain relationships. The resulting upset may be strong and leave bad feelings for many years.

The Letter *U* When Found in the Last Name

During the middle or second year of this transit, you may experience a sense of bitterness, anger, and malice toward individuals who, you feel, have caused you harm or pain. Emotions can be intensely negative and destructive. You may even attempt to gain revenge against those who have hurt you by creating and then passing along vicious rumors or lies. It can be an intense period.

The Letter *V* (A 4-Year Transit)

GENERAL MEANING

Regardless of the placement of the letter *V*, you will be called upon to pay past debts; likewise, you can also collect past monies due. Long-outstanding debts owed you may suddenly be paid off. This letter, extravagant by nature, could also cause financial strain later on if your impulses are not kept in check.

During the *V* transit, serious thought will be given to your life and obligations. You may develop the desire to live on a more practical level. Business and family matters must be placed on a solid financial basis. In business, more success will result through improving older forms of employment rather than beginning new ones. Frequently your business may not bring much pleasure or a feeling of satisfaction; nevertheless, positive lessons are being learned.

A desire for travel and luxury will make life somewhat more pleasant, but again you must be careful not to overspend.

The Letter *V* When Found in the First Name

When placed in the first name, the letter *V* attracts favorable situations. Generally, you will encounter some form of financial gain during the middle of the second and third years of its transit. Additionally, your health should also be good.

The Letter *V* When Found in the Middle Name

In the middle name, the letter *V* will bring experiences that enhance your growth both spiritually and mentally, with the result that your life will attract meaningful new friendships and associations.

The Letter *V* When Found in the Last Name

With the letter *V* in the last name, you will achieve a great deal of inner peace, and will ultimately possess a feeling of new-found wisdom and satisfaction. Significant spiritual growth should be attained during this period.

The Letter *W* (A 5-Year Transit)

GENERAL MEANING

The very shape of the letter *W* suggests that emotional highs and lows will be encountered during its transit. In the area of marriage and love affairs, certain events producing sudden change will bring upsetting conditions and shocks to the emotional system. Unexpected encounters could filter into other relationships, including business, and cause blowups and breakups. Promiscuous actions or overindulgence in sensual affairs could affect your health. Disagreements usually do not continue past the transit of the letter.

The letter *W* usually brings the chance for travel. Jobs related to mining, transportation, real estate, and underground projects, such as oil and ores, could bring financial gain. Unique opportunities will surface quickly and afford you the opportunity to make money.

In business, it is important to seek good advice and legal counsel before committing yourself to projects.

The Letter *W* When Found In the First Name

When the *W* is present in the first name, there can be sudden and unexpected moves, especially of your home. Domestic and financial conditions will vacillate, up one minute and down the next.

The Letter *W* When Found In the Middle Name

When the *W* is present in the middle name, there will be emotional upsets, especially during the middle part of the transit up until approximately your twenty-third birthday. At this point a major love affair may end and another one begin. In financial areas, the same fluctuation may exist.

The Letter *W* When Found In the Last Name

Little spiritual growth of any major significance will take place with the letter *W* in the last name.

The Letter *X* (A 6-Year Transit)

GENERAL MEANING

During the letter *X*'s transit, your life will be at a crossroads as to whether you lead a life of service or fall prey to temptation. This 6-year transit calls for a change in consciousness if progress is going to occur. While you may be pivoted before the public limelight, you will still be working for the benefit of others.

The letter X can bring on negative emotions and a sense of inner crucifixion if compassion and understanding are not shown to others, especially family members. Although travel and finances are generally positive, other aspects of life will be problematic if you are self-seeking.

Family relationships may be strained if compassion is not exercised. Strange involvements between family members and relatives could also develop, resulting in incest or other unhealthy alliances or behavior. Unusual attachments between mother and son and father and daughter could bring much emotional pain and strain to other family members.

During all phases of the X transit, you should not enter into secret, illegal, or underhanded business activities that may have a tendency to bounce back and crucify you emotionally at a later date. Watch carefully where your money is placed, since you should be prepared to spend funds, if necessary, for other family members. You must be willing to sacrifice for the welfare of loved ones.

Strokes have been known to occur during the X transit, as well as major breaks in family relationships. Conversely, attending to the needs of others both in family and business can bring far-reaching financial gain and recognition.

Extra attention should be given to children. Often a troublesome child runs away from home during this transit. Jealousy is frequently a major cause of the problem.

The Letter X When Found in the First Name

As a child, your emotional health should be watched. After the age of approximately twenty-one, nervous strain and misdirected energy could cause problems. You could do a great deal of traveling.

The letter X attracts fame, as well as infamy. Working for others will bring recognition. You should be careful not to attract negative publicity as a result of a loss of position or a fall from high office.

There will be many ups and downs during the X transit. You could be preoccupied with secrecy or become more withdrawn than usual. Financial profit is indicated.

The Letter X When Found in the Middle Name

The X in the middle name is not a fortuitous placement, since it has the tendency to bring emotional upset of a sudden nature. At times, you may feel burdened by one emotional crisis after another.

The Letter X When Found in the Last Name

Of all the X placements, the X in the last name holds the best possibility for emotional and spiritual growth. Because the letter X can vibrate over the entire line, growth may take place after a crisis or strain has existed for a while.

The Letter Y (A 7-Year Transit)

GENERAL MEANING

Like the letters G and P, there is a secretive element during the Y transit, and consequently, you may desire to spend more time alone in introspection. As a whole, you will be bored quickly with the outside world and tend to be annoyed with crowds or those living on the lighter, less serious side of life. A desire to study, learn, and interact on a more mental plane will bring contentment. Misunderstandings in marriage and romance could lead to upset and divorce.

Educational pursuits are important during a Y transit. A desire to learn more about the physical and spiritual laws of existence could lead you to study law and its operations, as well as philosophy, psychic phenomena, and spirituality. Financial increase will exist but not on a massive level. Interpersonal relationships and marriage may not necessarily be happy or entered into for love.

Affairs of a secretive nature are more prone to occur but should be shunned, since they will surely die out either midway or in the fifth year of the transit and result in much grief and pain. You will also value your privacy more.

The Letter Y When Found in the First Name

With the letter Y in the first name, some financial gain can be expected but not of major proportions. You should be extra careful, since you will be more accident-prone, especially midway through the transit.

The Letter Y When Found in the Middle Name

If the letter Y occurs in your middle name, you should avoid overindulgence in wine, drugs, or sexual activity, since it will cause problems. A desire to be alone will be more pronounced, coupled with a tendency toward an increased secretive nature. Clandestine, unusual, and unwise love affairs, while hot and steamy, and occasionally troublesome, will tend to die out around the middle of the transit, and the upset could affect your health.

The Letter Y When Found in the Last Name

Of all placements, the Y in your last name is the best, since it will bring a higher level of spiritual growth, coupled with less grief.

The Letter Z (An 8-Year Transit)

GENERAL MEANING

The letter Z in any position is going to bring a desire for prominence in business affairs and an urge to uncover the mysteries that govern universal law. Involvement with international, government, and influential institutions can bring forth prominence and recognition. Involvement in politics could bring authority as well.

Under the Z transit you should not engage in illegal or

underhanded activities. Success in all activities can be achieved only through the proper focusing of your efforts.

The *Z* transit will bring an interest and possible involvement in affairs of a psychic, occult, spiritual, and mysterious nature. An effort should be made to understand universal and metaphysical laws without overly attaching emotion to them.

Recognition and advancement in your position is possible if you engage in mental and scholarly pursuits. People of different cultures, as well as distant lands, will interest you. Travel to faraway places may be encountered. Knowledge of a specialized nature will bring financial profit. Communications, publishing, foreign affairs, and government work may also interest you during the *Z* transit and result in a rise in reputation.

The Letter *Z* When Found in the First Name

As a child, you will be driven to compete for good standing among your peers. One could say that your strong ego will make its mark. As an adult, you will be interested in entrepreneurial enterprises, aimed toward attracting a higher financial base.

The Letter *Z* When Found in the Middle Name

The *Z* in the middle name brings a warning that you should not push your wishes, desires, or ambition for a higher station in life on others. Your ego must be kept in check, along with all self-seeking tendencies. A strong interest in the self will become evident, and marriage, if entered, may be for financial reasons.

The Letter *Z* When Found in the Last Name

The *Z* in the last name brings a warning not to engage in underworld, illegal, or unlawful activities. Not much growth of a spiritual nature will take place with placement in the last name.

After analyzing the letters in your name, you may find

that the general meaning, as opposed to the specific meaning, of the letter is applicable at any given time. According to the individual, the general meaning of the letter may vibrate over the entire mental, physical, emotional, or intuitive aspects of your life. It is always a good idea, therefore, to become familiar with the meanings of the letters in all placements, committing to memory the positive as well as negative ramifications.

CHAPTER 9
Living through the Letters of Your Name

As individuals, we live through the letters in each of our names. Each letter attracts experiences that help us grow and develop as individuals. You may say, Well, I didn't pick my name at birth; it was selected for me by my parents. Metaphysically speaking, however, each of us before we are born attracts the ideal conditions under which to be born. These circumstances include the ideal parents, from whom we learn the initial lessons of life, and also our name, which is subconsciously suggested to our parents. We pick all of these elements in order to work out many of the lessons and problems of past lives that still need attention.

Throughout the course of our lives, we live through the experiences as attracted by each of the letters of our names. In order to ascertain which letters are influencing our actions during any given year, we must first set up a chart. For computing purposes, the first thing that must be determined is which letter of each individual name—first, middle, and last—we are presently living in. Each letter of the alphabet carries a number value that operates over a specific number of years. For example, the letter *E* will be in effect for 5 years, the letter *T* will be

In effect for 2 years, and the letters *A* or *S* will each be in effect for 1 year, and so on. We call the passage through the letters in our name the "*Transit*." The final number total of the letters that we transit is called the *Essence*, which gives an overall description of the activities as outlined by the individual letters themselves.

In setting up the chart, it is important to place each of your individual names on a separate line. Let us now analyze the life of an imaginary friend, Mary Smith, who is presently thirty years old, born on May 8, 1960.

Rule: The Transit of the letters operates from birthday to birthday.

Unlike the Personal years, which run parallel to the Universal years and operate from January to December of each year, the Transit of the letters runs from *birthday to birthday*. More frequently than not, most individuals during any given year will be living between different letters in the name, because the birthday falls somewhere *within* the year. People born at the beginning and end of the calendar year do not have this problem.

Now, let us see which letters are presently affecting the life of Mary Smith. In computing the length of years of each Transit, it is essential to understand that the first letter, *M*, in Mary's name will run for four years, *from the age of zero to four*. During the first year of Mary's life she will be living in the time frame of 0 to 1. In actuality, by the time her first birthday has arrived, she will have lived one year. She will then transit the letter *A* in Mary, which is in effect for 1 year, during her fifth year of life, and will transit the letter *R*, in effect for 9 years, beginning in her sixth year up to and including her fourteenth year. Likewise, Mary will live through the *S* in Smith from the year 0 to 1, since the letter *S* has a Transit of one year, and will then move on to transit the letter *M* from the ages one up to and including the end of the fourth year.

After the letters in Mary Smith's names have been computed, the next step is to add together the number value of the letters to arrive at the Essence, or total number count.

In the name "Mary Smith" we can compute the name as follows and then take a shortcut later on:

0	1	2	3	4	5	6	7	8	9	10	11	12	13	14
M	M	M	M	A	R	R	R	R	R	R	R	R	R	Y
S	M	M	M	M	I	I	I	I	I	I	I	I	I	T
—	—	—	—	—	—	—	—	—	—	—	—	—	—	—
5	8	8	8	5	18	18	18	18	18	18	18	18	18	9

15	16	17	18	19	20	21	22	23	24	25	26	27	28
Y	Y	Y	Y	Y	Y	M	M	M	M	A	R	R	R
T	H	H	H	H	H	H	H	H	S	M	M	M	M
—	—	—	—	—	—	—	—	—	—	—	—	—	—
9	15	15	15	15	15	12	12	12	5	5	13	13	13

29	30	31
R	R	R
I	I	I
—	—	—
18	18	18

By looking at the chart above, we can see that Mary Smith at thirty years of age is currently living in the letters *R* and *I*. As a matter of fact, we can say that she is living in the fifth year of the letter *R*, and that the total letter value of the Transit at her thirtieth birthday is 18 (the total of the letters *R* and *I*). As you can see, all the letters in each of her names begin and end at different times. Nonetheless, she will live through all the letters in each of her names and will begin again.

The total number value, or Essence, of these letter Transits is also going to be important. In Mary's case, the 18/9 Essence is going to bring the experiences of the number 18 and also the experiences of the number 9, since number 18 is a higher octave of the number 9. If this number value 18/9 occurs for Mary in a 9 Personal year, the double 9 is going to bring problems, trouble, sacrifice, and loss. Frequently, the middle and the final year of Transit for a letter will bring important experiences and destiny changes. Knowing ahead of time that these changes can occur can help to explain or prepare you for the shift that may take place.

Like the experiences that govern each of the letters, the total value of the Essence is going to attract specific experiences, too. By studying the Transit of the letters, and specifically the number Essence for any given year, you can develop a fairly accurate picture of which kinds of activities and events you may encounter.

The Number 1 Essence

The number 1 Essence will bring a change, sometimes dramatic, into your life and will represent movement in some new direction that will improve your life. But for this new beginning to take effect, the old way of life will first have to terminate. For this reason the 1 Essence can bring both birth of the new and the death of the old, honor and loss at the same time. The 1 Essence forces decisions that must be made and requires leadership, initiative, organization, and supervision in order to launch new beginnings, a new environment, or new aspects to old lines of work.

Under the 1 Essence, sudden occurrences are frequent, sometimes even a total upheaval in your life results, from which lifelong lessons are learned and new opportunities are embarked upon. After the upheaval, when all the dust has settled, the changes will usually be seen to have worked out for the better. Under the 1 Essence, therefore, you will begin projects and set long-range goals.

The Number 10 Essence

Under the 10 Essence, decisions will be made that test your inner faith and desires for their true value. Possessing a higher force of the number 1, the general description of the 1 Essence will be present in a more forceful degree.

The Number 19 Essence

The 19 Essence is going to bring many individual tests

of character. Life will force you to make choices that will test your integrity and ability to distinguish between right and wrong. Many positive, unforgettable lessons will be learned. Under the 19 Essence, unusual occurrences may take place that will push you to attempt to break free from existing conditions and overcome past obstacles. You will feel a need to exert your will to be independent and establish a new order, but must be careful not to abuse the rights of others. Forcing change because of feelings of restlessness could bounce back and cause problems. Moreover, impulsive actions could cause loss in every aspect of your life.

Emotions at times could run high during this Essence, because of feelings of resentment over existing conditions or just from the impatience that accompanies a desire to change. You are advised to choose your relationships carefully and to stay away from unwise associations. Be cautious with your words, move slowly with your activities, avoid impulsiveness.

The 19 Essence can bring an increase of money and may find you living more on the extravagant side of life. Moreover, at times you will be unsure of yourself and may tend to vacillate before coming to a firm decision.

The Number 28 Essence

This essence often occurs when there are four names in the proper name. It should be interpreted as being similar to the 10 Essence.

The Number 2 Essence

The 2 Essence brings the opportunity to receive help and to work in association with others, but it does require cooperation. Basically a peaceful vibration, the number 2 Essence brings gradual growth along the lines of your present activities. The affairs of your life will move slowly, allowing you time to cooperate with others and assimilate what you have learned. Impulsiveness can bring problems; it is better to go slowly.

The affairs of life will bring strong associations and

partnerships that offer rewarding opportunities. The 2, being a domestic vibration, will require that you keep the peace, cooperate, and live harmoniously with others in order to improve family and business conditions.

The 2 Essence requires that many small and large details be taken care of in order to achieve success. Moreover, you may have to exercise patience, tact, and consideration for others. In domestic conditions disagreements will usually be quickly settled. There will be pleasure and popularity and much to gain by socializing. Although it is a rather slow-moving vibration, the worst that can happen during the 2-Transit is boredom. It is important not to push your affairs out of a desire to force change. This aspect of the 2 vibration could bring trouble and rupture.

The Number 11 Essence

The 11 Essence can bring sudden eruptions and unusual events that can make or break certain relationships. Unexpectedly and out of the ordinary, a sudden marriage or divorce could take place. Simultaneously, existing situations may bring misunderstandings, causing you to step back and make a decision about an important issue in your life.

The 11, being a number of slow growth, can also bring delays and fear of financial loss. A more spiritual outlook can alleviate this type of worry and set you in a new direction of patience and inner peace as a result of decisions made during an 11 Transit.

The Number 20 Essence

The 20 Essence, as a higher octave of the 2, brings many of the conditions of the 2. The circumstances and affairs of your life will need time to develop. At worst, a sense of boredom will exist.

The Number 29 Essence

The 29, as a higher octave of the 11, will bring many

conditions that are similar to the 11 Essence. Associations, partnerships, and unions, especially of a commercial nature, will bring much activity and growth along the lines of business. Many advantages will come your way if you are open to the ideas of others and make an attempt to agree upon important issues. Read the description and meaning of the number 11, too.

The Number 3 Essence

The 3 Essence is going to bring a more pleasant, colorful, and creative level of existence. It will be a very personal time, affording you an opportunity to enjoy yourself and experience a more pleasant environment that includes enlivening your social life and broadening your base of activities. Love affairs and emotional experiences may occur fast and furious and are common during the 3 Essence. Personal affairs can bring great happiness, new friendships, and trips that broaden your horizons and improve your old way of life.

The 3 Essence is an emotional time. You may experience unfortunate situations if you speculate too haphazardly, overindulge, or live extravagantly. Selfishness and a critical attitude could also cause conflict in personal relationships. Advancement will come if you cultivate the creative and imaginative side of your personality through hobbies, art, writing, lecturing, and travel. The number 3's downfall is often caused by scattering personal energies in many directions and taking what is said by others at face value. It is best to investigate what is told you instead of taking it as gospel truth. Engaging in too many activities and being overly trusting can bring great loss of both time and finances. Foolish actions, overspending, and engaging in gossip should be avoided.

The 3 Essence brings the opportunity to travel and establish new and different friendships, sometimes of an unusual nature, that emphasize the cultural aspects of living. Music, art, and literature can be cultivated to bring a more creative and harmonious way of living.

The Number 12 Essence

The 12 Essence is a fine period of time for fun and creativity and for enjoying the lighter side of life. You will have to guard the tendency to scatter your forces. Emotion must be kept in check; avoid repeated negative thoughts or indulgence in introspection. In order to establish anything of a lasting value, you must organize your time wisely and stick to tasks. There will be a tendency to leave activities unfinished. Often, nothing of a lasting nature is developed under the 12 Essence, but life will be enjoyable.

The 12 Essence can bring arguments and attract emotional upsets especially with loved ones, but problems will eventually blow over without any negative results.

The Number 21 Essence

The 21 Essence brings a warning to refrain from scattering your forces or your money, but you will also have greater potential for achievement, coupled with some emotional confusion. You will be more amenable to gambling on certain ventures. Close friends and relatives may cause emotional upset by attempting to take financial advantage of you. Financial hardship could result if you do not use good judgment. All financial loans should be made in a businesslike fashion, or you could run the risk of loss.

The Number 30 Essence

The 30 Essence is basically a higher order of the 3 Essence and usually occurs when there are four names in the proper name. In this instance, the general description of the 3 Essence will apply.

The Number 4 Essence

The 4 Essence brings a period of practical order and structure into your life. It represents movement toward a more organized and systematized manner of living. Affairs will be pared to their solid bases, emphasizing the need for practical living by means of budgeting and taking care of family and business situations. The 4 brings concern for family, children, home, property, health, and a desire to put affairs in good operating order. If you are building a home, business, or anything of importance, make an effort to use good judgment to bring about practical improvements and a more systematic existence. A great deal can be accomplished under this Transit if you maintain a responsible attitude. An irresponsible or illegal approach will be met with severe suffering. You usually will pay the full price for your mistakes.

While the 4 Essence brings a feeling of restriction and is slow-moving by nature, it will also allow you to live on a more matter-of-fact, no-nonsense level. At times there will be a concern over finances, since those close to you may make demands, but much good will come from working within the limitations that this Essence imposes.

The Number 13 Essence

Like the 4 Essence, the number 13 will slow down the pace of life; you will feel an inclination to conduct your affairs on a practical level, using good financial judgment. Some form of inner confusion may accompany this lull, however. Important decisions will be made during the Transit, since the number 13 represents a transformation to another level of living; often some element is terminated or completed, either a relationship or some form of work. In health matters, you are advised always to seek a second opinion and to refrain from unnecessary operations. This Essence tends to bring an increase in misdiagnosed ailments and operations that could be postponed to a time when conditions would be more favorable.

The Number 22 Essence

The 22 Essence brings the opportunity for a spiritual awakening within you, especially in terms of what you are capable of accomplishing. While a financial increase usually accompanies this number, especially from older, more well-established occupations, you may find yourself involved simultaneously with the demands of two activities, two obligations, two occupations or interests. It is best to embrace responsibilities with optimism and not with resentment, for to do the latter could cause emotional problems or illness. Some emotional confusion may be present during the number 22 Essence; sometimes relationships are broken. Basically, you will be more inclined to share what you have with others. Because the number 22 consists of a Master number, more self-awareness and knowledge will result, along with some form of spiritual awakening.

It is important during the 22 Essence that you pay any outstanding bills and debts that may have been incurred. By employing a universal attitude, more money can be earned to meet these obligations.

The Number 5 Essence

During the 5 Essence life will take on a more colorful, exciting, and adventurous overtone. Unexpected events and situations can force change upon you. Most often these events, although not desired at the time, bring about a more positive way of living and act as a steppingstone to a new direction and a better future.

Socially, you will be actively involved in travel, both nationally and internationally. The new, the different, the kooky, the progressive in any field of endeavor, will be of interest; and the opportunity will be present for you to explore more advanced practices and ideas. Sales work can result in a large increase of money.

The 5 Essence, being a publicly active period, often finds you interested in any number of activities. In business, you will have a number of coals in the fire. Too many projects occurring simultaneously, however, can cause confusion and loss. You are warned, therefore, not to be overly speculative or careless with free time or money. Any overindulgence on the physical plane, involving drugs, sex, or overeating, can also lead to danger. Any breaking of the law will also be strictly enforced and will make you miserable.

The 5 Essence affords you the ability to break loose

of conditions that were formerly of a confining nature. You will still notice, however, a feeling of restlessness, which can lead to sloppy behavior and illegal involvements. But more often than not, the 5 Essence will allow you the chance to move forward in life, with a greater amount of mobility and freedom.

The Number 14 Essence

During the 14 Essence, you will be able to overcome difficulties by striving to make harmonious agreements with others. There will be a tendency toward some misunderstandings and unnecessary competition, both on the job and at home, but these drawbacks can be alleviated if you keep your demands to a minimum and try to compromise as much as possible. The 14 Essence may bring more emotional upsets and disagreements than the straight 5 Essence, coupled with an increased vulnerability of the senses. Keep a keen eye on your financial situation. Finances may fluctuate, but do not attempt to offset a downward trend by unwise and frequent speculation, overspending, and gambling. Moreover, take care of your health. The 14, being a karmic transit, will bring activity that invites the tendency to misuse one's freedom by overindulging in food, drugs, alcohol, sex, and gambling.

The Number 23 Essence

The 23 Essence brings with it long-range travel, progressive living, and sometimes a twist to the existing career or a totally new career. The different type of work experienced during the Essence will be coupled with many people making demands on your time and finances. Negative emotions are likely to involve your feeling overburdened by the weight of the demands, but the degree of sickness or financial loss will not be apparent. As a result of promising opportunities, unusual and unique changes can be expected, and if you are involved in a dedicated marriage, positive results can be attained.

The Number 6 Essence

The 6 Essence brings with it the opportunity to enjoy and experience the rewards of sharing and being responsible for family members, children, in-laws, and spouse. High ideals must be maintained. In exchange for the love and compassion shown to others you will experience protection of a spiritual, physical, and monetary nature. Financial gain will be accompanied by greater demands than previously experienced.

You may respond emotionally as a result of being burdened by caring for others. Watch your negative reactions. While you are advised not to carry an unnecessary load, still you will have to accept some form of responsibility. Any form of selfishness will bring about resentment and loss, even possibly divorce. Marriages that maintain the high ideals of love, sharing, and giving will bring rewards.

The financial success acquired during the 6 Essence is usually a result of inheritance, aid from a spouse, or operating a business that looks out for the welfare of others. It can also come through the admiration of the opposite sex.

Often love and romance during the 6 Essence reaches a higher plane. But when love is given selfishly, resentfully, or is betrayed, the emotional loss and attendant problems will be significant.

The Number 15 Essence

Domestic responsibility will be present, but more freedom will also exist. From time to time problems may suddenly appear within the immediate or extended family that will cause emotional upset and require attention. Financial strain or responsibility may exist on account of loved ones. At times, you may feel that you are being asked to shoulder too much domestic responsibility. Nevertheless, once you realize that you are accountable, and accept it, things should settle down. The 15 Essence, however, is a very positive vibration within which to begin a marriage.

The Number 24 Essence

The 24 Essence carries more responsibility of an immediate and of a more restrictive, confining nature with regard to loved ones. Family obligations will demand a great deal of time and attention, with less opportunity to pursue one's personal pleasures, hobbies, or endeavors. However, the 24 Essence does not carry the negative problems or emotions that tend at times to accompany the 15 Essence.

The Number 7 Essence

The 7 Essence brings the opportunity to study, specialize, and deeply analyze life or your profession on a microscopic level. You will be able to advance by taking advantage of educational and literary pursuits. Often metaphysical, philosophical, and religious subjects can move you toward an improved way of living, especially emotionally. The 7 Essence affords the opportunity to dive into the mysteries of life, to explore strange and unusual events and repercussions.

Study, specialization, and writing, coupled with educational pursuits, usually make the 7 Transit an interesting one. Psychic phenomena can accompany such a transit, but be careful not to become overly emotionally involved; rather, take an intellectual approach.

Life during the 7 Transit will also impose more economic restrictions, as in the 4 Transit, but they will result from other interests costing money. Quasi retirement from the mainstream of life and from social engagements will evolve as more scientific, specialized, and educational activities interest you. During the 7 Essence, it is important to refrain from worry as much as possible, since it can lead to agitation and depression. It is important to refine and direct your thoughts into concentrated studies that will improve the quality of your life.

The number 7 carries a spiritual attraction; money can be made through quiet, specialized pursuits. In order to benefit from a 7 Essence, however, you must live on a higher plane. Marriage and home life are blessed if all parties undertake a more harmonious existence. Your health should not be neglected, as ailments may tend to be of a more mysterious and serious nature. Turbulent relationships should be avoided.

The Number 16 Essence

The 16 Essence is karmic in nature and may entail a test or the giving up of something during the Transit, not necessarily a physical thing, but even an attitude or way of life that must end. Relationships can blossom almost overnight and fall apart just as quickly, bringing emotional upset and drastic changes in your life. Introspective thoughts and behavior can bring feelings of loss. Since there is much knowledge to be gained during the 16 Essence, you will benefit greatly from educational and specialized pursuits.

Under the 16 Essence, karma will be collected for previous irresponsible acts, sometimes even acts that took place in past lives. You may feel as if you are living and existing within a fog, unsure of where you are heading, but nevertheless, movement will be made in the right direction. After this period is over, you will generally be in a much better situation than when you began.

The Number 25 Essence

The 25 Essence is very similar to the 7 Essence, but with particular emphasis on heavy investigations of a specialized nature. Often some sort of writing accompanies this form of analysis. The 25 Essence does not carry any of the negativity and emotional crisis of the 16 Essence but brings a more harmonious way of life, particularly in specialized professions. You may want to reread the general meaning of the number 7.

The Number 8 Essence

The 8 Essence brings the opportunity to advance and be recognized through big business, property, community and civic affairs, in buying, selling, and publishing. While the number 8 brings with it certain privileges, you will also be required to bear a heavy responsibility. More money will flow into your life, but expenses will be high as well.

The 8 Essence brings advancement through hard work and much effort. It is a great time to engage in the affairs of the community, and running for public office could bring recognition. Travel and romance will often take on business overtones, becoming less romantic in nature. There may be financial strain, which is always a potential problem under all 8's. Delays of one form or another can also be expected, but if these are met with efficiency and good judgment, rewards will follow in the end.

The 8 Essence brings the opportunity to engage in the management of property, either buying, selling, or supervising, as well as printing, publishing, and commercial interests. You may be exhausted because of the constant effort that must be exerted, but the rewards are great and will be worth it.

The Number 17 Essence

The 17 Essence is probably one of the finest of all Essences from a business standpoint, but the demands are high. Finances must be attended to constantly, with an eye to paying the bills and balancing the budget. Abundant financial rewards usually accompany the ownership and operation of property that must be attended to.

The Number 26 Essence

The 26 Essence is usually the worst for finances, because so many other people are relying on you for support. Most often a good amount of money must be paid out for the benefit of others, with little left for you alone to enjoy. Additional debts may account for a large chunk of lost income. In any event, expenses will be high, due to obligations owed to family and those close to you. This number commonly shows up among people who employ four names.

The Number 9 Essence

The 9 is a dramatic Essence, which must be lived on a highly compassionate and broadly universal level. Great strides can be made along the lines of your business or professional life, in acting, music, and religion, but a broader outlook must be cultivated.

While some kind of progress can be expected, it can also be a time fraught with delay, sorrow, and emotional loss. People no longer necessary to your development will go out of your life, either through death or by moving off in their own directions. It is best to simply view these situations as part of life. If they are considered a real loss, emotional problems could result.

While experiencing a 9 Essence, you should not try to hold onto things or people that resist it; it is best just to let go and to move on with your life. You should live on a higher plane, try to assist others, and avoid being self-seeking or selfish in any way.

The 9 Essence brings a greater tendency to argue; disagreements can be frequent, resulting in unhappiness, sorrow, separation, and divorce. Romantic relationships, if self-seeking, can be short-lived and negative in nature. Marriages begun in the 9 Essence can be painful and disappointing, resulting in divorce, separation, and emotional loss. Love affairs that are clingy, demanding, or that expect too much from others can cause problems. For this reason, love and romance, if entered into during a 9 Essence and not based on high ideals and a true sense of sharing, are often a disappointment.

Others may try to take advantage of what is not rightfully theirs, resulting in legal disagreements. But the chance for financial gain will be available, along with varied and favorable opportunities. Big business can be interesting and abundant during the 9 Essence, bringing the opportunity to advance your reputation and acumen. You will find an unlimited capacity for greatness if you seek to take care of the needs of mankind. Money is often made, retained, lost, only to be regained. Legal involvement becomes pronounced when honesty is not maintained in business.

The Number 18 Essence

The 18 Essence, as a higher vibration of the 9, incorporates all the characteristics of the 9, with the added element of activity with large corporations and institutions.

The number 18 Essence brings the possibility of a position of authority and power. Greater financial increase can bring even higher recognition, public exposure, and authority, but it sometimes follows a legal struggle because of the dishonest actions of others. During the 18 Essence, you can advance in reputation and career, achieving a sought-after level of personal satisfaction, but the basic, often heavy-hearted emotions and drama of the 9 Essence will remain and have to be handled, possibly contributing a feeling of loss and emotional strain.

The Number 27 Essence

The 27 Essence combines both the characteristics of the 18 and the 9, bringing the possibility of excellence in unusual occupations and long-distance travel. Under the 27, you must attend to all health matters and make sure that nothing is left uninvestigated, since there is a greater chance of chronic disease forming. There is also the increased possibility of sustaining accidents, which might leave permanent injury, especially those caused by machinery, such as automobiles and mechanical devices. You should not operate these conveyances if under emotional stress or strain of any kind.

When the number of the Essence matches your Personal year in question, the doubling effect of the vibration has the tendency to turn negative and result in negative experiences. It is always important, therefore, to exercise special care and precaution during these periods. The following occurrences are possible:

Personal Year	Essence	Description
1	1	Spinning wheels in too many directions, overactivity, nothing accomplished.
2	2	Bad health, excessive nervousness, loss, disappointment, reduced finances.
3	3	Severely stressed nerves, scattered activities.
4	4	Tremendously heavy work load, burdened by limitations.
5	5	Irresponsible sexual activities, negative use of free time.
6	6	Too much responsibility, acrimony at home.
7	7	Locked in, with no chance of movement, depression, withdrawal, feeling limited by environment.
8	8	Overworked, insufficient money, overstrain, financial loss.
9	9	Sacrifice, loss, oppressive emotions.
11	11	Severe mental strain, very bad nerves.
22	22	Feelings that one is losing his mind, severe mental strain, fear of nervous breakdown.

CHAPTER 10

Double Whammy: The Double Letter Transits

Throughout our lives, we transit each letter in each of our names, and when we finish a name, we go back to the beginning of that name and begin again. After setting up the chart for the Transits, sometimes we see a doubling or tripling effect, the Transit of two or three of the same letters on two or three lines. This phenomenon frequently occurs when there is a double letter in the name, such as in the name "Betty," or when one letter ends and the same letter begins in another name. When this happens, the effect of that letter and the experiences it highlights are doubled.

Rule: When two or more of the same letters appear in the same year, the effect of that letter is intensified and is viewed as dual or negative in nature.

The dual qualities of the letters can bring obstacles and conditions that must be looked after carefully. It is important for you to know, therefore, what to look out for and what to expect. Sometimes advanced planning can help alleviate some of the stress caused by negative situations. A good rule of thumb would be to take advantage of the good aspects when they appear and not panic during the rough spots. A good suggestion during a double-letter Transit would be to just sit back and make no major moves during the Transit until the trauma, or the test, has passed. Remember, many of us have lived through double Transits a number of times and we're still here functioning marvelously.

Before we discuss the meanings of the double-letter Transits, let us look at a name such as Danny DeVito. Without even knowing his birthdate, you can see that for four years, from birth to the end of his third year, Mr. DeVito lived through a *DD* Transit as he passed through the *D* in Danny and the *D* in DeVito. During that period of time, health problems could have plagued him. His chart for the first few years would have appeared as follows:

0	1	2	3	4	5	6	7	8
D	D	D	D	A	N	N	N	N
D	D	D	D	E	E	E	E	E
—	—	—	—	—	—	—	—	—
8	8	8	8	6	10	10	10	10

We can readily see that besides four years of a *DD* Transit, what followed shortly afterward was four years of a 10 Transit, consisting of two letters that carry the 5 vibration, *N* and *E*, appearing on the same line. While these letters do not double with the same letter vibration, they do double with the same number vibration, which could have resulted in accidents brought on by overactivity or motion.

Now, study the effects of the dual letters, and learn what you should be on guard for.

A-A The double *A* can result in overactivity, with not much accomplished of a concrete nature. During this type of Transit you should frequently check to see that a strong foundation has been laid beneath your activities. Go out and take the initiative, but make sure that you are not all motion, spinning your wheels in too many directions.

B-B The letter *B* is a sensitive and emotional letter. During the *BB* Transit, you should make every attempt to keep your emotions under control, since the elements will double and can have a negative effect. In health-related matters, there is the possibility of being overly tired, run-down, or anemic.

C-C The *C*, being a letter of motion, conviviality, and activity tends to carry with it an accidental nature. You should be on guard for accidents, especially related to falls, such as off high places or down stairs. Moreover, during this period your back area is prone to injury, so exercise care in movements.

D-D The *D*, being not too pleasant a letter with regard to physical conditions, could indicate bad health or reduced resistance to disease. You should keep a sharp eye on health matters; do not neglect nagging problems or allow them to linger.

E-E The letter *E*, being an emotionally active letter, tends to bring stress, nervous tension, and accidents of a moving nature. Since the *E* carries the tendency to overindulge in vices, such as drinking, gambling, eating, sex, and drugs, you should exercise restraint in these areas.

F-F The *FF* Transit could bring heart and ear problems. Family problems, heavy responsibility, and sorrow could overtax the heart.

G-G The letter *G*, as a secretive letter, could bring undiagnosable illnesses that tend to linger. During the *GG* Transit, it is better not to allow the body to get run down. Treachery from unsuspected sources is also possible. You should watch what you say to others: Maintain discretion both in what you say and to whom you say it.

H-H Since the letter *H* is a powerful letter, during an *HH* Transit you will tend to overstrain, overwork, and overstretch for success. Such tension can result in reduced or bad health. Serious problems could produce heart problems and blood disorders. Before jumping to unfounded conclusions, however, you should look to the total number line, or Essence, as well as the Personal year.

I-I The letter *I* is a very emotional letter. During the *II* Transit, there will probably be some sort of emotional turbulence. This heavy emotional stress could run down bodily functions and cause digestive problems as well.

J-J The letter *J*, being a mental letter and one involving increased responsibility, will bring a doubling influence in both mental and physical areas. You may feel burdened by the strain of caring for others and handling too many problems. This overactivity could exhaust the body. The *JJ*, while it usually isn't associated with the intimidating duality of the other letters, does bring heavy responsibility and some overstrain. Regardless, you will be able to carry the load.

K-K The letter *K* is an emotionally charged letter and oversensitive in many areas. The *KK* Transit will bring a fear of breakdown and shattered nerves.

L-L The letter *L* is an action letter and may involve you in activities related to motion. You should be doubly careful about avoiding accidents during this Transit. Since the letter *L* also affects parts of the body that deal with sinus and throat ailments, it is best to attend to problems in these areas as well.

M-M The *MM* Transit is similar to the double *D* in that both Transits carry the heaviness and restrictive qualities of the 4. Nagging health conditions should be checked and not permitted to become chronic. Serious illness is possible during the double *M* Transit, but recovery is usually a full one, with no lasting mental or physical effects.

N-N Like the letter *E*, the letter *N* is one of motion. The *NN* Transit could bring accidents of a serious nature, resulting in death or permanent injury. When operating any type of machinery or automobile, you should use double protection and be more safety-oriented.

O-O The letter *O* is an emotional letter. The *OO* intensifies inner and outer emotional responses, especially when dealing with family matters. Be sensitive to warnings: Check heart problems and related disorders that could be serious. Occasionally cancers could become evident, as a result of prolonged and deep-seated bitterness and sorrow. Check the number Transit and the Personal year for more accurate information. Again, you are cautioned not to jump to unnecessary conclusions, since other factors would have to be considered.

P-P The letter *P* is a mysterious letter. It is connected with things hidden and secretive. During a *PP* Transit, you should be on guard for negative health conditions resulting from incorrect or undiagnosed ailments.

Q-Q The letter *Q*, even more than the letter *H,* brings high-intensity conditions, usually resulting in overactivity and strain. Exercises that release stress and reduce pressure are advisable. Like the letter *H*, digestion problems could manifest themselves.

R-R Basically the *RR* Transit is a nasty one. You will be very accident-prone. Your standard of living should be watched carefully. Overindulgence or substance abuse could result in sudden and severe accidents and sometimes even death. Theft while traveling is possible, so guard possessions carefully. Migraine headaches and nervous tension could also take their toll.

S-S The letter *S* is a very emotional and vacillating letter. The doubling in intensity could cause a nervous breakdown. Additionally, lung problems could cause illness and bad health.

T-T The *TT* Transit could bring deception, treachery, and betrayal in relationships, as well as sudden death. Headaches should be attended to.

U-U The *UU* Transit, carrying the double 3 vibration, could intensify problems related to the throat and speech organs. In women, problems with the female organs should be checked. During this Transit, a tendency to overindulge could become excessive because of unhappiness. Therefore, you should keep a close eye on your personal habits.

V-V The *VV* Transit, like the *DD* and *MM* Transits, can have a very bad effect on your health, even worse than the *DD*. You should use extra precaution to protect the limbs of your body, since a loss or a crippling effect is possible. The *VV* personality also tends to be overly trusting when receiving medical opinions. A second medical opinion should always be sought before making major decisions. Intestinal and spinal problems should also be watched.

W-W The *WW* Transit, like the *EE* and the *NN*, can be excruciatingly cruel in that it carries the heaviness of the *VV* and the problems brought on by the *NN*. Always get a second medical opinion before making major decisions. When traveling in moving vehicles over long distances, use extra care, since serious accidents are possible.

X-X The *XX* Transit could bring some type of emotional or physical cross to bear. It is wise to avoid involvement in any of the sciences dealing with black magic. Emotional suffering intensifies during a double *X* Transit.

Y-Y The letter *Y* is an introspective letter. The *YY* will compound this effect and add elements of brooding and depression. A feeling of loneliness and aloneness may exist. Again, you are cautioned to guard against accidents.

Z-Z Like the *HH* and the *QQ*, the *ZZ* Transit is going to bring an excessive dosage of drive, stress, and pressure into your life to get ahead and be a success. This Transit could double the possibility of acquiring the ailments associated with the *HH* and *QQ* Transits. Stomach problems of a serious nature should be attended to immediately.

Before you run off and panic, it should be noted that many of the conditions listed may not necessarily develop, but you should remain alert that they *could* occur. Moreover, I have seen any number of individuals live through double Transits, including myself, without harm. While the effect of the double letters is intensified and negative, still, valuable lessons are learned that sometimes force an individual to let go of negative habits and live in a more constructive fashion.

CHAPTER 11

What Really Motivates You: The Soul Urge

The *Soul Urge* represents what you are really like and aspects of your inner self that are uniquely your own. Your Soul Urge represents your wishes, desires, how you feel, think, act, and which interests really motivate you. Unlike your *Quiescent Self*, which represents your daydreams and how others view you, or the *Expression*, which represents how you must live, your Soul Urge represents the real you, what you are like, what abilities you can count on to get ahead in life, as well as which traits have been developed and carried over from past lifetimes. If you want to discover what another individual is really like, it is best to study his Soul Urge.

The Soul Urge can also be likened to the spark of light or central spot within each and every one of us that becomes the driving force for recognition, ambition, and accomplishment. It is the Great Motivator, what we really want to do and how we really want to live and what we are really like.

Often the Soul Urge is so powerful a force that it overrules all the other important elements in a person's life. As representative of the very essence of our being, the Soul Urge identifies quite accurately our outlook on life and in what manner we will view certain experiences, people, places, and events that happen within our environment. As the blueprint containing the development of our soul in past lives, it contains the key to positive character traits that we can count on when the need arises. Consequently, the Soul Urge is frequently not that aspect of our personality that we show to the world. Many of us hide the direct and forceful aspects of our personalities behind cheerful façades, as seen by the *Quiescent Self*. But when we need to draw from inner strength in order to accomplish a certain task, we draw that personal power from our Soul Urge number.

The Soul Urge is also called the *Heart's Desire*, because it clearly represents what lies within each person's heart in the form of ideas, ideals, attitudes, ambitions, goals, and desires.

When considering your compatibility with another, it is a comparison of your Soul Urge with that of another that will point to similarities and differences in personal likes, dislikes, attitudes, and goals. No matter how you mask your yearnings publicly, when the chips are down, it is your Soul Urge that is going to surface and get you out of a tight spot. It will always reveal the true inner nature and character that you possess.

Computing the Soul Urge

To compute your Soul Urge, simply add up the numbers representing the vowels in your name, and reduce your answer to a single digit or Master number. It is best to add up the totals of each name separately so that you do not miss a Master number.

The vowels used for computation purposes are *A, E, I, O, U,* and sometimes the letter *Y* if there is no other vowel in the syllable. For example, if your name is May, the letter *A* would be computed as a vowel in the Soul Urge but not the letter *Y*, because there is already a vowel in the syllable. In the name Randy, however, both the *A* and the *Y* will be computed as vowels, for in the second syllable of the name there is no other vowel except the letter *Y*. Later on it will be important to remember in what sense you are using the *Y*, so that if you use the letter *Y* as a vowel in computing the Soul Urge, you cannot use it later on in computing the Quiescent Self.

Some numerologists also consider the letter *W* a vowel when it is united with another vowel, as in the name Matthew. I do not use this method, since the syllable already has a vowel that can be used for computation purposes. I just include it here to show you that some numerologists think otherwise.

In computing the number totals for the vowels in each of your names, it is always a good rule of thumb to reduce your answer to a single digit or Master number at the end, and not reduce each name separately to a single digit and then add your totals together. If you reduce your numbers before you reach a total, you can, and often will, miss a Master number, which is always going to have important significance.

In choosing which names to include in your computation, use all the names given at birth that appeared on your birth certificate. Limit the names used to four. If you were given more than four names at birth, use the four most often included in your signature or legal papers. Do not use baptismal names or Confirmation names unless they were given within days after your birth. If your name does not appear on the birth certificate, then it is best not to use the name.

If you are adopted and don't have a name on your birth certificate or the name reads just "Baby Doe" or "Girl Baby," then use that name and then compute your adopted name. The Soul Urge on your birth certificate will represent what you bring from past lives, and the Soul Urge number from your adopted name will represent the extent to which your Soul Urge must grow in this life. Your adopted name will represent how far you must push to become the Soul Urge as represented by your total number. You will be amazed at how similar it is to how you view yourself.

Let us now compute the Soul Urge of one of America's

most famous stars, Michael Jackson. In computing the Soul Urge, we place the corresponding numbers *Above* the vowels in each name, then add the totals of each name, and reduce your answer to a single digit or Master number. If your total is a Master number, do not reduce your answer any further.

1	2	3	4	5	6	7	8	9
A	B	C	D	E	F	G	H	I
J	K	L	M	N	O	P	Q	R
S	T	U	V	W	X	Y	Z	

```
      9    1 5          1         6
   M I C H A E L    J A C K S O N
        15 + 7 = 22 Soul Urge
```

With Michael Jackson's 22 Soul Urge, he is capable of moving mountains and attaining a high level of accomplishment in any profession. By looking at the 15/6 of his first name, which vibrates to voice, and the 7 of his last name, which demands a great degree of specialization with a spiritual overtone, we can readily see how Michael Jackson became so famous as a unique rock star. The 22 in his Soul Urge represents that he was born with the knowledge of creating on a universal scale. I think we could all agree that he is a "larger than life" personality.

Let us look at the Soul Urge of another star, who although deceased for a number of years, still remains alive in the hearts of many Americans, Elvis Presley.

```
   5    9         5      5
   E L V I S    P R E S L E Y
   14 + 10 = 24 = 2 + 4 = 6 Soul Urge
```

In this situation, where we have computed the name of Elvis Presley, we do not use the letter *Y* as a vowel because the letter *E* in the second syllable of "Presley" already constitutes its vowel. Here we have a situation where Elvis's Soul Urge and Quiescent Self both vibrate to the number 6, the number of voice, beauty, and responsibility. When this occurs, it means that on the inside he is exactly as he appears on the outside.

Now compute your Soul Urge and learn what the real "you" wants to do.

THE MEANING OF THE SOUL URGE NUMBERS

1. With a number 1, your Soul Urge indicates that you are courageous and naturally desirous of leading others or being at the head of important projects. Gifted in your ability to begin projects and handle significant issues, you prefer starting projects and then passing the ball to others who will fix, mend, shape, and particularize all details. As a 1, you are a better starter than a finisher, with a natural dislike of taking orders from others.

Your originality, inventiveness, and ability to create can find recognition in all forms of executive and administrative positions, for it is in this field that you are able to display your true leadership skills. Recognition, appreciation, and respect are necessary if you are to continue to work hard and accomplish on a grand scale.

As a friend or business person, you are generally loyal and fair, preferring to work on projects where your strength and usefulness can be appreciated and praised. Moreover, you have the ability to work well with others or alone, as the situation warrants, as long as you are unhampered.

As a parent, spouse, lover, or child, your 1 Soul Urge will bring out the possessive qualities of your personality, and phrases such as "My wife," "My children," "My this or that" will not be uncommon as long as the person you are discussing sheds light on some proud aspect of your character. Since you are basically unemotional, romantic love may not be necessary for you to live happily and not having it would not detract from your developing a successful relationship.

As a negative 1, you have the tendency to be boastful, egotistical, headstrong, and domineering if your talents go unrecognized, or to stay hidden, remaining dependent, hesitant, reticent, and fearful of moving into a position of leadership and trust.

2. With a number 2 as a Soul Urge, your gentle, loving nature thrives more on living and working peacefully and harmoniously in union with others than it does by working independently and alone. Not as ambitious or driven as the number 1, nevertheless, you are capable of accomplishing greatness by following the leader and fastidiously watching all the details, accumulating knowledge and attending to the facts. You don't mind remaining in the background, allowing others to gain the recognition or the fame. You are more of a joiner, content with the smaller things in life, living and working in mutual harmony with others.

As a number 2, you have a wonderful grasp of the dynamics of important issues, but you prefer to work in a more gentle fashion, not stepping on the toes of others, attracting friends and exercising a more receptive attitude. You work well in areas in which diplomacy, tact, peace, and truthfulness are honored and deemed important. Your easygoing nature can act as a magical key that opens the door to successful associations and partnerships with others. This is no small accomplishment, for in order to achieve on any level, one must first learn how to cooperate, listen, and communicate effectively with others, being mindful of their feelings. Your timing is excellent in opening and closing important deals. With a highly developed ability to analyze detailed situations, you excel in areas requiring accuracy and perfection.

As a number 2, your sensitive and emotional nature acts as a magnet, attracting influential friends and business associates. Possessing excellent intuitive qualities, you could also excel in music or dance. Your friendly, shy, affectionate approach makes you a good companion for others, but you must be careful not to be used as a doormat. Soft and withdrawn, you may cry easily, but you won't suffer from an overly headstrong personality, either.

As a number 2, the spiritual side of your personality is more pronounced than many of the other numbers.

Your psychic abilities make you a good student of religion, philosophy, and metaphysical studies.

3. With a number 3 Soul Urge, you enjoy the happy, imaginative, and inspirational side of life, where you can express beauty, joy, and friendship. Others may misjudge you, seeing only the scattered and unfocused qualities of your personality, and failing to recognize the independent, fearless, and courageous nature that lies beneath the cheerful image that you project.

You enjoy projecting the artistic and expressive beauty that you see in life, as long as you don't have to handle any annoying details. Your need to express yourself optimistically brings the element of joy and conviviality to all of life's experiences. Like all number 3's, you excel in areas such as speaking, acting, writing, and art. If your feelings become repressed for any reason, emotional or physical sickness is possible.

As a number 3, your soul longs to be involved in large projects of an ambitious nature, where your independent streak has the opportunity to promote unique ideas. You are not afraid to take giant steps, either, in moving your projects forward.

In romantic and domestic relationships, you enjoy both giving and receiving love, being kind and helpful to others, but you do also need to be appreciated and admired. You have the ability to laugh at your failures and try again by making light of the tragedy that befalls all of us at some time or another. Children and loved ones will bring great joy, as long as they do not hold back your dynamic energy. As a 3, you prefer to be on the go and not bogged down by the technical or boring aspects of life.

If your personality is not given the room to express itself, you have the tendency to become talkative, boisterous, and flirtatious in an attempt to get attention through other means. You must always guard against a tendency to sacrifice more than necessary for others or procrastinate longer than you should.

4. Because of your number 4 Soul Urge, you are practical, dependable, a lover of work and order. Regularity

and consistency bring a sense of well-being and security into your life. Although not original or creative by nature, your strength lies in your ability to follow the directions exactly as laid out by superiors. You can be counted on to do the job as requested, thereby gaining the respect of those in charge.

Disciplined, loyal, and honest, you are not afraid to work long hours in order to get the job done. You are also reliable when it comes to finishing tasks and can't be accused of scattering your energies in too many directions.

Like the number 1 and the number 3, you are ambitious but more so when it comes to material accomplishments. You prefer to invest in an area that is tried and true, solid, consistent by nature, and possessing a positive track record. You want something to show for your hard work; you like to see results.

As a number 4, you are interested in structure and possess a strong mechanical side. You function well, therefore, with machinery of a technical nature. Because you are patient and can persevere with detailed work, you often excel in highly technical, scientific, mathematical, and industrial professions.

As a 4, you have a need to follow tradition and regularity; many surprises could make you nervous. You don't adjust to change well, and any form of major adjustment might bring about inner conflict.

While you are not unique, innovative, or speculative by nature, your friends and family appreciate your strength, dependability, and the steady, solid, and sincere image that you convey. You are the rock upon which a successful family unit or business enterprise is built.

On the negative side, you often find it difficult to make changes and will often cling to an old and outmoded method rather than adjust to something new. Your persistence could make you seem difficult, stubborn, and narrow in scope. You need to cultivate a less argumentative and more flexible nature. Additionally, despite the fact that your love of home, family, and country runs deep, you may have trouble displaying affection and may be hesitant before being demonstrative. You need to learn that it is all right to be sentimental.

5. Your number 5 Soul Urge denotes that you crave freedom, change, travel, and variety in your life. Adaptable and curious by nature, you enjoy staying busy on different projects and are always eager to experience the new and the different. Above average in intelligence, you are quick to grasp opportunities. As a number 5, you make the best salesmen, writers, and speakers. Employment that offers variety can help you experience life in all its different phases.

You dislike routine in any form and are irritated when boxed in by responsibility. This does not imply that you are lazy, but that you find systematic chores a restriction. You need to be free to change and move around.

As a number 5, you possess a magnetic personality and can be interesting to speak to. Sensual, progressive, and freethinking, you are generally seen sporting the latest style, especially one that represents youth and sensuality. Your dashing, daring attitude toward life could also get you into trouble and place you in harm's way, so be sure to curb your excessive nature.

Your ability to adapt quickly to all sorts of conditions makes you fun to be around. People find you witty, charming, and thoroughly interesting and exciting. Unfortunately, routine chores or obligations could really infringe upon your available time. You weren't cut out to stick to a schedule. Nevertheless, some form of stability, routine, and concentration should be developed to keep your restlessness in check. Having too many coals in the fire could reduce your achievement level. Moreover, you must watch what you say to others. Impulsive statements could leave deep scars and bring an end to friendships.

6. As a number 6, you are a lover of home and family. Often viewed as the cosmic parent, you are eager to serve humanity in a responsible fashion. Your loyal, loving nature revolves mainly around family and close friends, but you welcome anyone to come to you when they need wise, frank, and honest advice. Like all 6's,

you are interested in righting the wrongs of society and seeing that justice is done. Moreover, you have the power to heal others and make them well again. For this reason, you could be attracted to a profession in law, medicine, social work, or counseling.

As a number 6, you possess a number of strong opinions and enjoy voicing them on many issues. You make a convincing and persuasive speaker, singer, or artist. You are also viewed at times as argumentative, stubborn, and disagreeable, and for this reason, you could alienate those close to you. Your blunt speech, strong opinions, and curt voice could contribute toward your losing the affection and appreciation that you long for.

If there is a most admirable part of your nature, it can be found in the loyal and dedicated way that you serve others. Less ambitious than the other numbers and preferring to work in union with others, your ego does not need top billing or center stage; it just needs praise and appreciation. For this reason you usually achieve a good name, anyway.

At home you crave love and affection and can give generously to a fault. Your love is strong, deep, and often all-consuming. Family members could accuse you of smothering them with too much affection. Although you need to curb your opinions and keep your strong emotional nature in check, on the whole the family does generally revolve around your strong presence and kind, sympathetic nature.

7. If your Soul Urge is computed as number 7, you are more quiet, introspective, and philosophical than the other numbers. You prefer silence and solitude to change and variety, and for this reason, do not mind being alone, out of the mainstream, in a more studious and contemplative atmosphere.

Basically a serious and reserved individual, you are attracted to occupations and avocations that require deep thought. You prefer to ponder and test for results, rather than take things at face value. There is a need to analyze and study a subject from every perspective.

Although emotional in your search for wisdom and

truth, you naturally withdraw from loud noises, large crowds, and public displays. While you crave love and affection, seldom are you demonstrative in public. People find you mysterious, shy, and aloof, because they do not understand your basic meditative nature.

You long for peace and tranquillity and often find it in peaceful natural settings. It is here that your intuitive side can balance itself and awaken your higher analytical, scientific, and intellectual centers. When operating on this keen mental level, others find you intelligent and a bit of a perfectionist. You will be called upon often to share your knowledge or render a professional opinion and will be respected for the wisdom and expertise that you possess.

8. With a number 8 as a Soul Urge, you are daring and courageous, with a healthy respect for power, authority, and success. Ambitious and progressive by nature, you have learned through sheer force and experience how to handle a number of projects successfully at one time.

You gravitate toward the source of power in large institutions of both a commercial and financial nature. You enjoy big business, feel comfortable regulating others, taking responsibility, and making important decisions. For this reason you often sit at the right hand of power and are respected for your balanced judgments. You give orders better than you take them, however, and must be careful not to lock horns with the wrong people.

Basically, as an 8, you possess a store of courage and force of personality that gives off a vibration of confidence and competition. You are usually considered an asset to any large-scale operation, since you love to manage, direct, and make things pay off. The bigger the operation, the greater the challenge, courage, and determination that you exert to make things happen. You are confident and powerful, especially in emergencies, and possess excellent judgment. The financial decisions you make in business, however, are better than the ones you make for yourself. Ironically, you can be lazy when it comes to finances and managing your own affairs.

As an 8, you have learned to take a more balanced

approach. Long ago you learned that chasing success, power, or money was really a vicious circle. It not only could have left you disillusioned but could have wasted your health as well. By now you have developed a basic philosophy and have cultivated a more spiritual side, which keeps your blind ambition in check.

Like all 8's, you must cultivate a softer image with loved ones; relationships must take on less of a business nature. Moreover, you must understand that not everyone is going to have the same devotion to work or be driven for the same measure of success as you.

9. With a 9 as a Soul Urge number, you possess a compassionate, sympathetic, and forgiving nature. Willing to submerge your own needs to serve others, you are loved and respected for your kindness. Possessing great wisdom, intuition, and appreciation for others, you give freely of yourself, with little regard for receiving in return.

A perfectionist by nature, striving often to serve others and make their life better, you can give on a universal level without thinking of your own needs, often to the point of exhaustion.

When it comes to emotional control, you can suffer and experience bad health as a result of feeling too deeply. You must cultivate a broader viewpoint and not allow others to sap your strength. You must learn to let go and not be affected by harsh words or thoughtless deeds.

Like all 9's, you want to broadcast your strong feelings to everyone so that humanity can benefit as a whole. Because of your giving nature, you are truly loved by everyone and respected for your wisdom and intuition. When you are not right, however, you can intensify your own suffering, because you want everything to be correct and perfect. Discovering something less than admirable about yourself, you are likely to be overly critical, angry, moody, and unjustifiably judgmental.

Your dramatic and artistic nature will always help you over the tough spots, and nothing will be lost forever. You will benefit by broadcasting your knowledge, experience, and expertise for the world to benefit. Seeking and giving universal love will bring more favorable results than demanding personal love, since you belong to the world and to no one in particular. Adverse conditions are often replaced by goodness and hope within a short period of time; nothing of a negative nature hangs around forever. You are often attracted to dramatic, artistic, or humanistic endeavors, where you are afforded the opportunity to serve others.

11. An 11 Soul Urge number indicates that you possess the abilities of the number 2 raised to a higher octave, in that you have high intuitive and inspirational qualities that are capable of raising the consciousness of the world to a more advanced level. Having a Master number, your superior intelligence and powers of revelation can be utilized as a counselor, psychic, visionary, religious leader, and celebrity. Your soul longs to be before the public in some way. It must never be locked up and utilized for the benefit of a few.

Since the number 11 consists of the double 1, you desire to lead, inspire, invent, and pass along the truth to others in the broadest possible way. For this reason you work well as a performer, artist, or TV and radio personality. You are a true champion of your ideals, and with your electric mind you are capable of remarkable inventions.

Sometimes you can fall down when it comes to interacting on a one-to-one level with others. You should cultivate, therefore, a more sensitive side when dealing on an individual basis. While you need a great deal of love and understanding, you will find that you get what you give to others.

Developing your finely tuned intuitive side will help in conveying your ideas. If you mingle more with the people of the world and follow your hunches, you will find that others will turn to you for the strength of character that you possess, as well as for your ability to act as the peacemaker and diplomat and visionary.

22. With a 22 Soul Urge number, you possess the high visionary quality of the number 11, coupled with your own innate talent to build, organize, and lead in a masterful way. Desirous of erecting lasting structures for the benefit of mankind finds you attracted to all fields of

government service, and national and international dealings.

Possessing a massive supply of energy and power, you are less of a dreamer than the 11 and are capable of working on a broad scale to put your ideas into concrete form. Your inventive mind allows you to excel in any field open to mankind, as long as the practical, theoretical, and inventive aspects of your work benefit the masses. Taking one step at a time, you are able to move clearly and convincingly in a logical fashion. At times you may lack confidence, but your strong organizational qualities and practical mind get you through the rough times.

One of the attributes you possess is the sheer power and excess energy to make things happen. Others are aware of your dedication, practicality, and universal outlook, and you are respected for the contributions you make. Within you lies the qualities of all the numbers, for you represent an old soul who has come to serve the masses and offer a better way of life. As such, the responsibility placed upon your shoulders is awesome, but you are able to live up to your superhuman reputation.

THE CHALLENGES TO THE SOUL URGE

Although the *Soul Urge Challenge* is frequently not discussed, it is important to know what it represents, for it will highlight which challenges or roadblocks exist within you to hinder you from achieving what your soul desires most.

The meaning of the Soul Urge Challenge is the same as the general meaning of the Challenge numbers, which are computed from the Life Path numbers.

Locating the Soul Urge Challenge

To find the Soul Urge Challenge simply subtract the value of the first and last vowels in the name from each other, the lower number from the higher number, and apply the general meaning of the number.

For example, let us use the name George Washington to compute the Soul Urge Challenge. First, it is helpful for us to compute his Soul Urge, so that we know which good qualities he has brought over from past lifetimes and what his soul longs to continue developing in this life.

$$5\ 6\quad\ 5\qquad\ 1\qquad 9\qquad\ \ 6$$
$$\text{G E O R G E}\quad\text{W A S H I N G T O N}$$
$$16 + 16 = 32 = 3 + 2 = 5\ \text{Soul Urge}$$

To find the Soul Urge Challenge, we subtract the value of the first vowel, *E*, from the last vowel, *O*: $6 - 5 = 1$. George Washington has the Soul Urge Challenge of 1. As such, in order to achieve the freedom, change, and variety that he desires, George is going to have to contend with people, maybe from his family, who try to force their will power or desires on him. He may also have to deal with powerful superiors who feel that he should conduct himself in a certain way. We know from history that George Washington did achieve a large measure of success with his troops, and was able to mingle and mix successfully with all types of people, a number 5 quality. Not knowing the demands of his family life but knowing some aspects of his life from history, one can safely assume that George was able to maneuver diplomatically and tactfully by using the positive aspect of the sensitive 2's found in his birthday.

In computing the Challenge to your Soul Urge, you will note that there are no Master Challenges, since the letters in our names are given the number equivalents of 1 through 9.

1. You must learn to develop leadership, originality, the ability to begin projects and work alone, and an ambitious nature.

2. You must learn to cultivate tact, diplomacy; be the peacemaker and mediator, one who brings others

together in association, a joiner, a good partner, and a friend.

3. You must learn to bring out your creative and self-expressive abilities; be ambitious and courageous, friendly, cheerful; and bring joy to others.

4. You must learn to be organized, a hard worker, practical, patient, persevering, methodical, and a builder of strong foundations.

5. You must learn to move on and let go of the old, outdated, and no longer useful; cultivate variety and a progressive spirit; be a good salesman and promoter; learn to accept freedom and change.

6. You must learn to adjust to circumstances and situations, be a humanitarian, serve others, be responsible, be a just and good adviser.

7. You must learn to seek wisdom and truth, be analytical, look beneath and beyond the superficial, develop a philosophical and scientific attitude, become a specialist, and get a good education.

8. You must learn to be materialistic yet practical and spiritual, cultivate a desire for success and attainment, live in a balanced fashion, develop good financial judgment, be able to work hard and succeed in serious undertakings.

9. You must learn to be kind, caring, generous, a big brother and good friend; be detached and give service to others.

CHAPTER 12

How Others See You:
The Quiescent Self

We are all curious to know the impression that we make on others. Whether we like it or not, a positive first impression can go a long way toward attaining a desired result, and a negative one can hold us back for years. In the study of numerology, this outer appearance or impression that you make on others is called the *Quiescent Self*, or the Secret Self. In appraising your own and the Quiescent Self of others, you must be careful, for what you see isn't exactly what you're going to get—it's just the first impression that you encounter.

It is important to note that the Quiescent Self is not the true or the real you—it is just an appearance. In many circumstances, however, appearances can be very helpful in getting you where you want to go. A well-balanced Quiescent Self can be a major asset in acquiring a specific job. Unfortunately, if your Soul Urge or Life Path number can't carry the requirements of that job or you have not developed the necessary skills, your true qualities, or failings, are going to be discovered, and you will be out of luck in the long run.

Most people are hoodwinked by an individual's

Quiescent Self, especially in romance. What often happens is that an individual will meet another and immediately be impressed by a certain appearance, believing that the appearance represents the true values, traits, and qualities of the individual. Unfortunately, later on when it is too late, he finds out he has totally misjudged the person and is sorely disappointed. This occurrence is an experience that most of us can identify with at some point in our lives, because we mistook the Quiescent Self of another for the true person—a trait basically discoverable by means of the Soul Urge.

The Quiescent Self also represents the "daydreaming" side of your personality, what you become in your fantasies. But your daydreams are only momentary lapses into wishful thinking—all puff and no substance, unless you exert a great deal of will power to make them happen. You may, from time to time, strive to carry out the hopes of your daydreams, but most often they will remain just mental escapes to a pleasant place.

Discovering the Quiescent Self can lead to accurately predicting the most personal items, down to the type of clothing that you will feel most comfortable wearing. For example, a 5 Quiescent Self will wear racy, progressive, sensual clothing, whereas a 4 Quiescent is going to show up in a sturdy, tailored suit.

Computing the Quiescent Self

Locating the Quiescent Self is easy. It is computed from the consonants in your name. To calculate the Quiescent Self, first compute the consonants of each name separately and then add the totals of each name together. Reduce your answer to a single digit or Master number. In this manner you won't lose a Master number. When figuring the consonant totals, be sure to place the numbers below the names. Let us compute the Quiescent Self of real estate tycoon and developer Donald John Trump.

1	2	3	4	5	6	7	8	9
A	B	C	D	E	F	G	H	I
J	K	L	M	N	O	P	Q	R
S	T	U	V	W	X	Y	Z	

```
D O N A L D        J O H N        T R U M P
4   5   3 4 + 1    8 5 + 2 9      4 7
   16 + 14 + 22 = 52 = 5 + 2 = 7 Quiescent Self
```

As you can see by interpreting the 7 in Donald Trump's Quiescent Self, he will be viewed as analytical, and a perfectionist. From the 22 consonant count in his last name, "Trump," we can see that Donald will enjoy being a superstar, living before the public, engaging in the building of large superstructures. The 14/5 consonant count in his middle name, John, will find Mr. Trump engaged in the activities of buying, selling, entertaining, and promoting spectacular events. With the 16/7 consonant count in his first name, "Donald," Mr. Trump would be advised to live as much as possible within the realms of responsibility to his wife and family. To become deeply involved in extramarital love affairs or forget about the duty he has to his wife, children, and mankind in general will result in bad press and represent a fall from grace in public opinion.

Now set up your own chart and discover how you appear to others.

The Number 1 Quiescent Self

You appear to have a dominant personality, creative, original, and forceful, possessing leadership qualities. Others see you as courageous, driven, and not afraid to promote unique ideas or instigate taking action. You are viewed as a successful individual. With a 1 Quiescent Self, you should make an effort to stand tall, neat and dignified in straight-lined clothing, but, with many 1's, you may have to struggle to maintain a proper weight. Your home reflects your outer personality and possesses furnishings that are bright, clear, and cheerful. Your daydreams find you traveling down unexplored paths as the leader who attains success in unique fields.

The Number 2 Quiescent Self

You appear to get along well with others as a good partner and companion, and to prefer to work in association with others rather than alone. You appear to allow others to maintain the dominant position and lead. Outwardly, others see you as quiet, laid back, and protective, taking care of friends and family in peaceful, elegant surroundings, such as a home base. When it comes to your clothing or home furnishings, you pay great attention to detail, matching and gracefully coordinating all accessories. Loud, off-beat garb is not your style, since you prefer to remain modest and quiet in your clothing, as well as in your approach to life. Preferring to dwell in a peaceful, comfortable environment, you do everything in your power to blanket those around you harmoniously with love. Your daydreams find you in positions where you play the role of peacemaker or the spokesman for important projects and people.

The 3 Quiescent Self

You outwardly appear bubbly, sociable, popular, and friendly. Your creative side is accented by colorful, fashionable, and unusual forms of dress. Your clothing is highlighted by distinctive jewelry. Sometimes you can go too far in your attire, and you must guard against dressing gaudily or with too many frills. You are applauded for your creativity and the way you throw sunshine everywhere. Your daydreams find you entertaining the world through acting, writing, decorating, or other imaginative vocations.

The 4 Quiescent Self

You perceive yourself as a pillar of strength to others, the rock upon which strong foundations are built. You can be depended upon to work hard and shoulder much responsibility. You like to look dignified in straight-lined, tailored clothing, with plain, simple designs, consisting of durable, sturdy fabrics. This style reinforces your stable appearance. Conservative and practical, you are viewed as a tireless, steady worker who doesn't often get distracted. Others know that they can count on you in a pinch. Your daydreams establish you as the founder of many a great cause.

The 5 Quiescent Self

You are seen as flashy, popular, youthful, up-to-date, loving the kooky and different, and accepting change at every bend in the road. Your sensual side tends to be emphasized, and people see you as possessing a magnetic personality. You enjoy the opposite sex and are able to converse well; you may even flirt, if appropriate. The perennial cheerleader, bubbly, bouncy, small, short, and perky, you appear the free spirit who enjoys traveling and hates to be loaded down with many obligations. Your love of people and gift for words could find you conversant in many languages and knowledgeable in many fields. Your dreams establish you as a Renaissance person, possessing something of interest for all people.

The 6 Quiescent Self

You appear the cosmic parent: caring, sympathetic, harmonious, responsible, and attractive-looking. Your love of humanity attracts people, who gravitate to you for advice and wise counsel. Basically a family person, your ideals concerning love, sharing, and caring take precedence over everything else. Desiring to live a harmonious existence, you surround yourself with loving family members, and with the accouterments of an agreeable existence—flowers as well as comfortably artistic creations. In dress, your clothing suggests neatness, design, and expensive taste. Your daydreams place you in the ultimate position of authority and responsibility as the cosmic father or mother looking after everyone.

The 7 Quiescent Self

You are viewed by others as wise, knowledgeable, studious, quiet, often reserved. Favoring peaceful surroundings, you prefer living nearer to the flowers and green grass than to crowded streets and bustling activity. Friends and associates seek solace in your wisdom, trusting that your knowledge comes from another plane. Although you appear reserved and shy around strangers, those close will consider you charming.

In dress you are not considered flashy but always appear well groomed, wearing carefully selected material and conservative styles. Your home may possess expensive and mystical furnishings. Your polished, perfected personality accents the demure, subtle side of life. Others may consider you unflappable, appearing at perfect rest or more at peace with yourself than the average individual. Your daydreams find you making major discoveries or expounding upon your philosophies.

The 8 Quiescent Self

Forceful and energetic, you appear never to take a back seat to anyone or to settle for second-best. As an 8, you enjoy being at the forefront of activities and are seen as powerful, successful, persuasive, and ambitious. Your demeanor, especially in times of crisis, gives off a cool, well-balanced, and efficient impression. You can pull off appearing rich even if you haven't got a cent to your name. Your home and business are furnished elegantly, suggesting power and status. You will not accept objects made of inferior quality. In clothing and attire, you give a wealthy appearance and can be seen wearing tailored or sports clothing of good fabric. Your daydreams establish you as the boss, expert, or authority, who sits at the right hand of power, making major deals in complicated business and corporate environments.

The 9 Quiescent Self

You are seen by others as a big brother: caring, forgiving, generous, and sympathetic. You are dynamic and forceful, but sometimes you fall short in carrying through on projects—appearing to possess more drive and less follow-up. Emotionally, you can comfort others and actually feel their pain, so a more detached attitude must be cultivated. Others view you as truthful and sincere, one who does not put himself first but who works for their benefit. People will contact you when they are troubled or need help. You appear to have many friends and to be quite loved and respected. In dress you appear artistic, yet comfortable. Unique colors and creative designs take on great import, and your clothing may more resemble a work of art. Your daydreams make you a crusader for humanity or an unusually forgiving person.

The 11 Quiescent Self

As the 11, you appear an idealistic dreamer, who is able to communicate with divine knowledge. On most days others are impressed with your ability to inspire and guide. Because you are desirous of revealing the truth or a better way of doing things, the outer world views you as a leader of important causes. People are attracted to the spiritual and electric side of your personality, but care must be taken lest you appear a martyr. In clothing, you look best in and prefer wearing soft, smooth materials of a fine texture that give you a soft, delicate appearance. Your daydreams find you being honored with pomp and ceremony as you lead the world to bigger and better achievements. As an 11, you must guard against appearing unfaithful, unreliable, vacillating, tense, and nervous.

The 22 Quiescent Self

As the 22, you give the impression of being an expert in any field where dreams and aspirations are capable of taking on material form. Practical, efficient, and well-rounded, like the number 4, you give the appearance of accomplishing on a huge scale, building for the benefit of mankind. In public, others see you as a practical reformer, doing the correct thing, creating for humanity, and adding beauty as you go along. Your taste runs to comfortable clothing that is correct in color and style. The fabric you select is durable. Your daydreams place you at the helm of huge, masterful undertakings, where you command the respect of others and are capable of reaching great heights. As a 22, you must remember to keep your feet on the ground and not appear hard, cold, or repressed.

THE CHALLENGES TO THE QUIESCENT SELF

Like the Soul Urge and the Expression, the Quiescent Self also has a Challenge that presents obstacles which must be overcome in order for you to promote a positive self-image.

Computing Your Quiescent Challenge

The *Quiescent Challenge* is found by locating the first and last consonants in the name and subtracting the number equivalent of the smaller consonant from the number equivalent of the larger consonant. Using again the name "Donald John Trump," the Quiescent Challenge can be found by taking the first consonant *D* and the last consonant *P* and subtracting the value 4 from the number 7. Now, compute your Quiescent Challenge, and work toward overcoming the negative traits of your Challenge number.

1. With 1 as your Quiescent Challenge, you must guard against appearing self-possessed, indulgent, and selfish.
2. With a 2 as a Quiescent Challenge number, you must guard against being viewed as duplicitous, crass, tactless, or, conversely, overly sensitive.
3. With a 3, you must control overeating and going on

hinges Additionally, jealousy could create problems, either because you feel it of others, or they are envious of you, thinking you have no cares or worries. You must watch where you place your affection or whom you confide in.

4. With 4 as a Quiescent Challenge, you must avoid over-eating, must watch your weight, and guard against becoming heavyset. You must refrain from appearing stubborn, narrow, and cheap.

5. If 5 is your Quiescent Challenge number, you must resist appearing impulsive, irresponsible, or excessive in your sensual appetites.

6. With a 6, you must keep from appearing opinionated, dominating, and bossy or smothering.

7. If your number is 7, you must forgo appearing restrictive, fixed, moody, and aloof.

8. With an 8, you must be careful not to appear dominant or aggressive.

9. If a 9, you must be careful not to appear overanxious to please, careless, or as someone who always forgets.

CHAPTER 13

How to Be Successful: The Expression

If someone informed you that by living a certain way success was almost guaranteed, wouldn't you be eager to know what that path was? Well, uncovering the way you were meant to succeed is as simple as computing your *Expression* number.

Everyone in this life has an equal chance for success, regardless of birth, race, or creed. Every day we see people overcoming incredible odds, to attain and achieve on a lofty level. The struggle, however, can be reduced substantially by following the advice of the Expression number.

The Expression number is often called the *Destiny* number because it points the way to your mission in life, why you are here, how you have to live, and what you were meant to do. You've already seen that you are given the promise of success if you follow a specific major highway called the Life Path number. So, too, are you commanded to journey upon that road in a certain fashion if you are to follow your true destiny. Unlike with the Life Path number, you are *not born* with this characteristic. The Expression number describes what you must do, the kinds of people you will work well with, and how you must cooperate with others in attaining your destiny. It does not highlight the characteristics that you were born with, but the qualities and manner of living that you must develop.

Computing the Expression

The Expression is found by adding together all the numbers in the total name. The total number count of each name should be computed first, since these totals will be important in discovering certain aspects of the Expression. It will also help you avoid missing a vital Master number, which could shed enormous light as to why you do things in a specific manner.

In analyzing the Expression, the number total of your first name represents personal qualities about you and discloses aspects about your disposition, feelings, personal attitudes, and traits. On a spiritual level, the number total of your middle name reveals the inner strength and reserve that you can call upon when needed. The number total of your last name represents your family's inherited characteristics, both good and bad.

Let us now compute the Expression number for Nicholas David Rehbock.

1	2	3	4	5	6	7	8	9
A	B	C	D	E	F	G	H	I
J	K	L	M	N	O	P	Q	R
S	T	U	V	W	X	Y	Z	

```
      9     6 1       1 9        5    6
   N I C H O L A S  D A V I D  R E H B O C K
   5  3 8 3  1      4  4   4   9  8 2  3 2
```

Soul Urge 16/7 + 10/1 + 11/2 = 37 = 3 + 7 = 10 = 1 + 0 = 1
Quiescent 20/2 + 12/3 + 24/6 = 56 = 5 + 6 = 11
Self
Expression 36/9 + 22/4 + 35/8 = 93 = 9 + 3 = 12 = 1 + 2 = 3
number

You will notice that first each of Nicholas's names are *computed separately*. Although the reduced number total of each name is indicated by use of a slash, we do not add together the reduced numbers for each name but the larger numbers instead.

In this example, we can clearly see that while Nicholas David Rehbock possesses a good amount of native independence, creativity, and inventiveness as seen by his number 1 Soul Urge, nevertheless, there will be a great deal of nervousness and inner turmoil present, indicated by the 11/2 Master vowel count in the name Rehbock and the 22/4 Master total in the Expression of David. As a child, he will appear nervous and fidgety, but by the time he reaches adulthood, Nicholas will devise remedies to correct this situation.

In order for Nicholas to be successful in life, he must first learn how to master the art of self-expression, a requirement of his number 3 Expression. He must learn to live creatively and in a fashion that brings others happiness. His outlets to achieve this success will be through art forms, music, writing, speaking, or entertaining. He will be viewed by others as expressive, unique, and a bit of a showman early in life. Since the number 3 signifies someone who enjoys friendship and a sociable atmosphere, Nicholas could benefit by working before the public in some way. His 1 Soul Urge ought to assist him by supplying the drive and leadership skills necessary to get him where he's going, along with the help of some close friends.

Living up to the meaning of your Expression number might be difficult at times. You may truly want to do one thing in life while your Expression number points in an entirely different direction. When this happens, you will be able to relieve the stress and the tension by satisfying your desire to both work and play.

For example, let's suppose that your Expression is a number 4, which is a more work, management, nose-to-the-grindstone vibration; and rather than working, you want to play tennis, go out with some friends, or read a good book. A viable, initial solution to the problem will be to *first* do some work, as the vibration indicates, and *organize your time wisely*. As the number 4 reveals, you must attend to obligations first for a specific period of time and then go out and play. By following this schedule, the practical and efficient side of the number 4 will be in less conflict. As time passes, you will see the results of your work and will be propelled to work longer and harder to achieve your goal. Working, organizing, living systematically, and in an orderly fashion will present security, financial reward, and the emotional and material comforts of life if you live according to the dictates of the number 4 Expression. You may even become a bit of a workaholic.

Always remember that one way or another, you must live according to your Expression number *if you are to be successful*—and by successful is meant whatever your original birth name indicates as your destined mission in life. Since you selected your name subconsciously before you were born, as well as selecting your parents, for that matter, it must be for your highest good that you live in this fashion, so don't look over your shoulder to the other fellow and wish you had his number. His number won't do you any good at all. His number may only get you into trouble. As the expression goes, You'll never get ahead playing another's game. Perhaps in this life it is time for you to live a more orderly, systematic existence. Remember, there is no such thing as a bad number; all the numbers lead to success. It is important, however, to follow *your own Expression number*. As the sum of your Soul Urge and your Quiescent Self, it is the total of who you are; it is everything that you've got to work with in order to live productively.

Remember, in computing your Expression number always compute each name separately, add the *unreduced* totals of each name together, and *then* reduce your answer to a single number or Master number.

MEANING OF THE EXPRESSION NUMBERS

1. Life requires that you be independent and cultivate a pioneering spirit. Your greatest successes will come by

first taking independent action toward your own goals and transforming your unique, creative, original ideas and talents into concrete achievements. You could find yourself running your own business or being at the head of a large enterprise. In either event, your destiny requires that you push your ambitious nature, remain self-reliant, and use your personal power to think for yourself. You must be in charge of your life. There will be times when you fear rejection for being different, having given up the old or established way of thought in favor of investigating new and better ways of doing things. Success will come if you take the lead and create and promote the new, different, and unusual. You will have to exercise a great deal of will power, but destiny will send you the needed courage.

Watch out for appearing egotistical, domineering, pushy, aggressive, wimpy, or dictatorial.

2. Your destiny demands that you be the "bridge over troubled waters" throughout your entire life. As you are friendly, persuasive, tactful, and a lover of peace, your friends will ask you to "troubleshoot," make things better, arbitrate, and bring warring factions together in a cooperative spirit, in order to live harmoniously and in association with others. While not necessarily viewed as the leader, your value lies in your ability to collect important facts, handle details, and bring others together for a common cause, being careful not to offend or step on toes. Success will revolve around fraternities, associations, partnerships, and marriage—aspects of life that will emphasize working in harmony and sharing your good fortune. Additionally, artistic, musical, and dramatic pursuits that emphasize timing and rhythm will bring rewards, happiness, and recognition.

Watch out for appearing overly sensitive, arbitrary, emotional, or uncooperative.

3. Life requires that you exercise your natural ability to entertain, create, and express the happier side of life. As the joy giver, you will find rich rewards by arousing inspiration, optimism, and laughter in others by means of writing, speaking, acting, or involving yourself in occu-

pations that emphasize the brighter side of life. You will have the benefit of many friends, a nice supply of money, ample luck, and a colorful environment as a reward for bringing happiness to others. Training your mind to be a cheerful leader in creative enterprises could find you climbing the ladder of success in the fields of entertainment, theater, children's activities, literature, art, and cultural organizations. Being a friend first will bring necessary contacts into your life, who will help you at important crossroads.

Watch out for scattering your energies in too many directions, taking life more seriously than is necessary, or not concluding projects.

4. Your fate will require that you be orderly, systematic, self-reliant, and conservative in outlook, attending to your affairs closely for practical results, and leaving nothing to chance. As a builder and manager of life, your great disciplinary talents will aid you in establishing lasting structures. As one who admires a good day's work, you will build from the bottom up, slowly, in an organized fashion, taking no shortcuts in the pursuit of your goals, since haste will surely make waste, and require that you begin all over again. Because of your sense of realism and knowledge of what patience can produce, others will look to you for guidance and protection. You will be required to take responsibility for others. At times, the routine, solid work, and heavy responsibility may be a drudge, weighty, and a hassle. If you can remember that you possess the gift of making life better for others in a sincere, honest, and loyal fashion, while silently teaching the virtues of perseverance, patience, and hard work, you will have lived a good life. Keep in mind that no matter what field of endeavor you choose to follow, you represent security and stability to others because you are the builder of firm and lasting foundations. You will be required to live a life of good moral fiber. It will be important to pick your friends wisely and remember that nothing in life can exist without the help of your qualities.

Watch out for a stern, repressed appearance, contrariness, brooding, and an argumentative attitude.

5. Cultivating a free spirit will bring exciting activities and change, affording you the opportunity to experience a life of variety, progress, and freedom from restrictions. After learning to explore different methods and ideas, you will be required to use your acquired knowledge to promote a better way of living for others. Cultivating a sense of versatility and interest in the new, clever, and up-to-date will assist you in letting go of the old, outmoded, and useless. If you don't learn to keep moving with the flow and accept progress, life will force change upon you in some other fashion. With the number 5 Expression, opportunity to advance lies in working before the public, promoting ideas, and mixing with people from all walks of life. Professions such as law, publicity, advertising, entertainment, and merchandising will afford an interesting and exciting life if you accept the challenge of seeing your projects through to the end. The establishment of roots and some routine planning will still be necessary, so be sure to plant your feet somewhere and call it home.

Watch out for jumping from place to place without finishing projects, overindulging in sensual activities—gambling, drugs, liquor—and refusing to accept responsibility.

6. Your mission in life calls for you to serve others, especially those who are weak and needy, and to live responsibly both at home and on the job. Every aspect of your life requires that you perform humanitarian service and bring beauty, companionship, sympathy, and most of all love and guidance to those who cross your path. You must act as the cosmic parent or teacher, emphasizing truth, justice, and the rewards of doing the right thing. People will flock to you for advice and guidance and be attracted to your stable, understanding nature. You may also possess an artistic side, which, if developed, will bring rewards by showing others how to live a more colorful, harmonious, vibrant way of life. Whether you involve yourself in music, decorating, design, floral work, or become a doctor or welfare worker, responsibility and

duty to others will follow. The tone of your voice will be attractive, your opinions respected, and your ideals praised. The rewards will be an abundance of luxury and material wealth.

Watch out for being overly opinionated, self-righteous, jealous, stingy, and interfering in the affairs of others.

7. Your mission in life will be to seek wisdom, truth, and the meaning of your existence. After acquiring the necessary knowledge and skills, you will be required to educate the world by uncovering the hidden aspects of life. Your purpose will be to dig deep, study, and test your theories, and then live by the knowledge and the skill that you possess. As a loner, deep thinker, and more sober individual, at times you may be considered difficult, different, and strange to others, but that is only because they do not understand you. Do not become overly involved in your emotions, since life will require that you take a more serious, purposeful, and less emotional and sentimental path, exposing your wisdom and skills for others to follow. You are meant to be calm, wise, truthful, skillful, philosophical, and scientific. Others will come to you for answers, since you are viewed as knowledgeable. For the understanding, knowledge, specialization, and expertise that you possess, you will be revered, respected, and acknowledged. Be sure to keep your emotions under control.

Watch out for moodiness, sarcasm, coldness, living with too much intensity, and aloofness.

8. Life will require that you involve yourself in big business, government, publishing, civic affairs, or large organizations. Your attainments will come through hard work, determination, and financial wisdom; often you will accomplish your goals by the sheer strength of your personality. Admiring success and possessing the ambition to achieve it, you will work long and many hours to get the job done. Others may try to take advantage of your expertise, but for the effort you exert, you will be recognized as an authority. Others will admire you because of the superior manner in which you efficiently

execute, organize, and direct both the personal and business affairs of your life.

You will accomplish and be successful by establishing a consistent work ethic. Do not take shortcuts or trust to pot luck. Yours is not a lucky number but one of masterful accomplishment, because of your strong character and ability to see projects through to completion. The rewards of life will be many, among them material success and wealth, but you will get nothing that you do not work for. To court money for its own sake will be to dance with disaster. Fulfillment of your fate will require that you live a more philosophical and less judgmental existence, one that stresses the joy of accomplishment for its own sake, always maintaining balance between spiritual and business affairs.

Watch out for greed, arrogance, temper tantrums, scheming, and overspeculating.

9. Destiny will require that you work for the brotherhood of man. You will be called upon to let go of the need for personal love and strive to serve others in a more impersonal fashion. You will be called upon to act with compassion, kindness, and understanding toward others who seem to gravitate to you when in need. The scope and breadth of life will be open to you, affording much opportunity to express your loving nature. All areas of art, philanthropy, acting, advising, writing, composing, and serving as the healer will bring rich rewards.

Because of the magnetic quality of your personality, there will be many opportunities to achieve greatness, but following through on your plans will be necessary. As the world's social worker, becoming overly emotional in the affairs of others will reduce your effectiveness and shatter your nerves. Objectivity may be a difficult principle to understand at times, since the 9 is a highly emotional vibration. The ability to let go and distance yourself from the problems of others, however, will help you to evaluate, discriminate, and serve in a more meaningful fashion. You can be sure of achievement and greatness if you think of others before yourself.

Watch out for overly identifying emotionally with others, bitterness, withholding love, and possessiveness.

11. As a higher vibration of the number 2, your number 11 Expression requires that you live on an idealistic level, willing to illumine mankind along the lines of spiritual and inspirational attainments. As a Master number, there will be times when it will be easier and more productive to operate on the level of a number 2 to attract meaningful associations. At other times, especially as you enter adulthood, developing the role of inspirational leader, teacher, or philosopher will bring recognition. All aspects of the stage, television, radio, and aviation, as well as involvement in large groups and associations, will supply a meaningful environment and bring rewards.

Whether people will look to you for the truth or view you as having your head in the clouds, your electric personality will magnetically attract a following. Many will trust in your ability to improve the quality of life. More spiritually, psychologically, and religiously oriented, you will find greater satisfaction in areas uplifting the plight of mankind than you will in the commercial world, which demands a less idealistic and more exacting approach to life. It will be important that you view both sides of an issue before making a decision. You must avoid being used as a doormat or as a dumping ground for everyone's problems.

Watch out for duplicity, extremist attitudes, moodiness, and vacillation.

22. Possessing the ability to turn the dreams and aspirations of the number 11 into a reality, your number 22 Expression requires that you create for the benefit of mankind on a large, broad, and universal scale. Organization, efficiency, and a practical approach must be employed, in order to guide and direct the affairs of big business to a successful conclusion. You will be seen as a master builder, an expert in his field of endeavor, endowed with realism and power. Success will come on an impressive level if you beautify the world as you build for its benefit. All international and national activities will bring great success, especially if good management

principles are followed. People will view you as an extraordinary being, one who backs up his word with deeds—the one to support in order to make dreams come true. If you live to broaden the scope of humanity, great riches and rewards are yours.

Watch out for neglecting those close to you, sloppiness, lack of organization, lack of application, and stubbornness.

THE CHALLENGES TO THE EXPRESSION

Living according to the dictates of your Expression number will not always be easy. Since you are not born with the attributes of your Expression number but must cultivate them, it is only natural that life will throw you a few obstacles and curve balls along the way in order to build character. In order to uncover the Challenge to your Expression number, first you must locate the Challenges to your Soul Urge and Quiescent Self. You will find the means of locating these other Challenges in the previous chapters on the Soul Urge and the Quiescent Self.

After you have located these two Challenge numbers, simply add them together and you will have uncovered the *Challenge to the Expression*. The Challenge to your Expression represents what you must *learn to do* in order to live by the dictates of your Expression number. Now, compute the Challenge to your Expression, and discover what you must do to accomplish your destiny.

1. You must learn to be courageous, daring, original, independent, a leader, and one who begins things.
2. You must learn to be diplomatic, detailed, tactful, a peacemaker, a good partner, a joiner, a sharer, and one who brings others together.
3. You must learn to be creative, artistic, entertaining, friendly, ambitious, happy, and a bringer of joy to others.
4. You must learn to be organized, methodical, reliable,

a hard worker, a builder of strong foundations, practical, patient, and persevering.

5. You must learn to be progressive, versatile, aware of the new and different, free, a promoter, and a good salesman.

6. You must learn to be able to adjust to circumstances, responsible, honest, just, a humanitarian, a good adviser and counselor, a voice among the people, and one who responds to the call of duty.

7. You must learn to be truthful, analytical, philosophical, scientific yet spiritual, knowledgeable, wise, and a deep thinker.

8. You must learn to be balanced, materialistic yet spiritual, successful, recognized, an authority in your field of endeavor, a good judge of character, and a hard and steady worker.

9. You must learn to be brotherly toward others, caring, generous, kind, detached and impersonal, yet compassionate; you must learn to let go of circumstances and move on.

You will want to note that there are no challenges in the Expression that result in Master numbers.

CHAPTER 14

The Purpose of Existence: The Achievement Number

Everyone is born to achieve some goal, to accomplish something special. The *Achievement number* describes precisely what that "something" might be and represents your primary reason for living, or your chief mission in life. The significance of the Achievement number is awesome and can't be emphasized enough. It carries tremendous importance and should be understood and improved upon early in life, so that it does not become a stumbling block. Until the Achievement number has been successfully assimilated as a permanent asset into your life, it will forever remain a thorn in your side, an example of negativity, or a hindrance.

The Achievement number represents your first Pinnacle in life and is found by adding together the month and day of birth. For many individuals, this first Pinnacle can be difficult, because you are working with negative behavior patterns and challenges that seem to creep up and make attainment difficult. Nevertheless, if you understand, accept, and strive to attain the true value and positive qualities of your Achievement number early in life, its attributes will definitely act as a guiding light for latter-day successes.

Locating the Achievement Number

To locate your Achievement number, add the numbers representing your month and day of birth, and reduce your answer to a single digit or Master number. By doing so, you will uncover what you must accomplish in this life. For example, if your birthday falls on April 20, 1950, you would find your Achievement Number as follows:

Month + Day = Achievement Number
4   + 20   = 24 = 2 + 4 = 6 Achievement Number

The meaning of the Achievement number is exactly the same as the meaning of your first Pinnacle number. Refer to your number by reading the chapter on Pinnacles.

THE ACHIEVEMENT CHALLENGE

As has been stated previously, no success is possible without first overcoming a challenge. While the lifetime Pinnacles have the lifetime Challenges to contend with, the Achievement number has the *Achievement Challenge* to contend with. The Achievement Challenge is not the same as the major Challenge but is an additional Challenge, especially present during the earlier years of life, and must be reckoned with in order to attain any lasting goal. The Achievement Challenge will be a major Challenge or obstacle to your mission in life.

Computing the Achievement Challenge

The Achievement Challenge is found by subtracting the Achievement number from the number 9. For our friend who was born on April 20, 1950, the Achievement Challenge is found as follows:

Achievement number = Month + Day of birth
Achievement Challenge = 9 − Achievement number

Month + Day   = Achievement number
4   + 20   = 24=2+4=6 Achievement number

Number 9 − Achievement number = Achievement Challenge

9 − 6 = 3 Achievement Challenge

This individual, therefore, will have an Achievement number of 6 and an Achievement Challenge of 3.

If your Achievement number is:	Your Achievement Challenge is:
9	0 or all the Challenges
8	1
7	2
6	3
5	4
4	5
3	6
2	7
1	8

Meaning of the Achievement Challenges

0. To work within the general meaning of all the Achievement Challenge numbers. For older souls, who don't find a need or possess the drive to go after any solid goals in life, the Zero Achievement Challenge could be to cultivate more of a zest and enthusiasm for life. For younger souls, this Achievement Challenge could present a number of obstacles that must be dealt with early in life. A number of Achievement Challenge numbers could require work at one time, creating difficult childhood experiences.

1. To learn to stand on your own two feet, individuate, become self-reliant without being overly domineering or pushy.

2. To remain receptive, cooperative, and tactful without

allowing oversensitivity and lack of confidence to block success. Also to allow your confidence to grow.

3. To cultivate an optimistic, enthusiastic, and creative life style in spite of heavy obligations and responsibilities.

4. To maintain a semblance of constructive and economic order, as well as a solid work ethic within a lifetime of constant change. Also to cultivate some form of roots.

5. To plan and allow for change within a structured and somewhat restrictive environment. Also, not to get stuck in a rut but to learn to move more with the flow of life, especially after growth has taken place.

6. To understand that life is not always going to be a happy-go-lucky joy ride but will also require that you shoulder your obligations responsibly both for yourself and for others.

7. To remain hopeful and cultivate faith in yourself despite your eccentricities and supersensitive feelings. Moreover, you must develop more of an analytical and philosophical attitude.

8. To develop your personal magnetism and power in a way that will enhance your individuality. Further, to cultivate a positive and more balanced attitude toward material, financial, and business matters.

9. There is no 9 Achievement Challenge.

CHAPTER 15

Dress for Success:
Your Best Colors

Dressing for success is a big business today and commands the expertise of a master who possesses a keen eye in determining whether a color enhances or hurts your image. But applying numerology can also help you select your best colors.

Color is sound made visible; it makes a statement. If you wear the color of your Soul Urge, chances are favorable that you will feel relaxed, at ease, and attract friends that will inspire you, because the color activates or awakens the personal vibrations that motivate you. If you wear the color of your Life Path number, you will attract favorable opportunities that demonstrate your natural talents in an easier manner. If you wear the color of your Expression number, you will enhance the strong aspects of your personality and broaden the scope of your activities. And if you wear the color of your Quiescent Self, you will attract people who see you in a certain way, a quality that could be a real asset if you are looking for a specific job. Additionally, by wearing the color of your Reality number, you could enhance your ability to attract successful opportunities into your later years of life.

Specific colors vibrate to certain numbers, and whether

you are looking for more money, romance, job opportunities, or just peace and harmony, wearing a color that will enhance these situations can help you over the hump, especially if you happen to be lacking a specific number vibration. The following colors vibrate to specific numbers.

Color	Number
red, crimson, flame	1
coral, salmon, orange	2
yellow	3
green	4
light blue, turquoise, aquamarine, pink, cherry	5
dark blue, navy, indigo	6
violet, purple, lilac	7
rose, beige, black, gray	8
all colors, pastels	9
silver, gray mist	11
deep earth tones, reddish gold	22

It is important to wear your favorable colors on Personal Days, Personal Months, and Personal Years, as well as on days involving big decisions. For example, if you are in a 4 Personal Year and you are going to an important business meeting, you might benefit by wearing something green, which enhances your organizational skills and adds to a practical, stable, and honest appearance. If you cannot wear green, for whatever reason, it would help to wear a green accessory, such as a handbag or tie, to complement the mood.

Additionally, you can benefit by wearing gemstones that vibrate to specific numbers. Wearing these gemstones on important days can likewise add the necessary color vibration. If your Expression or Soul Urge is a number 4, green could be your favorable color, and you would wear an emerald on important Personal Days.

A word of advice: Never wear black alone as a solo color on a 9 Personal Day, Personal Month, or Personal Year. These days are emotionally loaded, and the color black will only compound the heaviness and add nervous tension.

The following gemstones vibrate to specific numbers:

Gemstone	Number
ruby, garnet	1
moonstone	2
topaz	3
emerald	4
aquamarine, turquoise	5
pearl, sapphire	6
alexandrite, amethyst	7
diamond	8
opal	9
platinum	11
coral, reddish gold	22

CHAPTER 16
Eating by the Numbers

The food we eat can be a great asset, not only in maintaining and improving our overall health, but also in replenishing the body with the nutrients that it sorely lacks. This goal can be accomplished by eating foods that vibrate harmoniously to a specific Personal Day, Month, and Year, by eating foods that vibrate in *color* to a specific Personal Day, Month, and Year, and by replenishing the body by eating the foods that vibrate to the number or numbers that we lack.

Colors	Numbers
red, crimson	1
coral, salmon, orange	2
yellow	3
green	4
light blue, blue-green	5
dark blue, navy, indigo	6
violet, purple	7
beige, rose, black, brown	8
pastels, all the colors	9
silver, gray mist	11
reddish golds	22

Color, which to many is considered sound made visible, is all around us and vibrates with its own vital energy. Unfortunately, most of us are ignorant of the many ways that color manifests itself and can be utilized to enhance our lives. The colors of the clothes we wear, the homes we live in, the cars we drive, and the foods we eat all affect us in a multitude of ways, many of which are subconscious. Each number possesses a corresponding color or colors that can be substituted for the number vibration when necessary. The chart on p.268 lists the colors that vibrate to the numbers we have been discussing. By utilizing it, you can readily see the colors that help to maintain good health.

You should always eat foods that correspond in color to the number vibration you are lacking. For example, if you have no 3's anywhere in your name, you will want to eat foods that contain yellow, such as corn and custard. If you are missing the number 4, you will want to eat lots of leafy vegetables, peas, string beans, and foods with the color green in them. Using this guide will be especially important on number 4 Personal Days, Months, and Years. By doing so, you will supply the body with the vibrations it lacks.

Foods also vibrate to specific numbers and can be eaten on days that vibrate to your Personal Day, Month, and Year vibrations. For example, on a 6 Personal Day, Month, and Year, a bowl of spaghetti or an orange, both of which vibrate to the number 6, may balance your body chemistry more favorably than snacking on junk food. The following is a list of foods that can be eaten on specific vibratory days. Remember always to replenish your body by eating foods for the vibrations you lack.

1 Personal Day, Month, and Year

Eat: chocolate, baked beans, lobster, salad, halibut, meat loaf; or foods that are red, such as red meats, tomatoes, strawberries, raspberries, cherries, beets, apples, radishes, or watermelon.

2 Personal Day, Month, and Year

Eat: breast of lamb, walnuts, fowl, eggs, steak, shrimp, biscuits; or foods that are orange, such as oranges, mangoes, pumpkins, tangerines, apricots, cantaloupes, or nectarines.

3 Personal Day, Month, and Year

Eat: tomatoes, duck, grapes, romaine, potatoes, clams, liver, bread, Caesar salad, doughnuts, hamburger, asparagus; or foods that are yellow, such as bananas, yams, pineapples, lemons, grapefruit, eggs, cheese, corn, or peaches.

4 Personal Day, Month, and Year

Eat: veal, ham, grapefruit, carrots, strawberries, honey, coffee; or foods that are green, such as peas, pears, vegetables, lettuce, asparagus, avocados, or artichokes.

5 Personal Day, Month, and Year

Eat: cucumbers, beets, bass, apples, lettuce, celery, raspberries, melon, onions, beans, broccoli, chili, celery; or foods that are blue, such as blue plums, blueberries, or loganberries.

6 Personal Day, Month, and Year

Eat: spaghetti, pork, rye bread, bananas, peaches, oranges, fish, almonds, crab, dumplings, *guacamole,* beets, crackers, pizza; or foods that are navy or indigo, such as blueberries or plums.

7 Personal Day, Month, and Year

Eat: spinach, blackberries, herring, goose, omelets, anchovies, avocados, pancakes; or foods that are purple, such as purple grapes, eggplant, or blackberries.

8 Personal Day, Month, and Year

Eat: chicken, bacon, rice, apple pie, cereal; or foods that have beige, rose, pink, and brown in them, such as grains, bran, pink grapefruit, or oatmeal.

9 Personal Day, Month, and Year

Eat: Jello, cheese, beef, milk, caviar, applesauce, artichokes, Brussels sprouts; or brightly colored foods, but avoid foods that contain the color black.

On an 11 or 22 Personal Day, Month, and Year, follow the suggestions cited for the 2 and 4 Personal Day, Month, and Year.

CHAPTER 17
Health Conditions by the Numbers

Negative thought vibrations, as a result of bad temperament, overwork, emotional strain, sorrow, and anger, manifest themselves in physical conditions and health problems. We don't have to catch a cold, develop the flu, or suffer from blood abnormalities, however, to discover the type of physical disorders that we are more prone to; they are discoverable by the *number* of the day of birth.

Being aware ahead of time of the physical ailments that may plague you can help you take extra care and precaution when the signs of a budding illness begin to surface. Read the description below of the ailments that correspond to your birthday number. Then take positive steps to prevent these negative health conditions from erupting.

The Number 1 Birthdays (1, 10, 19, and 28)

With a number 1 birthday, accidents, disease, and infection will more likely attach themselves to the head and the lung area. Accidents can be avoided by being more aware of the potential for broken bones and knee injuries. Lung disease, sinus problems, and disorders of breathing can manifest themselves if you are unable to express personal desires or harbor negative emotions. Health conditions can improve by means of deep-breathing exercises.

The Number 2 Birthdays (2, 11, 20, and 29)

With a number 2 birthday, a sensitive system will cause disorders of the nervous system, brain, hands, and solar plexus area. Loud noises, hurt feelings, lack of confidence, and harsh conditions can also put the nervous system in distress, resulting in hair loss, trembling hands, and foot problems. Courses in creative visualization and self-visualization will ease tension and lead to increased feelings of self-worth. Education in proper eating habits will also work wonders, since food allergies could result from bad nerves.

The Number 3 Birthdays (3, 12, 21, and 30)

With a number 3 birthday, trouble with self-expression and fear caused by overstrain and worry will cause physical ailments of the throat, tongue, larynx, and organs associated with speech. Strained relationships, emotional problems, sorrow, worry, lack of association, or unpopularity will bring on ailments such as colds, strep, and sore throats. Improved communication, creative visualization, and exercises that help to reduce negative thoughts, excess worry, and fear will improve your health.

The Number 4 Birthdays (4, 13, 31, and 22)

With a number 4 birthday, stomach disorders of all kinds often bring problems due to a tendency to overeat or not eat the proper foods. Additionally, ailments of the right arm, right side, and blood pressure can bring headaches and heart disease of a sudden nature. An effective solution is to cultivate a less serious nature, get proper exercise, and avoid the continued consumption of rich foods. Maintaining a steady weight will also bring better health.

The Number 5 Birthdays (5, 14, and 23)

With a number 5 birthday, your health can suffer as a result of constant dissatisfaction with life, nagging criticism, improper consumption of alcohol and drugs, and overactivity. Having too many irons in the fire, impatience, and irritability can cause problems with the liver, left arm and side, and gall bladder. Accidents often occur as a result of overactivity, haste, and not concentrating on the activity at hand. Health improves by maintaining a positive attitude and not starting new activities until the old ones are completed.

The Number 6 Birthdays (6, 15, and 24)

With a number 6 birthday, problems with the heart, chest, skin, and blood result from domestic problems, negative love affairs, and carrying too much responsibility. Pathologies of the heart, chest, and blood will be of a more chronic nature. More understanding, approval, and appreciation, coupled with less responsibility, can improve the health dramatically.

The Number 7 Birthdays (7, 16, and 25)

With the number 7 birthday, health conditions are often weakened by disease and ailments of the sympathetic nervous system, spleen, left upper and lower side, glands, and white bloods cells due to bad diet, overstrain, repressed emotions, and allowing a general collapse of the body to take place. Ailments will be of a more mysterious nature and could be hard to diagnose at first. More sleep, quiet, better diet, and escape from the hard grind will improve the health.

The Number 8 Birthdays (8, 17, and 26)

With a number 8 birthday, your health is usually weakened by poor digestion, disease of the colon and lower bowels, ulcers, reduced vision, and bad circulation in the leg areas. Many of these conditions are caused by periods of prolonged stress, overambition, and engaging in a more intense way of life. Nervous headaches are often caused by a lack of inner calm. Health is usually more resilient with the number 8 birthdays and can improve quickly from more rest, outdoor exercise, stress classes, exercises, and frequent periods of relaxation.

The Number 9 Birthdays (9, 18, and 27)

With a number 9 birthday, diseases of the kidneys, bladder, and regenerative organs, coupled with problems due to negative habits, are ailments that can be expected to surface. Living in the fast track, overdoing alcohol or drugs, and allowing the imagination or emotions to overload could bring unhealthy conditions of a permanent nature or diseases that are hard to control. Because the emotions and imagination are so easily disturbed, all 9 birthdays should learn to practice letting go and living less in emotion and more in practical reality. This pulling back will reduce the heavy emotional impact of disappointing episodes in life.

The number representing the month and year of your birth will also illuminate specific ailments that can manifest themselves during the Formative and Harvest Subpaths. After you have read the ailments that can affect you throughout your entire life, go back and review the ailments more common during your Formative and Harvest periods, and take steps to prevent their occurrence.

CHAPTER 18

Selecting Your Telephone Number, Address, or Any Other Number to Meet Your Needs

Given the unique personalities and temperaments that we all possess, it should not surprise you that there are certain numbers that are more harmonious and beneficial for telephone numbers and addresses than other numbers. Each person possesses a different set of favorable numbers. Certain numbers can assist you in establishing a specific set of conditions. Being aware of favorable numbers can go a long way if you are going to live successfully with a given telephone number, address, or any other important number in your life.

If you are desirous of moving to a new apartment because you wish to have a larger home, develop a relationship, and do a great deal of entertaining, don't select an apartment or home that vibrates to the number 7, as you just may never do the level of entertaining that you desire. The number 7 apartment or address is not going to bring solid activity or conviviality but a more quiet, contemplative, and meditative state. Likewise, if you are looking for some peace and quiet, don't select an apartment with the number 5, since you may not be there frequently enough to enjoy it.

The principles of numerology can be applied to telephone numbers. If you have a choice of which telephone number you can use, always select a telephone number that is harmonious to the specific business you wish to engage in. The numbers 1, 4, and 7 vibrate to mental activity; the numbers 2, 5, and 8 vibrate to outward expression and the masses; and 3, 6, and 9 vibrate to the emotions and the arts. A favorable telephone and address can be discovered from the number of your birthday itself. If your number vibrates to a 1 (1, 10, 19, and 28 of any month), you are more of a mental individual and may feel comfortable with a number that totals 1, 4, or 7.

If you are running an art school, a clothing store, or a design studio, it may be wise to have your shop address or telephone number vibrate to the number 3. If you are teaching a class in brain surgery, it would help if the classroom number or address of the school vibrates to a 7, one in which mental acumen, wisdom, and specialization are required.

Your area code also reveals a great deal about where you live. The area code for New York City is 212, a number that totals 5 and is a good indication of the bustling activity indigenous to such a powerful city. In the outskirts of New York City the area code is 516, a number totaling 3, which symbolizes a colorful, cheerful, and social place to live—and it is just that.

If you are doing any type of sales work over the phone, having a telephone number that vibrates to 5 or has many 5's in it is going to be beneficial, for the number 5 vibrates to sales, promotions, and all things progressive and fast-moving. If you are involved with a business that does structural work, such as building, having a telephone number that totals 4 or has a 22 in it will be helpful.

Remember, the rule of thumb in selecting an address and telephone number is to first determine the purpose or function of the number. If you want to live a secluded, meditative style of life without numerous visitors or callers and can select the proper address or telephone number, pick a 7. If you want to run an art school or socialize a great deal at home, select a number that vibrates to a 3 or an 11. (Don't select an address or telephone number that's the same as a karmic lesson that you possess, or the number may present more problems than it's worth.)

When selecting a telephone number or address:

1. First, consider the function of the number. Do you need it for a specialized business? Is there a specific purpose for the number? Remember, a number 7 house *already* has a 7 personality, so you had better enjoy the attributes of the number 7 or you will be miserable.

2. Select a number that will be harmonious with your Birthday number, Soul Urge, Expression, Life Path, Pinnacle, or Reality number so that it will vibrate favorably to who you are or how you think.

3. If your telephone or house number is the same as your Soul Urge, you will find a great deal of satisfaction and compatibility with the callers.

4. If your telephone or house number is the same as your Birthday number, you will be able to perform activities compatible with the way you think and the work you do.

5. If your telephone or house number is the same as your Expression, you will be able to move along the talents of your Destiny number without hindrance.

6. If your telephone or house number is the same as your Life Path number, if you make the effort, you will attract opportunities that will bring you success.

7. If your telephone or house number is the same as those of your Pinnacles of Attainment, if you follow the dictates of this number, success will come easier in that you are living according to the dictates of the Pinnacle numbers.

The following is a list describing the activities and opportunities that can be expected under each telephone or house number:

Number 1 House or Telephone Number:

Positive: originality, creativity, and leadership; determination and self-confidence.

Negative: selfishness, bossiness, or hasty actions.

Number 2 House or Telephone Number:

Positive: cooperation, partnerships, tact, sharing, diplomacy, religion, group activities, attention to details.
Negative: pettiness, dominance, waste, and untidiness.

Number 3 House or Telephone Number:

Positive: cheerfulness, friendship, happiness, and attractiveness; comfort, imagination, joy, art, and loyalty.
Negative: scattering energies, extravagance, gossip, and impulsiveness.

Number 4 House or Telephone Number:

Positive: order, practicality, truth, honesty, common sense, purpose and application to tasks at hand, planning, organization, economy, work, thrift, and personal integrity.
Negative: Narrow-mindedness, arguments, and over-caution.

Number 5 House or Telephone Number:

Positive: freedom, choice, activity, progressiveness, usefulness, variety, opportunity, and changing conditions.
Negative: impatience, irresponsibility, and criticism; haste.

Number 6 House or Telephone Number:

Positive: responsibility, family, duty, beauty, service, money, peace, tranquillity, family, and friends.
Negative: possessiveness, discord, and an overconcern for self-importance.

Number 7 House or Telephone Number:

Positive: quiet, studiousness, reflection, self-control, meditation, inner powers, receptiveness, wisdom, peace, and education.
Negative: noise, dependency, loudness or lack of refinement, and irritability.

Number 8 House or Telephone Number:

Positive: achievement, self-mastery, goals, business, efficiency, recognition, accomplishment, respect, strong character, and perseverance.

Negative: violence, verbal or physical abuse, strain, and an overconcern for money and materialism.

Number 9 House or Telephone Number:

Positive: brotherhood, love, compassion, attendance to the needs of others, philanthropy, caring, sharing, and tolerance.

Negative: emotional, bitter, or disappointing episodes.

Remember, if you are moving to another state or city, it is best to compute the Expression of the area to see if you are compatible with the dictates of the number. By doing so, you can save yourself a headache and a great amount of expense and heartache.

CHAPTER 19

Do You Want to Change Your Name?

We've all heard of situations where an individual changed his or her name and began to attract great fame, wealth, and opportunity. For a long time it has been felt that changing your name was the fastest way to get rich. There are some necessary ingredients, however, that must be taken into consideration if you are desirous of changing your name.

First, you must fully understand that the *original name as given at birth* is the name that fits the code of talents and opportunities that you decided to carry forth from a past life that will attract favorable situations in this life. The original name at birth points the way to necessary experiences that will guide you in the direction of success, growth, and happiness. You will never change the pattern of your birth name and the opportunities that it attracts, even if you change your name thirty times. It is your name, and that's it! While you may not like your original name and may never use it, still, from a numerological standpoint, it could contain some great vibrations.

Your name represents the true *you*. Even if you use a new name that you like better, this new name is not going to change the real inner you. If you live up to the demands and challenges of your true name, while using the new name, success will still be forthcoming, because you are living up to the potential in your true name. A new name is not going to change your self-image.

This mistaken notion—that a new name will lead to a new life—often occurs when movie stars, actors, and actresses, as well as businessmen, feel that their present names are not an asset in their work. I have personally counseled many entertainers, a number of whom have Expressions that vibrate to a 4 or 7. While these are not glamorous numbers, they are an asset to an individual who must work hard, study, and specialize in order to get ahead.

Nevertheless, when an individual has attained a certain level of achievement, it is not uncommon for them to set their sights higher and desire a name that commands more attention and perhaps has more zing, zest, and appeal. On these occasions, the first thing I ask the individual is to select a number of names that they might enjoy using. I then calculate each name to see what vibrational experiences can be expected by using the new name and determine whether or not the name will be favorable. I try to establish how much progress has been made to correct negative tendencies, as I'm careful not to attract more headaches.

I never create a new name for an individual. The individual seeking the name change must do the selecting for himself. Since it is the individual who desires a new name, it is the individual who must select a name that he feels he can live with. My job as numerologist is to explain and educate the individual as to the meaning of the new name and enumerate the types of experiences that can be expected from its use.

Before selecting a new name, it is important to be clear why you want a name change. Do you want to get married? Do you want to be a movie star? Are you opening up a new business? All these factors must be taken into consideration before you select a new name.

In order to choose a name that will be harmonious, it is important to analyze your birth name first to determine what types of positive traits are already contained within the name. The major positions of the Soul Urge, Quiescent Self, and Expression are important because they denote who you are, how you appear, and your path of destiny.

When selecting a new name, it is important that the name attract favorable experiences and not more aggravation. You can lose valuable time and miss important opportunities if you select a name that reflects one of your major Challenge numbers, unless you have already worked to overcome its hindrances. Moreover, you must also ask whether or not you are willing to meet the Challenges of the new name and live up to the opportunities presented. This can be particularly insightful if the new name vibrates to a Master number, such as 11 or 22. A full exploration must be made to make sure that you are willing to live under the additional demands of these Master numbers.

Still, many movie stars and budding actresses and actors, as well as other ambitious people, need an extra boost or desire the opportunities that a name change can bring. Many of them select names that vibrate to 11 or 22.

It is not always easy to select the perfect name, but attempts should be made to select the best name that is offered for examination. Things will be easier if the Soul Urge and Expression are the same numbers as the original name, for the inner motivation will be the same and opportunities will come quicker. Sometimes the larger the number, the more motivation will be used to get ahead.

The following is a list of suggestions that will help you to select a new name.

1. Select a name whose Expression vibrates to 1 if you want to lead an enterprise, invent something, express your individuality, or stand tall.
2. Select a name whose Expression vibrates to 2 if you are desirous of a partner, looking for a job where tact and cooperation are needed, or if you wish to smooth out and soften your image.

3. Select a name whose Expression vibrates to 3 if you are desirous of being more creative and self-expressive in any endeavor or undertaking.

4. Select a name whose Expression vibrates to 4 if you desire to present a practical, economical, solid image as a foundation type of person.

5. Select a name whose Expression vibrates to 5 if you wish to appear youthful, slick, sexy, bohemian, or progressive and up-to-date.

6. Select a name whose Expression vibrates to 6 if you wish to get married, receive more respect, appear more responsible, expensive, or artistic, or if you wish your views to carry weight.

7. Select a name whose Expression vibrates to 7 if you want to be considered smart, an expert, or if you wish to portray an intellectual and wise image.

8. Select a name whose Expression vibrates to 8 if you want to be considered efficient, executive, corporate, and powerful.

9. Select a name whose Expression vibrates to 9 if you want to be considered philanthropic, a big brother, artistic, humanistic, and tolerant of others.

10. Select a name whose Expression vibrates to 11 if you want to be considered enlightened, a movie star or entertainer, a spiritual leader, an informer of truth, or one who works before the public.

11. Select a name whose Expression vibrates to 22 if you want to be considered an earth-plane director, one who carries vast responsibility and carries out large projects, an entertainer, a master builder.

It is not necessary to make this new name legal, since you will always carry the vibration of your *original given name*. It may be wise to use the new name for professional purposes, but, if you can, stick to the old name for legal requirements. In this way you will attract better luck.

A new name for the first few years carries the *potential* for new and wondrous opportunities, but it is really still in the making. Despite the fact that new and better opportunities may present themselves rather quickly, it will take approximately five years before the new name is in full force and effect.

If you want to spend an amusing few minutes, read through the list of individuals below who have chosen to change or alter their existing names for personal or professional reasons.

New Name	Old Name
Woody Allen	Allen Stewart Konigsberg
Julie Andrews	Julia Wells
Willy Brandt	Herbert Frahm
Ethel Barrymore	Ethel Blythe
John Barrymore	John Blythe
Lionel Barrymore	Lionel Blythe
Ray Charles	Ray Charles Robinson
Fanny Brice	Fannie Borach
Chubby Checker	Ernest Evans
Perry Como	Pierino Como
Eldridge Cleaver	Leroy Eldridge Cleaver
Jack Benny	Benjamin Kubelsky
Red Buttons	Aaron Chwatt
George Burns	Nathan Birnbaum
Judy Garland	Frances Gumm
Bob Dylan	Robert Zimmerman
Kirk Douglas	Issur Danielovitch
Rodney Dangerfield	Jacob Cohen
Joan Crawford	Lucille Le Sueur
Carlton Fredericks	Harold Casper Frederick Caplan
W. C. Fields	William Claude Dukenfield
James Garner	James Baumgardner
Cary Grant	Archibald Leach
Dale Evans	Frances Butts
Zero Mostel	Samuel Joel Mostel
Marilyn Monroe	Norma Jean Mortenson
Ann Miller	Lucille Collier
Ray Milland	Reginald Truscott-Jones
Ethel Merman	Ethel Zimmerman
Karl Malden	Malden Sekulovich
Dean Martin	Dino Crocetti

Paul Muni	Muni Weisenfreund
Ricky Nelson	Eric Nelson
Peter O'Toole	Seamus O'Toole
Patti Page	Clara Ann Fowler
Pelé	Edson Arantes do Nascimento
Mary Pickford	Gladys Mary Smith
Stefanie Powers	Stefania Zofia Federkiewicz
Martha Raye	Margie Yvonne Reed
Mickey Rooney	Joe Yule, Jr.
Yves Saint-Laurent	Henri Donat Mathieu
Casey Stengel	Charles Dillon
Connie Stevens	Concetta Ingolia
Beverly Sills	Belle Silverman
Nathanael West	Nathan Weinstein
Robert Taylor	Spangler Arlington Brugh
Danny Thomas	Amos Jacobs
Leon Trotsky	Lev Davidovich Bronstein
Rudolph Valentino	Rodolpho d'Antonguolla
Shelley Winters	Shirley Schrift
Jane Wyman	Sarah Jane Fulks
Bobby Vinton	Bobby Vintula
Natalie Wood	Natasha Gurdin
Nikolai Lenin	Vladimir Ilich Ulyanov
Harry Houdini	Ehrich Weiss
Billie Holiday	Eleanora Fagan
Rita Hayworth	Margarita Carmen Cansino

CHAPTER 20

Picking That
Lucky Number

Knowing your lucky numbers can be an asset these days, since the lottery, Lotto, and number games bring in such large sums of money. If you think there is a secret, magical formula to finding your lucky numbers, you'll be surprised to find out that there is not. Further, it is easier than you think to locate your own lucky numbers. Most people who win the lottery or other number games do so by selecting numbers and dates that are important to them. These numbers are solidly implanted within their stream of consciousness as favorable in meaning and are positive for attracting money.

The first number that is important in selecting a lucky number is the Life Path. It supplies you with one of your most favorable vibrations, since it points in the direction of success. It is who you are—your intelligence factor—and is always a positive number.

The second most important is your Soul Urge number. It points to the inner urges, desires, and motivations and always represents what you want to do. In this instance, you want to select a lucky number.

The third important number is your Birthday number, the number that most people immediately identify. The

Birthday number is fairly easy to locate. It is the number of the day you were born.

The fourth most important number can be found from the Expression, the total number count of your full name. Since the Expression describes the exact manner in which you must live and experiences that you should move toward, your Expression will also be a lucky number.

The fifth important number is your Quiescent Self, since it points to how you appear to others physically and the ideals you dream about. You want to appear lucky to someone else, especially the individual who selects the winning numbers.

There is an additional number that is considered fair and can favorably tip an outcome in a positive direction. This number is your Reality number. Your Reality number is found by adding your Life Path number and your Expression together and reducing your answer to a single digit or a master number. It denotes what activities you will engage in during your 40's and onward.

After you have selected these six numbers, all the remaining numbers will represent negative numbers. You should not select these when gambling or playing lucky-number games unless you feel intuitively that the number may be lucky because it represents a special day or occasion.

When playing a lottery, we generally do not select six single-digit numbers, since the frequency of six single-digit numbers being selected is slim to none. For this reason, it is important to know the double-digit numbers behind the single-digit numbers before they are reduced.

Let's say that after computing your important numbers you find that the following numbers are important to you:

	Single Digit	Double Digit
Soul Urge	1	10, 19, 28, and 37
Expression	4	13, 22, 31, and 40
Quiescent	3	12, 21, 30, and 39
Life Path	8	17, 26, 35, and 44

| Birthday | 6 | 15, 24, 33, and 42 |
| Reality | 7 | 16, 25, 34, and 43 |

If the above numbers are lucky for you, so will be the double-digit numbers from whence they came. For example, your number 8 Life Path number could be as a result of four double-digit numbers: 17, 26, 35, or 44. When playing a card with several games on it, it is important to mix the numbers, selecting for each game some single- and some double-digit numbers. For one game you may select numbers 10, 21, 40, 8, 33, and 43, and for the next game select 19, 13, 30, 44, 17, and 34, and for the next game select some numbers from your first and second games, mixing single-digit and double-digit numbers.

If you are playing a three-digit number, you would take the initial three single-digit numbers and play the numbers in lucky combinations, and then take the second set of three numbers and play them in lucky combinations, too; and then maybe select any three of the total six numbers, and play them in combinations.

For example, your first three lucky numbers will pull favorably for you. In this situation, the numbers 1, 4, and 3 are the three luckiest numbers. Therefore, we can play 143, 134, 413, 431, 314, and 341.

Once again, don't be afraid to change the direction or the line-up of the numbers when making your number selection, and always play your "hunch." Your hunch represents information that you receive in a psychic manner. All too often people don't listen to or follow their instincts, only to be greatly disappointed later on. I know a woman who played her husband's prison numbers—all of them, that is, except the last number. The lucky lottery numbers turned out to be her husband's *exact* prison numbers. While she won nicely with this game, she still missed a fifteen-million-dollar prize because she failed to play the last number. Now, you may very well say, A *prison* number? Well, that prison number was lucky for her, since it meant something special: It represented her husband, and she loved him very much. Remember, if the number or numbers are important to you, it is best to play them.

Ø The Power Of The Mind

SIGNET Books You'll Want to Read

☐ **STARPOWER:** *An Astrological Guide to Supersuccess* **by Jacqueline Stallone with Mim Eichler. With a Foreword by Sylvester Stallone.** In this eye-opening book, packed with celebrity gossip, Jacqueline Stallone shares the astrological advice that helped lead her son Sylvester to fabulous wealth and success. (168437—$4.95)

☐ **THE CRYSTAL HANDBOOK by Kevin Sullivan.** Put Crystal Consciousness to work for you! The A-to-Z guide to the psychic energies of more than 100 cosmic crystals, gems, minerals, and healing stones. Throughout the years the crystals have acted as the natural channelers of enlightening energy between the material and spiritual planes. Now you too can tune into their transformational powers! (154916—$3.99)

☐ **SELF MASTERY THROUGH SELF HYPNOSIS by Dr. Roger Bernhardt and David Martin.** This breakthrough book shows you how to use hypnosis to improve your ability and performance in every area of your life with this fully tested, dramatically effective, 30-seconds-a-day method. (159039—$4.50)

☐ **THE DIVINATION HANDBOOK by Crawford Q. Kennedy.** A remarkably easy-to-use guide providing detailed instructions for mastering over 30 different methods of divination—the ability to tap into a subconscious awareness of events past, present, and future—including crystal gazing, palmistry, tarot reading and dream interpretation. (163664—$4.50)

☐ **PSYCHIC:** *Awakening the Powers Within You* **by Carol Kennedy.** A highly respected psychic offers a step-by-step program for developing the hidden powers of your mind. Learn where your natural talents lie—in clairvoyance, precognition, telepathy, psychometry, or psychic flow—and make that talent work for you. (162293—$4.50)

Prices slightly higher in Canada

Buy them at your local

bookstore or use coupon

on next page for ordering.

Ø SIGNET   (0451)

HIDDEN POWERS OF THE MIND

☐ **MANY MANSIONS by Gina Cerminara.** The most convincing proof of reincarnation and ESP ever gathered in one volume. A trained psychologist examines the files and case histories of Edgar Cayce, the greatest psychic of our time.   (168178—$4.95)

☐ **THE TUJUNGA CANYON CONTACTS by Ann Druffel & D. Scott Rogo.** The shocking true account of two women's terrifying story of a UFO visitation ... of aliens who abducted them and brought them aboard their strange craft ... and of the curious two hour "lapse of time" no one could account for. What really happened on that March night in 1953? Find out, as a veteran parapsychologist and an expert UFO researcher attempt to unravel one of the most startling and ominous UFO encounters in history....   (159683—$4.95)

☐ **MEDITATIONS FOR THE NEW AGE edited by Carol Tonsing.** This extraordinary day-by-day book of meditations spans the broadest range of New Age thought, revealing just how much of this varied and rich movement finds its roots in ancient philosophy, general literature, and modern thought. From Plato and Confucius to Theodore Roosevelt; from Shakespeare and Schopenhauer to Elizabeth Kubler-Ross, this fascination collection presents the opinions of some of the most inspiring thinkers of our time—of all time.   (158407—$4.50)

☐ **TRANSCENDENTAL MEDITATION: THE SCIENCE OF BEING AND ART OF LIVING by Maharishi Mahesh Yogi.** Overcome the crises of modern life through meditation. This classic work, a source of profound knowledge and inspiration, tells how to achieve greater satisfaction, increased energy, reduced stress and sharper mental clarity in all spheres of life. (153863—$5.99)

Prices slightly higher in Canada

Buy them at your local bookstore or use this convenient coupon for ordering.

NEW AMERICAN LIBRARY
P.O. Box 999, Bergenfield, New Jersey 07621

Please send me the books I have checked above. I am enclosing $_____
(please add $1.00 to this order to cover postage and handling). Send check or money order—no cash or C.O.D.'s. Prices and numbers are subject to change without notice.

Name_____

Address_____

City _____ State _____ Zip Code _____
Allow 4-6 weeks for delivery.
This offer is subject to withdrawal without notice.

⊘ SIGNET   (0451)

MIND POWER

☐ **POWER HYPNOSIS: A Guide for Faster Learning and Greater Self-Mastery by Pierre Clement.** Now, with this effective guide to self-hypnosis, you can learn to harness the hidden energy of your mind. With gradual conditioning exercises, you'll learn, step-by-step, how to hypnotize yourself in order to lose weight, stop smoking, or gain the self-control and self-knowledge to manage your life successfully.   (159195—$3.95)

☐ **THE POWER OF ALPHA THINKING: Miracle of the Mind by Jess Stearn.** Through his own experiences and the documented accounts of others, Jess Stearn describes the technique used to control alpha brain waves. Introduction by Dr. John Balos, Medical Director, Mental Health Unit, Glendale Adventist Hospital.   (163281—$4.50)

☐ **SELF HYPNOTISM: The Technique and Its Use in Daily Living by Leslie M. LeCron.** Using simple, scientifically proven methods, this guidebook provides step-by-step solutions to such problems as fears and phobias, overcoming bad habits, pain and common ailments, and difficulty with dieting—all through the use of self-suggestion therapy.
          (159845—$4.95)

☐ **DAVID ST. CLAIR'S LESSONS IN INSTANT ESP by David St. Clair.** Through astoundingly simple techniques, discovered and perfected by a recognized authority on ESP, you can learn how incredibly gifted you are—and put your gifts to practical and permanent use to enrich and expand your life.
          (168186—$4.99)

☐ **SELF-MASTERY THROUGH SELF-HYPNOSIS by Dr. Roger Bernhardt and David Martin.** A practicing psychoanalyst and hypnotherapist clears up many misconceptions about hypnosis (it is not a form of sleep, but actually is a state of heightened awareness), and shows how to put it to use as a therapeutic tool in everyday life.   (159039—$4.50)

Prices slightly higher in Canada

Buy them at your local

bookstore or use coupon

on next page for ordering.

⊘ SIGNET

(0451)

SYDNEY OMARR'S DAY-BY-DAY ASTROLOGICAL GUIDES FOR YOU IN 1992

- ☐ **ARIES** . . . . (169980—$3.99)
- ☐ **TAURUS** . . . . (169999—$3.99)
- ☐ **GEMINI** . . . . (170008—$3.99)
- ☐ **CANCER** . . . . (170016—$3.99)
- ☐ **LEO** . . . . (170024—$3.99)
- ☐ **VIRGO** . . . . (170032—$3.99)
- ☐ **LIBRA** . . . . (170040—$3.99)
- ☐ **SCORPIO** . . . . (170059—$3.99)
- ☐ **SAGITTARIUS** . . . . (170067—$3.99)
- ☐ **CAPRICORN** . . . . (170075—$3.99)
- ☐ **AQUARIUS** . . . . (170083—$3.99)
- ☐ **PISCES** . . . . (170091—$3.99)

Price slightly higher in Canada.

Buy them at your local bookstore or use this convenient coupon for ordering.

NEW AMERICAN LIBRARY
P.O. Box 999, Bergenfield, New Jersey 07621

Please send me the books I have checked above. I am enclosing $_____
(please add $1.00 to this order to cover postage and handling). Send check or money order—no cash or C.O.D.'s. Prices and numbers are subject to change without notice.

Name_____

Address_____

City_____ State _____ Zip Code _____

Allow 4-6 weeks for delivery.
This offer, prices and numbers are subject to change without notice.

Let Sylvester Stallone's superstar mother guide you to super happiness, love, and grand fortune!

STARPOWER:
An Astrological Guide to Supersuccess

by JACQUELINE STALLONE
with Mim Eichler

Foreword by Sylvester Stallone

Discover the secrets that brought fame and fortune to Hollywood Stars—

- Why Gemini Jack Kennedy had the perfect wife in Leo Jacqueline Bouvier
- Why Libra John Lennon was a fated soul mate for Aquarius Yoko Ono
- Why Leos Madonna and Sean Penn should have never even gone on a second date, let alone said, "I do"!
- Why Aries Warren Beatty is able to exert such irresistible charm over women

Learn about the Stallone Love Scale and how to make smart decisions which reap happiness, wealth, and power. Jacqueline Stallone shows how STARPOWER worked for her famous son and Hollywood's greatest stars—and how it can work for you.

Buy them at your local bookstore or use this convenient coupon for ordering.

NEW AMERICAN LIBRARY
P.O. Box 999, Bergenfield, New Jersey 07621

Please send me _____ copies of STARPOWER (168437) at $4.95 each (please add $1.00 to this order to cover postage and handling). Send check or money order—no cash or C.O.D.'s. Prices and numbers are subject to change without notice.

Name_____

Address_____

City _____ State _____ Zip Code _____
Allow 4-6 weeks for delivery.
This offer is subject to withdrawal without notice.